A Rhino in my Garden

A Rhino in my Garden

Love, life and the African bush

Conita Walker

With Sally Smith

First published by Jacana Media (Pty) Ltd in 2017

10 Orange Street
Sunnyside
Auckland Park 2092
South Africa
+2711 628 3200
www.jacana.co.za

ISBN 978-1-4314-2595-2

Cover design by Shawn Paikin
Set in Stempel Garamond 10.5/15pt
Printed and bound by Creda Communications
Job no. 003081

See a complete list of Jacana titles at www.jacana.co.za

"If you pursue with labour, the labour passes away, but the good remains."
Marcus Tullius Cicero. BC 106

Contents

Acknowledgements

THIS BOOK HAS BEEN A collaboration between myself and Sally Smith, a long time visitor to the bush camps of Lapalala Wilderness and to the rhino and hippo orphanage at my homes at Doornleegte and Melkrivier. Over the ensuing years we became firm friends with Sally and her husband Ashley, who today reside in McGregor in the Western Cape. My diaries, notes and early manuscript became the basis for this story and I am grateful to my husband Clive who helped Sally steer the final edit with facts and dates. Sally's contribution has brought this story to life.

I am further extremely grateful to so many people whom it has been my privilege to know and work with and if I have omitted anyone please accept my sincere apologies. No one ever achieves anything entirely alone and I am no different, for my journey was never alone.

My late, loving parents were an inspiration to me and my siblings at a time in history that should never be repeated again, the Second World War (WWII). It was during my flying years as a flight attendant, which enabled me to travel the world with so many wonderful flight crews, that I met my husband-to-be Clive, which was to change my conventional way of life forever and brought me and later our two boys, Renning and Anton, into a world of 'wild' country and wild animals. We have shared this journey for more than 50 years and this story is as much theirs as it is mine.

My late mother-in-law, Enid Walker – who was living in our home when I was bitten by a venomous snake and the uproar that created – was a singular inspiration in her own right.

The following, in no sense of order, deserve my grateful thanks for so much that has enriched my life and helped Clive and me in all our endeavours through the years. Words are inadequate to fully express my feelings.

Val Ford, Ma Zeller, Rose Smith, Cherylee Pretorius and Heather Cowie who manned our Johannesburg office; the field guides and educators of Educational Wildlife Expeditions and the Wilderness Trust; the board of Trustees of the Lapalala Wilderness School (1985–2003): David Beattie, Val Ford, John Young, Jane Zimmermann, Rob Schneider, Harry Boots and Richard Burton; the Ladies' Committee of the Endangered Wildlife Trust: Wendy Farrant, Joy Cowan, Anne Deane, Val Whyte, Jill Morrison and Jane Zimmermann; and Petra Mengel of the permanent staff of the Endangered Wildlife Trust.

Dale and Elizabeth Parker provided the opportunity in 1981 to establish what was to become the magnificent game reserve where much of my story takes place, home to the 'bush' school we created at Lapalala Wilderness and then the orphanage for rhino and hippo. Clive and I shared the next 20 years with Dale, who made our home his and Elizabeth's bushveld home until his passing in 2001. This story is also central to his memory.

His son Duncan, who took up his father's mantle together with Mike Gregor, took Lapalala to new heights of excellence in conservation.

We moved permanently to Lapalala Wilderness in 1993 and were supported by all our staff, Clive and Nikki Ravenhill, Glynis Brown, David Bradfield – head of field rangers – my son Anton, who managed Lapalala East, and his wife René Walker, field rangers and labour force. A special word of appreciation to Rosina and Fred Baloyi, Titus and Lazarus Mamashela, who were an indispensable element in the raising of the orphans in my care. It's one thing to keep an eye on cattle but a very different matter with a full-grown hippo who doesn't like men (except Fred and Titus), and a one-and-a-half tonne black rhino – both animals that are amazingly fleet of foot. For their heart-warming welcome to us, from as far back as 1981, we are grateful to Shelly and Arthur Zeederberg, Colin and Joan Baber, Charles and Nina Baber, and Peter and Janet Farrant.

Karen Trendler deserves special mention for her dedication in raising rhino calves and especially the black rhino bull, Bwana. Many thanks also to veterinarians Dr Peter Rodgers, the late Dr Walter Eschenburg, Dr André Uys, Dr Richard Burroughs and Dr Pierre Bester, and Daphne Sheldrick of Kenya, an internationally recognised rehabilitator of orphan rhino and elephant calves, for her advice on milk formula.

Finally, and perhaps most importantly, my gratitude goes to all conservationists – from veterans like Clive and myself to the very youngest ones who may only just be starting out in this most important of careers. Your passion for protecting and healing the natural world has been my greatest inspiration, and will remain my most enduring hope.

ONE

The road to Doornleegte

"My dearest Conita, I came close to losing my life to a wounded lion today..."

He was a game ranger in Bechuanaland's Tuli Block. On my map Bechuanaland Protectorate (now Botswana) was where South Africa ended and the Real Africa began. I'd never been there – I had no idea what kind of a block the Tuli was. I'd never before met any rangers. I'd heard stories though, full of daring and danger, always something life-threatening. Bush planes crashed, wild animals attacked, floods, fires, poachers; safari adventurers got into trouble and faced certain demise but for a last-minute rescue by one of those heroic rangers. Big and bearded, I assumed; a sunburnt, sweaty man who didn't talk much, but having saved the day, might down his whisky, shoulder his heavy-calibre rifle and stride off into the sunset. John Wayne, only younger, more handsome and not so American.

I lived in a bachelor flat in Hillbrow, Johannesburg. My bravest adventure to date had been to change careers from teacher to flight attendant. I wore makeup, perfume and a dressy little uniform. If I hunted anything at all it was a bargain in the great cities of Europe and the Far East. The only thing I knew about elephant, rhino and lion or anyone tangling with them was that they were best avoided.

The fates conspired. A friend of mine was to be married and she invited me to be her bridesmaid. The bridegroom invited a friend, a fellow student pilot, to be his best man. "Clive Walker," I was told. "You'll like him. Everyone does."

At the engagement party he turned up with unkempt hair and a sunburnt face, a fund of improbable stories and a determination to mark his rare emergence from the bush in as festive a manner as he could contrive with his host of friends. A helpful sort, he offered to take me to the airport two days later when I had to leave for Japan. A 3am pick-up. His promise to be on time, like his wild tales, did not convince me. I made back-up arrangements. At 3:15 I was happy to have been proven right.

Just before the flight was due to leave I was given an urgent message: a man was waiting at the airport fence desperately eager to apologise. Whatever his story, whether he'd overslept after his late-night party or had in fact come straight from the party, I wasn't interested. He was treated to a cool and distant wave from the aircraft. When we landed in Tokyo there was a telegram waiting for me: "Take special care." I took offence.

Back in Johannesburg I received a 15-page letter in which the main event was that hungry lion, and the bravery required to kill it in the nick of time, thereby not only relieving the unspeakable agony of an animal caught in a poacher's trap but also saving his own life and that of his gun-bearer. He didn't hold back on his feelings upon finding a magnificent male lion dragging the steel trap which had all but taken off its paw, and followed with a graphic description of the fitting retribution for people who set such traps or gave villagers financial incentives to do so. He appeared to have extremely robust opinions on the matter. As if to sweeten the macho image, he'd included a small and, I thought, exquisitely detailed drawing of elephants around a baobab tree. Art helps him to get through his evenings, he said – long, lonely evenings all by himself in the bush camp, deprived of company and comfort.

I wondered how close to those elephants he'd been. Not that I cared, of course. I replied by asking him not to look me up again.

Within days, another bulky envelope: pages and pages of his exploits in the bush, followed by an indignant postscript – What did I mean by telling him to leave me alone? Didn't I promise to accompany him to his cousin's wedding? I tried to wriggle out of it: It had been mere chitchat, I didn't think he meant it, I was sure he'd have forgotten all about it as soon as he'd got back to the bush.

Another lengthy dispatch. He feels hurt; he doesn't chitchat and he doesn't forget, and his mother had brought him up to believe that a promise was a promise. Was she wrong?

For his second and last chance he arrived early, impeccably dressed, impeccably mannered and full of admiration for everything: my pictures, my books, my small collection of stones and shells, my dress, my hair. The cousin's wedding was a happy, heartfelt family affair, as good a setting as you might find for a sincere and handsome young man to show to advantage. By the end of the day I was smitten.

That was August 1966. On 3 December we got married. It must have been love. He owned – apart from his game ranger's rifle and his persistence – a lion skull, a dog, a box of books, some art materials and a Volkswagen Beetle.

A quarter of a century later that was the man I wanted to blame for the situation in which I found myself. On a morning like so many others and yet unlike any of them, I opened my front door, raising its weight by that one millimetre between a quiet escape and a wailing creak that would reach the sleeper in the bedroom. I walked out under the kind of sky you'll only find in a wilderness area. Stars brightening as the quarter moon swung west. No breeze, but faintly from some distance away, a broom cluster fig's extravagant fruiting nearing its end; every year that same sticky-sweet, overripe smell of late summer as it ripens into autumn. One season reliably flowing into the next and on into the next one. I longed for the security of such a predictable rhythm in my own life – the comfort of being able to trust what comes next.

Around the corner of the house there was a slight movement of cooler air. I tightened the shawl around my shoulders and faced east. The bush was singing. For a while that was enough, but then I closed my eyes and tried to hear past the pre-dawn clamour of bird calls. Nothing. It wouldn't last. Something was coming that would disturb not only the natural peace that surrounded my home, but also derail whatever safe routines I'd become used to. Reason told me it would be hours yet before I'd hear anything – the heavy truck, bearing its cargo in a reinforced steel container, would only just have begun its long, slow journey to me. For weeks I'd been preoccupied with that cargo. What on earth had made me think I would be able to handle it? My initial cautious excitement had become tinged with nervous dread. So there I was, well before sunrise, listening.

The light grew and dark mounds turned into umbrella thorns. Something stirred, an impala ram picking its way across the floodplain. I could hear the river. I was tempted to walk down – the Palala was only 500 metres away. Just past the peak of the rainy season it ran full and fast. In a more optimistic frame of mind I might have been tempted to take that as a sign – a propitious omen in a part of the world where, at least if you were North-Sotho or Shangaan or Pedi, every natural element, every seasonal event conveyed messages of ancestral approval or disquiet.

If there *were* ancestors watching over that particular patch of African bushveld, they were unlikely to have been mine. I'm German, a daughter of missionaries. Like my mother before me I went where my heart took me. The calling I followed and made my own was my husband's. Clive might not have been a missionary in the religious sense, but his avowed passion for wilderness was no less of a calling. In those long love letters from Tuli he had made no secret of that. In truth, there was no one to blame for the crucible into which I'd leapt with such naïve enthusiasm. When I chose the man I chose the life.

After our brief honeymoon in what was then Lourenço Marques (now Maputo) in Mozambique, he was a responsible married man who had to think of more pragmatic matters than his love of the bush. Money, of course. I was tempted to fling my conservative scruples to the winds and go adventuring with my cash-strapped game ranger, but prudence – and a forthright mother-in-law – prevailed. We returned to Johannesburg and he began to look for work with respectable income-generating prospects. He didn't say so but we both knew it would be an interim arrangement.

Drawing on his training as an artist he worked as the advertising manager of one of the biggest paint manufacturers at the time, Herbert Evans. I was a senior flight attendant with Trek Airways (later to become Luxavia). But at the first opportunity that we could get our schedules to synchronise we piled some provisions into the Beetle – rather dashing, I thought, white with red leather seats – and headed for the Pont Drift border post. On both the South African and Botswana sides everyone seemed to know Clive. I'd never seen such popularity, or found myself so instantly and fondly included. All those tales of peril and adventure I'd disbelieved turned out to have been true.

Another revelation was in store for me. In that famed triangle of bushveld between the Shashe and Limpopo rivers, the Tuli Block, I saw my husband in his true *heimat* (homeland), and discovered my own. At a wide, slow bend of the Limpopo, full of clouds and washed blue sky, I watched a herd of elephant emerge from the shade of giant mashatu trees and stir up dust in their rush down the bank. I followed leopard spoor in the sand of the dry Motloutsi River. Under a full moon, somewhere far beyond the firelight, I heard lions roar. Close by, the furtive conversation of scops owls. There was an eerie cry. Black-backed jackal, Clive said. I had a fleeting glimpse, into the light and out of it again, of a little ghost of the night – a serval. A blood-red sun rose over the sandstone ridges of Mmammagwa and I realised: I'd become one of them – bush-baby, tree-hugger, *umweltfreak* (environmental fanatic). My husband was delighted to discover in his wife the heart of a conservationist. When we packed for our return to the city I held up my small camping mirror: no makeup, cheeks and nose flushed after days in the generous Tuli sun, wash-and-wear hair. *Frau*

Walker: Naturschützer (conservationist). I would never again feel completely at home except in the wilderness.

My new-found passion extended also to the creatures that terrified the living daylights out of me: spiders, snakes, crocodiles and the elephants that were Clive's obsession. In the 1950s he had shot elephant in Mozambique. The excitement of the hunt, he found, was not enough. He would continue to seek them out, not to kill but to study and admire, and to be able to introduce others to the experience of being in the presence of such great wild creatures. Instinct and the bush craft he'd learnt from his trackers kept him safe far closer to elephants than I had the nerve for. We struck a bargain – not the one I had wanted, but the one I could get. When I was around he would abide by *my* definition of safe behaviour, not his; when I was not around, since I was not able to control his actions, I'd much rather not know about them.

In between our bush breaks we were a young couple with a completely urban life. When the first of our two boys came along his daily pram excursions were on the sidewalks of central Hillbrow. It would have been difficult to find an environment further removed from the wilderness than that one. Clive didn't complain. Such were the contentments and rewards of love and family that we were thoroughly happy.

The lure of the bush, however, was insistent, irresistible and growing. He became more and more involved in conservation matters, and I with him. My flying days had ended, without any regrets, with the birth of my children. My family came first and my husband's causes had now also become mine.

The founding of the Endangered Wildlife Trust under Clive's chairmanship – a seminal event in South African wildlife conservation – dates from that time and so does my education in what it meant to be involved in the battle to protect threatened species and ecosystems. I was shocked to discover just how much there was that needed protection.

I also discovered that, however noble the cause, you had to be prepared to get your hands dirty. Literally.

Shortly after we got married, on one of our regular Sunday

afternoon "Just looking, I promise" stops at a second-hand bookshop, Clive discovered a treasure: a 1929 publication that had found its way there from Herald's Bookstore in Salisbury, old Rhodesia. Denis Lyell's *The Hunting and Spoor of Central African Game* was the only book he'd ever found which showed life-sized animal tracks for the purpose of identification. Another Sunday afternoon, another bookshop, another find. Dr Reay Smithers's *The Mammals of Zambia, Rhodesia and Malawi* with small animal tracks accompanying the text. I could see where we were headed, and halfway through dinner with a friend who said, "You've got to include dung," I pushed away my schnitzel and tried to accept my fate. Across the table Clive and Koos Bothma, Professor of Wildlife Management at Pretoria University, were enthusing over the prospect of a first-ever fully comprehensive authoritative field guide to the spoor and signs of the mammals of Southern Africa. I was making mental lists, beginning with rubber gloves, plastic bags and industrial-strength disinfectant.

In the course of the next few years it sometimes felt to me as if every animal that had walked anywhere between the Kgalagadi in the west and the iMfolozi in the east had had its spoor measured, photographed, described and identified. If it had defecated anywhere within the range of vision of Clive and the various scouts who accompanied us from time to time, the remains of its last meal found its way into my meticulously labelled plastic bags. If it had dug a deep hole or tunnel both my sons would volunteer to investigate. Renning was older and already fascinated by the natural world, but Anton being the younger was smaller and often won the right to crawl into that dusty unknown while I panicked about snakes, scorpions or indeed the owner of that hole which could still be lurking down there, foul-tempered and hungry.

For the boys it was an adventure that continued over many holidays. They became expert dung collectors, sharp-eyed and unflagging. I gave up on rubber gloves and joined in their contests: with our fingers thrust deep into elephant dung we'd each offer our best guess – this morning, last night, yesterday. The scout was the judge. He was usually also the one to keep watch and send us all racing madly back to our Land Rover station wagon to escape the ire of lion, rhino, buffalo or elephant that resented our poking around their ablutions.

The aftermath to our study and collection trips was much less fun, and with that Clive was on his own. Banished to a room as far removed from the rest of our living space as possible, he soaked the dung specimens in tetrachloride and then had them drying for days on end in grim little heaps on sheets of newspaper before they could be deposited in labelled glass jars. The boys and I resolutely refused to assist. Carnivore dung, especially, was bad enough out in the open air of the Okavango or Savute or the Klaserie Game Reserve; at close quarters in a Johannesburg house we found that the romance of the wild was utterly gone. It was dung, it stank and was wholly and solely Dad's affair.

Signs of the Wild was published in 1981 and is still in print to this day. Popular and useful as it is among safari guides and tourists, for me it has even greater value. I see two small boys with sun-bleached hair shouting their excitement to me as they run up with their hands full of animal droppings. And, striding up behind them, their father, laughing.

That might well be my favourite image of Clive: on foot in the veld, and since 1975 that is how he spent much of his professional time – walking in the wild.

We had created Educational Wildlife Expeditions by then, an organisation aimed at bringing man and nature closer together. EWE took small groups on walking trails into unspoilt wilderness areas. Sometimes I was able to go along, but mainly, together with the responsibilities of full-time motherhood and part-time teaching, I was part of the team that ran logistics support from Johannesburg. These days wilderness trails have become one of the mainstays of nature-based tourism. All flavours of trailing: backpacking, slack-packing, every possible variation of eco- and wild- and green-, horseback, elephant-back, every degree of indulgence from hard-core no-frills, to ultimate no-sweat with every luxurious attention to your comfort.

It was different then. The renowned conservationist Dr Ian

Player had introduced his pioneering Wilderness Leadership School trails in KwaZulu-Natal. There weren't many other enterprises of the kind, and his model was the one closest to what EWE wished to achieve. The goal was straightforward. People, ordinary everyday people, were to encounter wild nature on foot. No more, no less. The focus was not the splendid designer accommodation or gourmet cuisine – we aimed for basic campsite comforts and hearty refuelling after a day's trailing.

It was all about Mother Nature. Nature's sounds and silences; nature's rhythms; the dramas of the wilderness playing out without being scripted and coerced by humans, without being commercially packaged for consumption by humans. Elephant, buffalo, lion, rhino, leopard: they weren't the Big 5 – each one was a wondrous, irreplaceable component of the natural creation, along with rivers and rocks, trees and flowers and clouds and stars.

I began to notice something. Trailists might have arrived with no greater ambition than to have a fun holiday, an adventure maybe with a moderate helping of adrenaline on the side. But by the time they said goodbye their conversations had changed. They were talking about feeling part of the natural world in a way they hadn't felt before. I knew exactly what they meant. It was that same quiet miracle of transformation wrought by the wilderness that I myself had experienced. As a way to win converts for the cause of conservation it was and still is to my way of thinking, unsurpassed. Best of all, of course, if you can catch them young.

That was another of Clive's missions: environmental education. Together with some like-minded colleagues, he created The Wilderness Trust, with a similar aim to that of EWE but with children as the target. Children of all races who were to become the inheritors of this country and be responsible, in their turn, for preserving it in a way that was worth inheriting – with its natural environment, its glorious wilderness areas, intact.

The response from children to this kind of exposure to the wild was extraordinary and intensely rewarding. We were fired with a desire to reach as many children as possible, and to do so in a way that would make a wilderness experience not just a privilege for the already privileged, but one that was available for every child regardless of background or finances. At that time the political dispensation in South Africa, still in the grip of apartheid, wasn't ready to embrace any such goal. But I'd grown up on a mission station: I was schooled in the pursuit of big dreams and faith in large causes. When Clive started talking about the creation of a wilderness school as a centre for nature-based education he had an easy convert in his wife. We were living in a city, hardly the place for such a school, but no matter. We had no finances with which to acquire land and build such a school – no matter. Our own two boys were at school in Johannesburg and still needed us as hands-on parents. No matter, we would find a way.

Clive scouted bushveld areas for suitable locations. He returned again and again to a little-known area in what was then the Northern Province and is now named after the river which defines its northern border, Limpopo.

This was the Waterberg, one of the major mountain ranges of South Africa – 14 500 square kilometres of outstanding natural beauty and ecological diversity lying just about halfway between the urban sprawl of Gauteng and the silence and vast horizons of the great Kgalagadi. Halfway in more than geography too: with a kinder climate than the desert and therefore a less punishing environment for both man and animal, it was in some areas still wild enough to have the identifying stamp of true wilderness.

To the conservationist's eye the greater Waterberg area showed some worrisome signs: an erstwhile wildlife paradise had become badly degraded, hunted out, leaving in places little more than a maze of cattle farm fences. But there were encouraging signs too: some landowners had chosen another direction and begun to restore and protect pockets of wild Waterberg as private nature reserves.

After those trips Clive came home and one name started recurring: Dubbelwater. Five thousand hectares of rugged bushveld through which two rivers, the Palala and the Blocklands, had cut winding courses to their confluence in the north-western part of the property before continuing on north to the Limpopo.

He was ready to make a decision, but wanted me to see it. "Pack something," he said. "You might want to celebrate."

Early the next morning, while all of Johannesburg was commuting to work, we set off in the opposite direction, out of the city. First the tarred national road aiming straight north, then a narrow secondary road, less straight, heading north-west, then gravel. With every turn-off the road became narrower, the surface rougher, until more than four hours later we were on a little-used jeep track, crawling up onto a plateau where we ran out of road. Clive led the way to a game track disappearing into dense vegetation. Under the trees the air closed in. I could detect the smells of animals that had passed that way. There was zebra spoor, and kudu. Then the unmistakable twin pits made by small klipspringer hooves – a sure sign that we were in some high, rocky place. After a few hundred metres the gritty sand and stones underfoot gave way to solid rust-coloured rock and we emerged from the shade into brilliant light. I was standing on a cliff-top. Two hundred metres below was the bend of a river, and to the right, the flat-topped hill which had dominated every view of our approach.

"That's Malora," Clive said. "And this," his walking stick tracked the river as it snaked towards us, tumbled over black rocks and angled off to our left, "this is the Palala."

There, on those towering rocks, we had our celebratory picnic on what Clive told me was Lapalala, part of the Dubbelwater farm. I couldn't see any signs of development; it seemed completely wild, as if it had never been disturbed by humans. But that was deceptive. The area had once been settled by groups of the Nguni people – remains of their Iron Age stone walling could be found on top of Malora. Certainly in other places too, Clive thought, once one started looking. The archaeological record would add immeasurably to the scope of the curriculum one could offer at a wilderness school in such a place.

We clubbed together with our friends and colleagues of The Wilderness Trust and began to negotiate with the owners, a South African and a former Kenyan hunter, one Eric Rundgren, godson of Karen Blixen's husband, Bror Blixen. We paid over the deposit. The remainder of the purchase price had a deadline attached to it. As month followed month that deadline seemed to be approaching faster than our prospects for raising sufficient funds. But at that point Lapalala drew another player.

On one of Clive's EWE trails some years earlier, in the Okavango in Botswana, the group had included a couple from Cape Town, a businessman and his wife, Dale and Elizabeth Parker. Already predisposed by an interest in Africa's natural environment to be sympathetic to the cause of wildlife conservation, the Parkers expressed an interest in Clive's causes. It wasn't long before Dale became a trustee of the Endangered Wildlife Trust.

In 1981 Clive was in Knysna in the southern Cape Province. Through EWT he was involved in a last-ditch effort to save the rare Knysna elephant. These animals had assumed almost mythic status: in the dense indigenous forests they were extremely seldom seen. There had been no sightings for a considerable time. This was a survey to determine how many, if any, elephant remained. Dale Parker volunteered to fly some more people down to join in the search. They found evidence of three elephants. That was the good news. It was also the bad news: human pressures on their habitat had allowed the survival of only three elephants.

At the post-survey dinner that night, in the course of a discussion around strategies for the conservation of large herbivores, Clive mentioned what he'd seen in the Waterberg: landowners moving into wildlife conservation. The Waterberg was so poorly known at that time, some of the people around the table needed to have the place described to them. Clive did, and he didn't hide the fact that he'd lost his heart to one particular part of it.

The next morning Dale had to fly back to Cape Town, but first he wanted a private word with Clive. If he were to purchase this place, Lapalala/Dubbelwater, he asked, would Clive join him in developing it as a wilderness reserve, and take care of the hands-on management?

Clive didn't hesitate. They shook hands on the deal.

A month later the Parkers flew up from Cape Town to have a look for themselves. Clive took them to that same spot above the Palala. It was enough.

Lapalala grew. Additional land was acquired – eventually 18 farms in all – veld was rehabilitated, fences dropped, wildlife species re-introduced, infrastructure created, management and staff trained. The initial 5000 hectares grew to the 36 000 hectares of the Lapalala Wilderness Reserve, and in the heart of it, on the banks of the Palala, rose our wilderness school.

Be careful what you wish for, they say. I learnt to do with much less sleep. We were now living and working in two places several hours apart, Johannesburg and Lapalala. At the same time other conservation work had to continue. In the course of the 1970s Clive had become involved with investigating and on several occasions exposing threats to free-roaming wildlife. In the Kaokoveld in northern Namibia, for example, he discovered a situation perilously close to whole-scale slaughter of desert elephant and black rhino. The usual culprits of course, but in this instance the havoc wrought by poachers was further increased by elements within the government and defence force. Under such circumstances one doesn't walk away. Through EWT and the Rhino and Elephant Foundation Clive joined with others in fighting the battle on that front. In 1981, as we embarked on our work in Lapalala, that battle wasn't merely ongoing, it was intensifying. And not only in the Kaokoveld.

Privately, well out of the public view, I had my moments when it felt like a losing battle. It seemed that wherever I looked there was a red flag: some creeping devastation threatening the survival of some part of the natural environment. And often, by the time the alert went out, there was an all but irreversible fait accompli: a development green-lighted or even already half-built; a wetland laid waste; species numbers decimated; carcasses rotting in the sun.

Through EWT Clive was frequently the one who had to sound the alarm. He didn't flinch, although the sight of my husband on his soapbox was not always welcomed by authorities. I'd realised long before that I'd married an idealist, a dreamer. Now I discovered that his particular brand of dreaming was that of the crusader, the kind that caused wives to lie awake worrying at night. He seemed to be relentlessly positive. Both publicly and in private he resisted anything that resembled a defeatist attitude. There was always a plan to be made, some action to initiate or support. A battle was there to be fought, not to be lamented.

I learnt that, with conservation, you signed up for the long haul. The most effective strategies tend to be the ones with the long-term view. They may not make the headlines and they won't deliver in the short term, but they seed a future with more favourable conservation prospects.

Wilderness trailing with EWE was just such a strategy. So was the wilderness school. Lapalala also opened the opportunity for another. Dale was skeptical. I have to admit, it wasn't the kind of business plan that would have sounded convincing in a corporate boardroom. But at his request, albeit without his whole-hearted belief at first, we as EWE took over the three very rustic self-catering bush camps which had originally been established by a friend of Eric Rundgren. The camps operated on a somewhat unusual basis. For the most nominal of fees it was placed within the reach of ordinary people, families who would otherwise not have been able to afford an experience of that nature. This was only possible because Lapalala was privately funded, the owners were willing to absorb some of the additional costs and gracious enough to trust us with such an enterprise on their land.

Since EWE, operating from its base near our Edenvale home, was already a fully functional walking trails operation, we were perfectly placed to absorb these three camps. That soon grew to six rustic, unfenced camps in stunning locations. In time four more were added. Ten idyllic, wild hideaways. There was a single rule for guests: drive to your camp and then no more driving until the day you leave. Explore on foot, wherever you like, for as long as you like. No guards, no guns. There was also an unwritten guarantee: for the duration of your stay the expanse of wilderness around your camp (many square kilometres of it) belonged to you only and to the wildlife of the place. You could watch, quietly, a family of antelope or baboons or warthogs going about their undisturbed business for hours; you could lie basking in the sun on a black basalt slab in the middle of the river, or walk around all day in whatever state of dress or undress you preferred, searching for rock paintings or butterflies, photographing rare plants or spotting birds, or questing for inner peace. No one would notice except the wildlife, and as long as you didn't bother them, they wouldn't care.

Lapalala hadn't re-introduced elephant and lion, and buffalo were kept in separate sections of the reserve, but everything else was there. It was wild – a living laboratory for the encounter of man and nature. Lapalala soon had its regulars and devotees. Over the years, thousands of them. Parents would bring their infants to a favourite bush camp to meet the world into which they were born, and a new generation of conservation-minded children would grow up to become supporters and activists for the cause of conservation – taking on, if you will, the missionary mandate for Africa's wild places.

Our own children still had their primary home in Johannesburg, but whenever possible they were there with us, learning to enjoy and trust the bush. The Parker children's primary home was also in a city, Cape Town. But every year, on their family break in Lapalala, they too were exposed to the best the Waterberg had to offer. For Dale that meant the Palala: at first in Marula, overlooking a 150-metre pool which, like most of the other camps, was ideal for the Canadian-style canoes we had co-opted from our EWE operation in Tuli. Later the Parker holidays moved further upstream, to Lepotedi, their own special riverside camp at the foot of the cliff where in 1981 Dale and Elizabeth had had their first glimpse of the Palala.

The bush camps were the responsibility of someone who, up to that point, had been invisible and contented to remain so. On occasion visitors arriving in their heavily laden vehicles would come across a bush-weary Toyota Hilux that had pulled off the jeep-track to allow them to pass. The driver would exchange friendly waves and smiles with them. Many times, watching in her rear-view mirror, she would see a head suddenly whipping around to look back at her. She could guess why. The visitors would suspect, but not be quite sure, that the friendly little lady in her serviceable safari-wear and sunglasses behind the wheel of that Hilux must be the wife of the very much better known Clive Walker whose name was associated with the place.

There was the public Clive Walker. The one who, as CEO and founder or co-founder of several conservation organisations, got called for press statements about wildlife crises, the one who wrote his books and donated his wildlife paintings to raise funds for wildlife conservation. And there was the private Clive – the family man; the wilderness lover who walked every inch of Lapalala, and together with Dale Parker in their headquarters on the Doornleegte verandah, planned and dreamed the reserve into being.

Of Conita, the wife, there was only the private one. She shared those verandah dreams and managed the background logistics of family and homes and business. When she pulled off the jeep-track to allow the next intake of bush camp occupants to pass, it was because she had just finished checking that the water tanks, the beds, the gas fridges and freezers, the showers, the lamps, the first-aid box, the stacked firewood, the numerous other little attentions for their safety and comfort, were ready for them.

You might describe mine as the classic mothering role. Mothering came naturally – my two sons, Renning and Anton, of course and, although he might protest, Clive. So when in June 1990 he announced that he and Dale Parker were going to attend the annual wildlife auction in KwaZulu-Natal, "just to have a look," I agreed to hold the fort as usual and also as usual on similar occasions to pack the provisions, up to and including the beer ration they required per day.

I suppose I should have seen it coming. Some time previously Clive had organised for officials from the then Natal Parks Board to visit the Waterberg. They assessed Lapalala as suitable habitat for black rhino. There weren't any black rhino, nor any plans to bring them in, but a reserve large and ecologically sound enough for black rhino was a haven for myriad other fauna and flora. Good news therefore: an endorsement of the conservation work carried out by Clive and the reserve personnel, and a validation of Dale's faith and investment in the enterprise.

It so happened that that 1990 wildlife auction was rather a special one, the largest ever up to that point, drawing international as well as national buyers. For the first time in South Africa black rhino were to be offered for sale. But that was co-incidental – Clive and Dale were "just looking". I believe that for Dale, at least, that was true.

At Clive's instigation they drove to the viewing bomas at the iMfolozi where the black rhinos were being held. Five magnificent specimens – two males, three females. As with the EWE trails and the Lapalala bush camps the same formula was in operation: facilitate exposure, let nature do the rest. Dale had never before encountered wild black rhino at such close range. He returned to the bomas again and again.

Come auction day he and Clive, as mere non-buying members of the public, entered the auction room which was already abuzz with excitement. There was a massive media contingent – press, radio and television. After two hours the group of black rhino came up. The bidding stalled at one million rand. That didn't seem right. Dale thought perhaps the bidding only required a bit of stimulation to really get going. He leaned over to Clive and whispered, "What do we do now?"

Clive said: "Put up your hand."

Cameras and microphones scrambled to find the unknown, unregistered bidder. Someone rushed up with the required paperwork and a bidding disc. At the end of furious bidding the first black rhino to be offered on auction had gone into private hands. The press converged on Dale. But he, no less astounded than everyone else, had just paid 2.2 million rand for five animals – he slid out to recover in the parking lot. Their real prey having escaped, the media pounced on the remaining partner, the excited, slightly dazed managing director of a wilderness reserve who'd just seen a dream come true.

And several hours away, his wife – completely oblivious of these happenings – is unaware of the fact that something had been set in motion which, three years later, would have her shivering in her shawl in a pre-dawn panic attack, waiting for a truckload of responsibility.

After the auction there followed a busy and anxious two months for everyone at Lapalala. Permits, the design and construction of enclosures, additional specialised training of the reserve's field rangers, the logistics of transportation. Black rhino relocation is never a small matter. One deals with insurance, with the hazards of gravel roads, and with the wellbeing of powerful, highly strung and unpredictable wild animals confined in a six-berth transporter.

Fortunately it went well. But then, as the days passed, a small worry grew to a major concern: the veld was dry and the forecast was for late rains that year. Weather conditions, always a pre-occupation, became the focus of conversations and very often the reason for them. Dale would phone from Cape Town: Has it rained? Does it look as if it might? Is the Palala still flowing? How soon after the rains started would the veld have recovered sufficiently for the release of the rhinos?

Every day, after the lunchtime radio news, I listened to rainfall figures from areas further north or west of the Waterberg. To the east the Lowveld had had rain. So, further south, had the Free State. Scattered thunder showers even over the semi-desert Karoo of the Northern Cape. No mention of the Waterberg. Twice a day the rangers delivered freshly cut browse to Lapalala's first black rhinos waiting in their bomas. The Palala slowed to a trickle.

Meanwhile, in the other half of my life, our Johannesburg garden budded and flowered in its reliable, municipally watered spring and early summer. Then one afternoon the phone rang and I picked it up to hear Clive's voice: "Listen."

Drumming on the tin roof at Doornleegte – rain.

At the end of 1990 black rhino once again roamed a part of the Waterberg where for well over a century the only evidence that they had ever been there existed in ochre paintings on sandstone rocks.

TWO

Bwana

THE CLASSIC APPROACH to the Waterberg is from the south. From the tiny "tamed" tip of Africa explorers, vagabonds and fugitives looked north. On horseback or by 16-span ox-wagon they risked all on blind faith or bloody-mindedness and forged a way through trackless bush country until, after weeks or months, sometimes even years, of danger and hardship, there it was, the lovely southern arc of a 200-kilometre-long escarpment curving away further north, further into the hinterland. Day after day they watched those sandstone and conglomerate ramparts inching up from the distant trembling horizon, and named them The Seven Sisters. Beyond them they were to discover a wild, game-rich, water-rich country: the Waterberg. Some came to hunt and trade, others to hide, everyone chasing a dream – freedom, adventure, a fortune, a place to settle amid peace and plenty.

Today they still come, in ever-increasing numbers now and ever-decreasing discomfort – all it takes is a quick fly-in to any number of private airstrips, or less than half a day's drive on good roads. And we who are fortunate enough to live here know why they come and why many of them, like us, will find it impossible to leave again.

We don't have malaria – that trumps most other wildlife areas in South Africa. We have clean free-running rivers – that trumps all of South Africa and much of the world. We have vast swathes of true wilderness and, in a geological rarity known as the Waterberg Red Beds, the oldest geological evidence on earth of enough free oxygen in the atmosphere to support life. The archaeological record places man in these valleys and gorges for at least three million years. Our long history has left us with a polyglot society: Northern Sotho, Tsonga, Tswana, English, Afrikaans, even German. Side by side with the modern tourism draw-cards of 5-star lodges, art routes and big game hunting, indigenous cultures of the Bapedi, Tswana and Ndebele live on in more than two dozen rural villages. But it isn't the least of the Waterberg's attractions that, unlike far too many places in this country, the natural landscape still holds its own against the imprint of human enterprise.

Early in the 20th century the South African Prime Minister, General Jan Smuts, had been so struck by the unique ecological importance of the Waterberg, he advocated the preservation of most of it in a great national park stretching all the way up to the Limpopo – a treasure in perpetuity for all South Africans. As history records, that plan was short-circuited: in 1948 he was voted out, and the architects of apartheid voted in. The Waterberg wilderness lost a champion for its cause.

Many decades later, however, in a welcome reversal of fortunes, the area is gradually moving closer to Smuts's vision. At the time of writing, almost two million hectares are already managed according to conservation principles, a large percentage of it in private hands. Together with governmental agencies, individual landowners like Dale Parker have become the modern champions of the Waterberg wilderness. It is *their* patronage, their drive and passion that now protects much that is most in need of protection.

With Dale's 1990 purchase of black rhino Lapalala became a

sanctuary for this highly endangered species. Two years later I heard from Clive that he and Dale were again discussing a trip down to the Natal Parks Board's wildlife auction. This time Elizabeth and I thought it wise to go along.

There were the usual offerings: eland, blue wildebeest, giraffe, kudu, some nyala, tsessebe, waterbuck. There were also, again, black rhino. They'd been captured in the iMfolozi Game Reserve, flown in by helicopter to the reserve's holding pens, and had already settled down well. They'd be ready for transportation immediately after the auction.

2.3 million rand later Lapalala had acquired another five black rhino. One of them was pregnant. That was a surprise, as was the fact that she was considerably older than had been estimated prior to capture. The Zulu rangers called her "Makoko" (Granny).

Her name followed her to Lapalala, and I soon discovered that, as the oldest (human) female at the reserve, I'd also become "Makoko", customised to "Magog". But that old rhino cow was responsible for more than just my nickname.

On 31 March 1993 there was a convoy approaching the Seven Sisters. I was at Doornleegte. I knew they were coming. They knew I was waiting. All of us hoped I'd be ready. A few days earlier, driving that same road to the Waterberg, I had grave doubts on that score. A thousand times before I'd headed into the gap of Sandrivierspoort, but this time it was different. From that day on, the Waterberg would be my permanent base. I would have no other home but Doornleegte. A different life altogether. To say that I had no misgivings would be tampering with the truth.

I comforted myself with the fact that I'd had misgivings before, and been proven wrong. In 1981 when Clive returned from Knysna with the news of his discussion with Dale, he was inspired. This might be an opportunity to do something extraordinary, he said, something *real* for conservation. Meaningful and fulfilling work. A purpose larger than ourselves. It felt petty to question and object; petty to worry. I would take that leap of faith with him.

Ten years on I wasn't sorry. I'd toughened up. I'd become used to the regular commute between the two poles of our lives up to that point. I had a home and an office to run in Johannesburg, and a home and a wilderness school in Lapalala. Our initial dream was on track: busloads of young people were regularly being transported to and from the environmental school, beautifully laid out along the banks of the Palala. The bush camps too were thriving, booked up for at least a year in advance. A lodge had been added to the accommodation options: Kolobe Lodge had all the mod cons and hosted private guests as well as conferences.

The restoration of the veld, especially, was a source of satisfaction. Literally tonnes of garbage and farming debris had been removed, anti-erosion measures taken where necessary, game was again plentiful, including white rhino in the sour-veld areas, and of course there was now also black rhino in the rockier and densely thicketed sections.

Then came 11 June 1992. A group of Kolobe guests was enjoying a game drive. After the traditional starched-linen-and-crystal champagne breakfast at a jaw-dropping view site, the lodge manager, doubling as game ranger for his guests that morning, chose a circuitous scenic return route. Whatever the game scout spotted from his seat on the bonnet, the happily mellowed guests were delighted to investigate. Halfway down an incline he pointed to something close to the jeep track. They'd already seen warthogs on their drive that morning, and there was another one, squealing and shining in the morning sun.

The Land Rover pulled up, binoculars lifted, the excitement grew. That particular warthog was shining because it was wet. It was squealing because it wasn't a warthog at all, but a prematurely born black rhino.

Evidently the mother, Makoko, having just given birth, hearing the Land Rover's noisy approach up the rocky incline on the other side of the hill, took fright and bolted. By the time the vehicle arrived on the scene the only rhino to be seen was the calf, its little footpads and toes still with their soft skin covering that protected the mother while it was in the womb. The likelihood was that the newborn had not even had the vital first suckling that would have provided it with antibodies in the colostrum.

Lapalala's eagerly awaited first-born black rhino baby was premature, abandoned and unprotected against any number of infections that could attack and kill it within a matter of hours. It was winter. It was a Sunday. Clive was away.

I was at Doornleegte and followed Lapalala's shifting into high gear over the radio. The emergency was reported to the reserve manager, Clive Ravenhill, and he called Clive in Johannesburg. From there the SOS went to Dale in Cape Town, then to Onderstepoort, the veterinary facility attached to Pretoria University, and from there to the nearby Animal Rehabilitation Centre (ARC) and its manager, Karen Trendler. In the meantime everyone with access to a phone frantically tried to find expert advice for dealing with the situation, only to discover that such advice didn't exist – not at that time.

The lodge manager tracked down a colostrum replacement and this, together with the stroppy little baby, was raced out of the reserve to meet the animal ambulance despatched from Pretoria. At the end of that Sunday a student at the animal hospital had been moved out of her room to make way for the baby's first night while Karen was preparing her study to serve as a temporary rhino nursery.

Our rangers named him Bwana, the Big Boss. The media loved him. Bwana was world news, and with good reason.

Only the hardest of hearts would dispute the cuteness of a baby rhino. As a photogenic, defenceless orphan, Bwana's was a story that tugged at the heart-strings.

But there was a bigger story, one which, to my mind, illustrates perfectly man's apparently unlimited capacity to be utterly foolish. It also illustrates Africa's vulnerability to such foolishness.

As a small child in rural South Africa I had first become aware of the fact that this great continent of ours is poorly guarded against blows struck far from its shores. Germany, the homeland of my missionary parents, was for me no more than a fantastical place. It lived only in their stories. Yet suddenly it mattered to people who didn't know us that we belonged in some punishable way to that remote, unreal country and to the terrible conflict into which it had plunged the world. Someone else's war entered my life and because of that my father was removed from it. Not because *he* was at war, but because somewhere faraway other people were. It was a disquieting realisation: a family in Africa was as vulnerable to the shifting tides in European thought as it was to the ebb and flow of the Niger, the Congo, the Zambezi.

That was WWII, but it was no different before and it is no different now. To this day Africa seems to have no protection against ambitions and obsessions from other continents. From Europe, Asia or America such appetites inexorably reach across the vast geographical and cultural barriers that separate us to come and stir the grass of our savannah.

Whether it be a thirst for territory and mineral resources, for slaves or converts, for magical elixirs, Africa has ever been the quencher of great foreign thirsts. Sometimes that has meant war.

In the 1860s tantalising rumours began to reach the Britain of Queen Victoria: diamond deposits in South Africa. Rumours became reports. What promised to be a rich diamond field lay on the cusp between the Empire's Cape Colony to the south and the Boer Republic of the Orange Free State to the north. By 1877 the diamond fields were under British control, annexed to the Cape Colony. Less than a decade later there was more news: gold deposits in the Transvaal, another Boer Republic further north. By 1896 the Witwatersrand gold reefs accounted for 23% of the world's gold production. The new El Dorado.

Three years later the British Army sailed for South Africa. The Empire was playing to win and also called on soldiers from its far-flung colonies – Canada, Australia, New Zealand, India, Ceylon – to join the British and South African colonial forces. Two further appeals were issued to volunteers to join the armed forces in mounting Britain's greatest military campaign since the Battle of Waterloo in 1815.

The Boers, largely a farming nation, gathered together an initial resistance of around 87 000 men to face 448 000 soldiers advancing under the Union Jack. One of those soldiers was a 16-year-old boy from Hatton Garden in London. He'd lied about his age in order to enlist and join the adventure in Africa. In February 1900 the Empire's forces reached Paardeberg, just south of Kimberley – the epicentre of that alluring prize of the fabulously rich diamond fields. The 16-year-old Londoner, fighting in a Welsh regiment, had become a battle-hardened soldier.

After the devastating Battle of Paardeberg the defeat of the Boer nation was slow but certain. The Empire's loss of 22 000 soldiers, tragic as that was, was dwarfed by Boer losses, which extended well beyond the battlefield. Close on 30 000 Afrikaner women and children died of starvation and disease in British concentration camps. The real toll was even higher: many thousands of black people, who'd found themselves caught up in this conflict between Brit and Boer, also perished in the so-called "black" concentration camps. But that was not enough for the would-be conquerors. Even the possibility of survival in the rural areas of the Boer republics had to be obliterated: more than 30 000 farmsteads were torched, livestock killed and left to rot, water sources poisoned and crops destroyed in execution of the coup de grâce, Lord Kitchener's "Scorched Earth" campaign. On 31 May 1902 it was over. The Peace Treaty of Vereeniging was signed in Melrose House in Johannesburg, the city built on gold. The Empire had secured another prize.

The young man from Hatton Garden survived the war. Africa still promised adventure and, a civilian now, he chose to make a life for himself in the conquered territory. His name was Charles Walker.

Today his grandson, Clive Walker, is engaged in another war in which I find it impossible not to see dreadful similarities. Again it is fought on African soil, again the primary instigator is a foreign appetite for an African resource, again the opposing forces are unevenly matched, again it leaves devastation in its wake.

Ask people who are closely involved with wildlife conservation and they will tell you that the term "war" is appropriate. For more than 50 years I have been married to a conservationist fighting on the front-lines of that war. I have no illusions about just how brutal and bloody it can be. Ask conservationists what their true feelings are upon discovering yet another elephant carcass, or yet another dozen of them, indiscriminately mowed down by automatic rifles from helicopters, their ivory chain-sawed out of their skulls. Sometimes those are cows, matriarchs, their calves left traumatised and lost.

Now ask those conservationists about what has been dubbed "The Rhino Wars". Ask them about an animal staggering blindly, half its face hacked off – just one of many nightmare scenes left behind by ad hoc armed bands or well-organised internationally connected syndicates who come equipped with rifles, poisons, hi-tech immobilising drugs, pangas, axes and chainsaws and a total disregard for considerations of law, ethics or morality. Against them the rhinos don't stand a chance. Sometimes they are not killed first. Sometimes the cows are pregnant or nursing a small calf. Sometimes the calf doesn't escape: its hornbed is gouged out too.

Why? Because rhino horn feeds a fantasy which lives on the other side of immense oceans. It is *not* a magical elixir for restored health and sexual vigour, yet the myth persists. And Africa, defenceless against such an insidious invader, loses its rhinos.

Africa's most abundant rhino (abundant being a relative term here) is the southern white. Once plentiful throughout the natural grasslands of Southern Africa, by the beginning of the 20th century only a 100 or so survived in KwaZulu-Natal. It got worse. The species was 30 animals away from extinction when an unprecedented effort by the then Natal Parks Board managed to turn the tide.

Black rhino too were once plentiful throughout countries like Kenya, Tanzania, Zambia, Zimbabwe, Mozambique and South Africa. In the 1950s and '60s their numbers fluctuated between 60 000 and 100 000. Those days are now long gone. Over the last 60 years the black rhino population has decreased by over 90%. On the IUCN Red Data List *Diceros bicornis bicornis,* the Southwestern black rhino and the southeastern sub species, *D. b. minor* both of which occur in South Africa, are classified as

Critically Endangered. Extinction is a real possibility. The loss of a single black rhino is one step closer to that unthinkable eventuality.

Now there was Bwana. So rare, so vulnerable. So many hopes of so many concerned people invested in the survival of that fragile little life.

ARC's Karen Trendler was taking on a challenge. In terms of rescuing wildlife, a baby black rhino was a very different matter to, for example, antelope species. In Kenya two justly famed wildlife rescuers, Daphne Sheldrick and Anna Merz, had successfully raised black rhino calves, but never from such a young age. Bwana was premature and at 21 kilograms just half the weight he should have been at full-term. His survival would be of interest to wildlife scientists and conservationists well beyond the borders of South Africa.

The Onderstepoort veterinary facility partnered with ARC in the project and two commercial firms generously came on board. One of them, Nestlé, even going as far as stopping their production line in order to manufacture the first supply of 25-kilogram buckets of fat-free milk powder needed to prepare Bwana's feeds.

Karen was already known for her work in animal rehabilitation, but Bwana's arrival would prove to be a turning point for her too. As she nursed him devotedly through his battles with diarrhoea and polyarthritis, she gained the kind of experience and exposure that resulted in ARC, in time, becoming a wildlife rescue centre of choice, also for rhino calves.

Bwana stayed at ARC for eight months. In that time I went to see him there. So did Dale Parker. Whenever he travelled up from Cape Town he made the detour to ARC and watched the boisterous little animal in his small enclosed yard from which, once a day, he was taken on a short walk into a field. Then Dale would travel on to the Waterberg and, with his henchman Clive, gaze at the expanse of wilderness – ideal free-ranging black rhino habitat – at Lapalala. Then, inevitably, their gaze narrowed: they contemplated the area around Doornleegte. Behind the house was a rocky hillside, literally covered with the kind of trees and shrubs that black rhino love to browse.

A meeting with Lapalala staff was called at Kolobe Lodge and the dilemma explained: Dale and Clive wanted to bring Bwana home, but they could only do so if someone undertook to devote him or herself entirely to his care, to rear him until he was ready to be re-wilded. There was no lack of volunteers. Such a cute little animal – of course they'll adopt him.

Did they realise that this meant 24 hours a day for however many years while his needs have to come first, always? Oh.

I sat at the back of the room. I knew that what they were talking about was, essentially, motherhood. I'd brought up two sons, I did not volunteer.

"Conita? We were just wondering..."

They had to ask more than once. But not for the first time, nor the last, there was someone who wore down my resistance. I was told to be ready on 31 March.

For every doubt that approached via the Seven Sisters en route to Lapalala that day, I had several more. Their concern was on Bwana's behalf: even a few days' guidance from Karen Trendler couldn't turn a 55-year-old untrained caretaker into anything but a death sentence for this valuable little orphan. I shared that concern and agonised about a few others which, for the press and for Karen, were off the radar. I had a family that included dependants, and my husband's professional life, which I shared, was already very full and ranged well beyond the responsibilities at Lapalala.

My own tasks at the reserve included supervision of staff. It was probably that, as much as anything else, that convinced me of the truth of that clichéd preconception about the German temperament. We like to have things *right*. Almost-right is not good enough. Perhaps we are genetically predisposed towards a love of order, and a discomfort with sloth and half-measures. I was also brought up to admire diligence and discipline, and to enjoy the rewards of hard work. When someone like that is placed in charge of people whose performance or lack thereof would directly reflect on her own performance, it is a recipe for wakeful nights.

Thank heavens for Glynis Brown. She had been Clive's secretary at EWT and had been persuaded to trade her Johannesburg office for a rustic stone and thatch building surrounded by Waterberg bush. As director of Lapalala's bush camp operation I would have been lost without her as our manager. She was immensely popular with guests for many of whom she was the first introduction not only to Lapalala, but to the Waterberg. Still, even with Glynis as my right hand, responsibility for personnel was the least favourite part of my life at Lapalala. I expected much of people, even more of myself, and now my innate urge to do my best, to have things *right*, was to have an additional focus where lack of performance would be a matter of life and death.

I feel compassion now for that poor, under-slept, anxious woman waiting with her pages and pages of research and advice, schedules and feeding charts, her kitchen turned into a hyper-hygienic feeding station with buckets of formula ingredients and outsize feeding bottles, her laundry turned into a cleaning and sterilisation unit, and her office space for record-keeping positioned in such a way that she could keep her charge under observation.

Outside, Doornleegte had also been customised. Fenced and gated sleeping quarters led into our front garden which now had a generous mud-pool, a large pile of sand and troughs for drinking and feeding. The enclosure also opened into a fenced 10-hectare area at the back of the house where, it was hoped, Bwana might in due course be introduced to his natural environment.

Around lunchtime I was on the verandah, listening to the sound for which I'd been waiting since before first light that morning. Vehicles going slowly, then speeding up a little as they reached the bottom of the rutted and rocky incline that brought them from the plateau down into the Palala valley. The easier run on fine gravel and sand. The slow-down for the sharp right onto the track winding its way through a stand of knob-thorns until the view opened up. Ahead of the visitors and to their left they'd see the floodplain's umbrella thorns. To their right: the house and the woman waiting for them.

I debated my options. I could wait on the verandah – dignified, self-possessed, unflustered by the arrival of guests, whatever their number and importance. But that might seem unwelcoming, disinterested, even timid. I could walk down and meet them at the gate. That would certainly be welcoming and show enthusiasm. It might also betray things I'd rather keep hidden: my anxiety, and my need for approval. I was annoyed with myself, a grown-up woman ruled by her insecurities.

"Come, sweetheart," Clive had appeared behind me. Together we started down the verandah steps. The first vehicle drove into sight, then another and another. Then a heavy truck, with more vehicles behind it. Hands waved to us as we, halfway between verandah and gate, strolled up to welcome them.

There were flashing cameras and plenty of goodwill. Everyone had something positive and encouraging to say. Karen Trendler looked assured, but to my eyes also concerned. She accompanied Bwana right to the gate of his enclosure. He looked so small. Robust, sturdy, highly alert. But small. A baby after all. And right there was our biggest worry. Baby rhinos attach themselves very closely and exclusively to their mothers. For Bwana, that was Karen. If he was to survive, he would have to do the most unnatural and unlikely thing: accept a new mother. Me.

THREE

Matriarchs and motherhood

ABOUT AN HOUR'S DRIVE from Lapalala is Vaalwater, a mixed blessing of a country town with which I've enjoyed a love-hate relationship for more than 30 years. Way back when we first got there this tiny commercial hub of the central Waterberg was a telling picture of the market forces operating in the district. No competition at all for the single farmer's co-op, supermarket and café, but at opposite ends of the narrow strip of gravelled main road there were two fuel stations vying for business, and two churches doing the same. A minuscule police station managed to keep the peace.

In the ensuing years Vaalwater has grown into the kind of town of which visitors, after an embarrassed hunt for something complimentary, might declare: "The people are *very* nice."

The place isn't entirely charmless, but it is the awkward charm of a gangly teenager overtaken by growth and not yet sure of direction. It sprawls in inelegant angles, its gentler contours hidden behind a utilitarian purposefulness. Vaalwater frowns and flexes commercial muscle. It doesn't aim to be pretty, it aims to be useful. Function above form.

It didn't take me long to realise that, for someone who lives in the Waterberg bush, Vaalwater was a lifeline. It was where one took things that broke (a limb, a drive-shaft, freezer, water-pump), stocked up on essentials (food, fuel, candles for power outages, first-aid supplies for smaller emergencies, whisky for bigger ones). It was where you dropped off donations for the school, the church fête, various charities; where you collected your mail, the latest news, and passengers needing a lift to neighbouring farms. It offered community – essential contact with the world beyond the bush. It was all I needed it to be and I was staunchly loyal in my support. But when I suddenly found myself with a hungry baby rhino on my hands my expectations of Vaalwater escalated.

After the excitement of Bwana's arrival the previous day, Thursday 1 April dawned and with it the realisation of the size of this animal's appetite. I stood in the kitchen and stared at my notes. Bwana required five bottle-feeds per day, seven litres at a time – 1050 litres just for his first month at Doornleegte. I counted, again, the buckets of fat-free milk powder I'd stacked ready for use. While the Nestlé sponsorship was in place our supply was assured, but it would be unrealistic to expect that to continue until he was weaned – usually at around 18 months for black rhino. What then? I was all for supporting local trade, but in my mind's eye I saw Vaalwater's supermarket shelves with, on a good day, a small stack of half-kilogram packs of milk powder. As eager to please as Vaalwater was, local wouldn't do it – I'd have to look further afield for an alternative.

Bwana didn't only need milk, he was used to consuming basins-full of fruit and vegetables. In a more urban or peri-urban environment one could draw, as Karen Trendler's Animal Rehabilitation Centre did, on plentiful leftovers from greengrocers for items like watermelon, pawpaw, apples, grapes, salads and wholewheat bread.

An almost daily there-and-back foraging drive to Vaalwater would not be sustainable, even if I could assume, which I couldn't, that the shops there would be able to supply sufficient quantities and do so on an uninterrupted basis. Bwana's nutritional needs would not be a matter of negotiation due to seasonal availability of shop-bought produce, or labour strikes, road conditions, fuel shortages or any of a number of contingencies that are the realities of life in the bush.

I walked to the back door and looked out. The spiny thickets of *sekelbos*, so pretty and oriental-looking in early summer with their fluffy yellow and pink flowers, were now laden with nutritionally rich brown bunches of curled-up seed pods. There were many other species, including horn-pod trees, the common spike thorn and wild pear. My research had told me that was black rhino browse. Bwana's mother would have taught him that that was his food.

He was a black rhino at home in black rhino country – we'll be fine. Step by step, but we'll be fine. That's what I told everyone, hoping that if I heard myself saying it often enough I'd start to believe it myself.

My lessons began as soon as Bwana's did. He learnt that I was now the source of his food and I learnt that he didn't like waiting for it. He liked his milk, he wanted lots of it and he wanted it *now*. I didn't mind as I knew that the feeding routine was the first key to him accepting me.

As soon as I could I coaxed him into the front garden, a safe and shady semi-wild environment with plenty of scope for exploration and play. He stayed very close to me, right from the beginning. Wherever I wandered he did too, but every so often he would simply stop and lean heavily against my legs. After a while I got the message. The preferred habitat for black rhinos is dense bushy terrain. A small calf follows closely on its mother's heels, for protection and so as not to get separated from her and lost in the thickets of shrubs and trees. Bwana was signalling his instinctual need for that behaviour: I was to walk in such a way that he could follow as closely as he liked in order to feel safe and comfortable. I was expected to behave as if I *was* his mother.

I stood there with the solid, well-muscled, remarkably weighty little animal almost pushing me off my feet. If anything more was needed to win me over, that was it. It was an excellent beginning. Lapalala echoed to a collective sigh of relief.

Then came the moment everyone dreaded and many of them expected. Bwana became ill. He suffered the worst diarrhoea and try as we might we could not arrest it. Day after day I watched his weight drop and his boisterous manner fade into a listless, weakened state. I consulted every expert I could reach. I didn't sleep. As mothers do under such circumstances I prayed rather a lot.

Somehow, for some reason, Bwana got better. For a while.

Karen Trendler had warned me to be on the watch for certain stress-related conditions, and perhaps that was a factor. That first severe attack of diarrhoea was followed by other similar attacks, extremely dangerous for him and intensely worrying of course for me. Wildlife vets and veterinary scientists were generous with support and advice and twice, to my intense gratitude, Karen came to Doornleegte to help me.

We were never able to identify a cause, but after taking himself almost to death's door every time, Bwana would rally and we could all breathe again.

One day, just after he'd recovered from his latest bout of illness, Bwana and I were on one of our dawdling walks around the garden. I'd climbed into a tree and was bending down the thinner branches for him to sniff, hoping that he might venture onto a first nibble. He did. Tentatively, to be sure, but it was a beginning. A baby black rhino beginning to do what black rhinos do: browse on natural vegetation.

As I sat in that tree, my hands and arms scratched by the branches I was urging closer to his inquisitive face – his pointed, prehensile upper lip lifting and twisting for the grip – I couldn't bear the thought of him getting so desperately ill again. All the regimes we'd put into place for his wellbeing had been scrutinised and vetted over and over again, but still we'd been unable to prevent recurrences of that first dreadful diarrhoea attack. Who was to say there wouldn't be any more?

I had been made aware of my shortcomings as a non-scientist, as someone who did not possess the requisite knowledge and experience to perform wildlife rescues with any kind of confidence. All true, of course. I had no argument with that. But now there were just the three of us: Bwana, Lapalala and me. We had to figure it out for ourselves.

There were many trees in our garden and I was up in them for a long time that day, encouraging Bwana to investigate each new kind of food while I tried to find some encouragement for myself. I thought I knew what I had to do, but I wasn't sure if I had the courage of my convictions. The courage born of necessity would have to do. *Mut verloren, alles verloren,* my mother used to say – without courage, you've lost already. It was the voice of dearly bought experience.

Gertrud Anna Franziska Hagens (née Schröter) was a modest but resourceful woman of enormous fortitude. She needed to be. As the brand-new bride of a Lutheran missionary sent out in the early 1900s by the Berlin Missionary Society to work in rural South Africa, she travelled with her exquisitely hand-embroidered trousseau linen to a remote part of what the white people knew as the Transvaal, and the black people as the chiefdom of King Sekhukhune. They arrived at Lobethal, the small mission station, in the middle of the night. Paraffin lantern in hand, she followed her husband through a cold rambling house. Their first furniture would need to be constructed from the packing crates of their luggage shipped from Berlin.

A year later their son was born. Their second child, a girl, died in infancy. When I came along, it was February 1938, the same month that marked the first arrival in Britain of the "Kindertransport" from Berlin – Jewish children between the ages of five and 17 who were sent from Germany, Austria and Czechoslovakia to escape the darkness that was settling over Europe. When I was two weeks old the German Army marched into Austria – the beginning of the "Anschluss". In September, when I was seven months old, four European leaders sat down in a great European city and debated the fate of ordinary people. It was the Munich Conference and

Germany's Adolf Hitler, Italy's Benito Mussolini, Britain's Neville Chamberlain and France's Edouard Deladier negotiated the ceding of Czechoslovakia's Sudetenland to Germany.

Chamberlain returned to Britain and announced that they had achieved "peace in our time". But before I was 18 months old Germany invaded Poland and Chamberlain made another speech: "I am speaking to you from the Cabinet Room at 10 Downing Street ... I have to tell you that this country is at war with Germany."

WWII. And suddenly all of that European politicking affected us on our little mission station in far-off Sekhukhuneland in Africa. My father was only a missionary, but he was a *German* missionary in a country that was to join forces with the Allies. He was sent to the internment camp at Baviaanspoort near Pretoria. While more and more of the globe got drawn into the war, my mother was left to manage, on her own now, all the responsibilities that came with mission work: family, of course – the youngest of whom was a baby, her fourth child – but also the mission's school, clinic and church; she had to keep up her community classes in midwifery, needlework, food gardening and bible study; she had to diagnose ailments and in that remote location somehow obtain medicines for them.

Fifty kilometres from the nearest shop – an Indian trading-store – she had to feed her family from her vegetable garden, her chicken coop and the few cows on the mission. When shopping became an unavoidable necessity it was by donkey-cart.

She wrote letters to her husband telling him all about us, his children growing up without their father. He was able to read the censored letters in the presence of a guard. Then the letters would be confiscated and he would rush back to his room to write down everything he could remember from the letters. Once or twice a year my mother could visit him in the internment camp. After every visit he would again write down everything he could remember of their conversation.

Those little wartime notes of his became a treasured family archive, particularly precious to me because they record parts of my life that I was too young to remember. Like my mother's recurring malaria attacks. Many years later I read, in my father's handwriting, my mother's words:

"Conita behandelt mich zo liebevoll..."

"Conita treats me so tenderly and brings me her dolls to hug and water to drink; she strokes my face and brings me cold face cloths for my feverish cheeks and asks her dear Jesus to make me better quickly, that I could sleep."

This is also how I discovered that as a toddler I would walk up to his photograph on the wall, and ask him when he is coming home, begging him to make it soon; that an eye-infection blinded me for a time, until by some miracle American missionary doctors were able to obtain antibiotics, and I got my vision back; that I had a little black friend with a white name, Regina, and that she taught me to eat black people's food: flying ants, grasshoppers, plump mopane worms roasted over an open fire.

I was to wait for that man in the photograph for five years.

In June 1944 the South African government offered the internees the option of returning home. Home was war-time Europe. Still, overwhelmingly, the internees chose to be repatriated. My mother was given a date to board a ship in Durban. She packed up her household, and after a final few minutes at the grave of her second child, left Lobethal for ever. The internees from Pretoria were transported by train and brought right up to the ship. We had no way of knowing if my father was among them. My mother gathered up her three children and boarded anyway. I am chilled when I think of the kind of desperate faith that made her do that. She got us settled and then she began to search the ship, deck by deck.

I remember waking from an exhausted sleep to see my brother and sister in the embrace of a bearded man. Older than the man in the photograph and there was the unfamiliar beard, but it was him. We were a family again.

All the world was at war. It took six months for us to arrive at our destination. First that interminable ocean voyage and then progressing from one quarantine camp to another, one bomb shelter to another, from Portugal all across Europe to Berlin. We arrived the day before Christmas. In Africa it would have been mid-summer; war-ravaged Berlin was freezing in winter snow. We had the almost unimaginable joy of a family Christmas with grandparents and Christmas decorations and treats and presents, but when the sirens sounded we had to hurry down into dark, crowded bunkers while the bombs rained down.

I contracted scarlet fever and had to be kept separate from the others. In the coal cellar I could still hear the sirens, but not the bombs any longer. There is a memory that has stayed with me far more acutely than the sirens or the bombs. It is the picture of small children being made to stand in a circle, shamed and mocked for their fear which caused them to wet themselves during the bombings. One of the children was my baby sister. I couldn't bear to see that and rushed to hold her.

The bombing raid would finish, the all-clear would sound and we'd go up into the day to see the smoke drifting over the ruined city.

The most remarkable thing was that I wasn't afraid. I felt so secure in the love and care of especially my mother during that time, that I didn't know fear. Somehow she managed that.

As Bwana and I progressed from tree to tree through the Doornleegte garden I was struck by the parallels in the lives of mother and daughter, and humbled too by how puny my challenges seemed against hers. Now her challenges were over – she had passed away the previous year taking a major part of the anchoring of my life with her. But in the immutable way of mothers and daughters some of her example must have imprinted on me. If her kind of mothering could have kept me happy and secure in the midst of the greatest war this world had had to endure, I thought, perhaps I might manage sufficient mothering skills to help a little orphaned wild animal thrive.

I also had another role model, one which, were it not for her warmth towards me, I might have found very intimidating. My mother-in-law.

Clive's father, the son of that young British soldier who'd come to Africa to fight in the Anglo-Boer War and afterwards found he couldn't leave again, had died unexpectedly when Clive was eight years old, his brother six. The family business, a construction company, waited for the young widow, just 27, to decide on the way forward. She was a dental nurse; she knew nothing about the construction business – in 1940s South Africa that kind of business was in any case almost exclusively a male preserve.

Enid Florence Walker buried her husband, walked into the offices of a company whose operation she didn't understand and informed the 40-strong all-male staff that it would be business-as-usual. She was taking over. When Clive first introduced me to her she'd been successfully running that company for 21 years. She was to do so for 40. She never expected her sons to join the business to help her, but insisted that they should have their own independent lives. Her last project before she retired as Chairman of C.A.Walker & Sons was to build a house for herself on an acre of land in a Johannesburg suburb.

I had much to live up to. However loving and accepting our mothers-in-law might be of us, we'd prefer not to fail in their eyes.

So with two matriarchs looking over my shoulder I climbed down from the last wild-pear tree, resolved on my course of action. The next day was my new beginning with Bwana. Most importantly at first, I thought, was for him to be completely assured of having me as near to him as he needed, all the time. He had to be able to trust that constancy.

I don't remember that Clive interfered with the changes I made. I do remember some odd looks and a word, "molly-coddling". But more vividly I remember the many times he joined me for a cup of tea or a sundowner in our deck chairs near Bwana's feeding area. Both of us would talk quietly to the little rhino and he'd be so totally relaxed, he'd come right up close to our faces, nudging and pushing at us to be hugged. He was remarkably vocal, squeaking and softly moo-ing his hints for whatever attention he wanted.

As with elephants, some vocalisations of adult black rhino are infra-sonic, capable of travelling considerable distances over densely vegetated terrain. Such loud audio bursts are mostly at very low frequencies – below the threshold of human hearing. Bwana's baby squeaks, though, were very audible indeed, and I learnt to squeak and moo and moan right back to him.

My records from that time chart his steady progress. Measurements, weight, strength, changes in behaviour. His health held.

Our walks soon extended well beyond the front garden. I loved taking him up the hill behind the house. Time-consuming outings, but I'd trained as a teacher – I understood the virtue of patience. I'd dawdle in front and on my heels Bwana would slowly and loudly sniff his way up the rocky slope. Black rhinos have an acute sense of smell and he needed to smell *everything*. Herbal plants were a delightful discovery and after a cautious taste he started eating them, a little bit here and there, more each day.

He was becoming familiar with the shrub and tree species that provide the natural food for Lapalala's wild black rhinos. Twice a day the field rangers, en route to and from their reserve sections, stopped by at Doornleegte with all the freshly cut browse a growing young rhino could possibly need. At first Dale was unsure about this daily harvesting, worrying that it could have a negative impact on the vegetation. But it turned out to be no problem at all, being as it was simply the provision for one more black rhino who'd have browsed in the reserve anyway, and the rangers taking due care with their pruning.

With dung from some of the wild black rhinos, we created what I hoped would be a reasonably convincing rhino midden where Bwana could smell others of his own species, and learn to use the midden himself. At first the strange smells scared him, but then instinct took over and it worked wonderfully. This was more than potty training. Black rhino are solitary animals, and their communal excretion spot serves as their communications hub. It tells them who's around – male, female, one known to them, or a stranger.

Bwana was steadily acquiring the appropriate behaviours that made our ultimate goal of releasing him into the wilderness seem possible, so I had to look ahead to fostering his independence. He would have to be weaned, not only off his supplementary milk feed but also from his foster mother. He'd have to get used to other carers and accept my absence from time to time. In the main I was helped by two allies. Slender, good-hearted Rosina Baloyi, her skin the colour of Lapalala's basalt rocks, had a sense of responsibility that sat well with my German work ethic. She lightened the treadmill burden of bottle-feeding and, more importantly, was accepted by Bwana. Titus Mamashela, a young Shangaan, was the proud possessor of a newly minted Grade 8 certificate, able to speak both English and Afrikaans in addition to his mother tongue, North-Sotho, and diligent to a fault. Whether it was cleaning Bwana's enclosures, or painstakingly measuring his water intake, or joining me in watching closely to establish his food preferences, or be on the lookout for the first sign of an abnormality in dung or change in mood, Titus was invaluable.

In addition to my extensive daily rhino-care records, I also have records of another kind. My legs are covered in scars from lacerations acquired during excursions with Bwana. We'd meander up our rocky hill and he, bold enough to explore a few metres away from me, would suddenly discover that we were not the only animals around. A grasshopper would send him on a frightened dash back to mother. Or straight back *into* mother, and mother into thorns, a rock or spiny branches. I learnt to dodge and brace myself, although this very often still meant thorns and rocks and broken branches and a fresh crop of scratches and scabs by the end of the day. We met mice and mongooses on that hill, and rabbits, a variety of small buck, the odd kudu. Sometimes Bwana's full-tilt charge stopped just short of my bruised legs, but not always.

There was the memorable day when he encountered termites. He was engaged in a deeply satisfying head-rub against a termite mound when he got what seemed to me to be the fright of his life. Hearing is a black rhino's best developed sense and the slightest little sound would always bring him to a totally alert upright stance, his large ears swivelling to focus on the direction of the sound. I could imagine what the disturbance he'd caused inside that termite mound must have sounded like to him. He took off down the hill and raced straight into his enclosure. I was close behind to reassure and comfort him, but was delighted. He didn't flee to me first – it was a step towards independence.

Virtually from the first day at Doornleegte Bwana lived up to his name, the Big Boss. Playful, naturally, as befitted his age: rolling on his sandpile with legs in the air and then jumping straight up and down on all fours as if it was all just too much fun to be able to hold still; messing around in his mud-pool, covering his entire body with rust-red mud and then, only the whites of his eyes showing, heading straight for something to rub against – his rubbing-pole, a tree, the house wall, the verandah railing, or me. Then, galvanised by a sudden burst of adrenaline, he'd race around the garden or around and around the corners of the house at an astounding speed, to the imminent danger of any human who might be passing by. It was easy to believe the often-cited statistic of a black rhino's running speed being 45 to 50 kilometres per hour.

He'd get it into his head that a log or rock needed pushing and, nose down and eyes rolling wildly, he'd manoeuvre that heavy object from one corner of the garden to the other, or down the driveway and back up again and into a shrub, and then lose his temper in a way that fully illustrated the black rhino's reputation for aggression and danger.

We didn't dare leave the back door open. The damage a determined rhino calf can do in a house has to be seen to be believed. It wasn't just the mess. Whatever he pushed, moved. If it couldn't move, it dented. If it couldn't dent, it broke.

We were doing as well as could be expected. When I had to be in Johannesburg with my two boys who were still living in our house there and both studying, Rosina and Titus could hold the fort. On occasion Glynis Brown was kind enough to take a break from the camps management office and come to Doornleegte to substitute for me. Provided I wasn't away for too long, Bwana seemed to be happy with his growing independence.

Re-wilding, though, was still some way off. With black rhino, particularly males, this has proven to be very difficult. Males compete, they fight for supremacy. And with black rhinos being the immensely powerful and dangerous animals that they are, such fights are a serious matter.

Natal Parks Board offered us another young black rhino male, a problem animal which they needed to relocate. I was not at all sure about the wisdom of putting the two males together, but the experts assured me that because they were still so young there would be no danger. I allowed them to meet on a daily basis, but it was soon clear that the problem male was going to be a problem for Bwana too. He was prepared to kill him on sight. It wasn't long before the newcomer's vicious temper necessitated a re-think. He was released into the reserve and I had a strong sense that Bwana had dodged a bullet.

FOUR
Mothlo

There is an old piece of film in our family archives: Bwana is playing in the mud, his firm, chunky little body, over-sized ears, ancient-looking young face caked with rust-red blobs and drips and smears. Small dark eyes, bright and alive. The man doing the filming is Dale Parker. Off-camera there is the odd comment or chuckle from Clive.

I treasure that little film for a number of reasons. As with one's own children, it's a pleasure to be reminded of the cute and enjoyable phases, especially if you're no longer dealing with the very much less cute realities of exhaustion and smells and illness. It also reminds me of the joint pleasure we, the Walkers and the Parkers, had in witnessing Bwana's progress, vindicating the decision to bring Lapalala's orphan back home. Vindicating also another decision of Clive's.

Back in the '80s when we first moved half our lives to Lapalala, I was reminded of my parents, half a century before, arriving at the Lobethal mission station in the middle of the night and having to make a home out of what they saw in the light of their paraffin lamps. I viewed each of my five small rooms by daylight: they were blindingly cheerful. Walls in shrill pink, blue, green and yellow teamed with linoleum floors in even louder shades of the same plus one with scarlet squares and I seem to remember another in a sort of mottled purple. We, boringly, opted for something more sedate: white walls, neutral flooring. After that, a number of trips to second-hand furniture shops in my trusty Toyota, an epic tiling session by myself and a friend which ended in an exhausted bath at sunrise, and the Doornleegte farmhouse was home.

Clive was appreciative, but wouldn't rest: life in the bush required a verandah, preferably one stretching all along the front of the house and overlooking the garden in which he had planted more than 30 trees. He was right. It became our favourite spot for meals, sundowners and meetings. A stereotypical colonial verandah it sported antelope horns, elephant and buffalo skulls, and a camelthorn rhino rubbing post from Savute in Botswana. It was an ideal vantage point too for keeping an eye on Bwana and filming him as he played a few metres away while, beyond the garden, the wilderness waited for him.

That single-reel home movie is also a record of such naïveté. Principally mine. One makes these unthinking assumptions about the horizons of your own life. You can only do so much. When your days are filled to capacity there's no room for more. You can say No.

How wrong I was.

On 10 April 1994 I was busy writing up my Bwana records when I heard the radio crackle. A field ranger was calling the reserve manager: "… in the water. Screaming its head off."

"The mother?"

"Just the baby. Not looking too good – there's a lot of blood."

"Where are you?"

"Blocklands crossing."

"Stand by."

I returned to my writing. Another Lapalala baby was in trouble; winter was approaching; it was Sunday; Clive was away in Johannesburg. Déjà-vu.

The radio crackled again. "Doornleegte, Doornleegte, come in."

The reserve manager, now on the scene himself, had determined three things: the mother was gone, the baby needed emergency rescuing, and it was extremely hungry. Could I get some milk ready? Oh, by the way, not for a rhino – it's a hippo.

There was still a small supply of Bwana's fat-free milk powder which I kept for emergencies. I had no idea if that would be appropriate for a hippo calf. As little as I had known about the rhinoceros a few years earlier, I knew even less about the hippopotamus. It lives mostly in water; it feeds on underwater vegetation; it grazes on grass when it comes out of the water at night. It's considered highly dangerous: most humans who are killed by wild animals in Africa are killed by hippos. To my embarrassment, that was about it.

Ten kilometres from Doornleegte there was a fully catered tented camp on a tributary to the Blocklands River. Rhino Camp was run by my younger son, Anton, and his wife, René. They responded to my radio call in typical fashion, Anton being a wildlife manager and René the kind of gentle-hearted person who would rescue and hand-rear baby birds fallen out of nests. They picked up my two bottles of milk en route to the rescue.

With the radio in one hand and a duvet cover in the other I walked over to the storeroom, hoping that I'd hear reassuring news that would make my just-in-case preparations unnecessary. But I stuffed straw into that duvet cover to total radio silence. Back in the house I heard that Clive was on his way back. He had in the meantime managed to get hold of Karen Trendler at the Animal Rehabilitation Centre, but no, she had not dealt with baby hippos before. A very competent lady in the Kruger National Park had though. The very competent lady's phone just rang and rang without being answered.

A couple of hours later Clive pulled in at Doornleegte. I offered tea and waited. It wasn't long. He began to hint, cautiously, that an injured baby hippo was unlikely to last the day, let alone a cold night, without the warmth and protection of its mother.

There was history behind his caution.

Along with most of its other big game species, the Waterberg, rich as it was in watercourses, had lost its hippos. Then in the early 1980s the first hippos to be re-introduced into the area were brought from Lake St Lucia in KwaZulu-Natal and released into the Palala. In Lapalala's other river, the Blocklands, there were no hippo.

One day Clive was contacted by a game dealer who was in search of blue wildebeest. He could pay in hippos. He had five of them, acquired from a Texan zoo, living in his swimming pool. Tasked as he was with the restoration of Lapalala's ecosystems, Clive contacted Dale Parker in Cape Town and suggested they do a swap: spare blue wildebeest for the pod of hippo. Expert opinions were not on his side even though the Blocklands had a fairly large dam, ideally suited to hippo, along its course. The unarguable fact was that both the Palala and the Blocklands harboured thriving populations of crocodile.

Dale thought it a risk worth taking and agreed to the swap. Now there was a badly injured baby hippo – possibly due to a crocodile attack – in the Blocklands, and Clive was waiting to hear: "Told you so."

He stirred his tea and without looking up wondered if it might not be a sensible idea to get ready to help out, "Just in case, and just for the night."

I led the way to the laundry. In the centre, like a four-poster bed, was my straw-stuffed duvet cover snugly shaped as a mattress between the four legs of the laundry table; on top of the table was the collection of lamps with which I intended to keep the room at a cosy temperature. Clive said he was happy to have married a German girl.

Anton's Land Rover drove up and we hurried down the verandah steps. An almighty noise erupted from the cab. With my hands over my ears I peered in. On René's lap squatted 20 kilograms of exhausted, hungry, bleeding and complaining hippo. René smiled: "Her name is Mothlo."

She was a heart-rending sight. Her face was scratched, her back ripped open and oozing blood. The rest of her body was covered in blood blisters – evidence of the way hippos sweat to protect themselves against sun exposure and over-heating, and of the fact that this little one had been exposed to the sun for far too many hours.

She'd had no nutrition for goodness knows how long. Despite the reserve manager's valiant attempts at feeding her with the bottles I had sent ahead she'd taken nothing. But settled into her four-poster in the laundry she greedily and messily drank as much as I felt was safe. Exhaustion overcame her and she was out for the count. That night she had more sleep than Clive and I, a few metres away. Every once in a while a grunt – of contentment, I hoped – reverberated through the walls and when, well before morning, she was ready for her next feed she made sure we knew it. While preparing her bottle I tried to pacify her with what I hoped might sound like hippo "talk". If Clive was laughing he did it in the bedroom where I couldn't hear him.

Another 24-hour-a-day job had arrived at Doornleegte. By sunrise work had begun on turning the back garden into a hippo-friendly environment. Until such time as Mothlo was ready to be introduced to the Palala, she needed a plunge pool. Even in winter the sun would be too hot for day-long exposure. She also needed to be in water to relieve her initial constipation. Hippos are born under water and are habituated to defecating in water – a behaviour which is of benefit to the river systems within which they occur.

While her pool was being excavated and cemented we made do with hosing her down at regular intervals. She took to this as readily as she did to being paraded around her new dominion in stately fashion beneath a huge black umbrella.

The kitchen was re-converted into a milk-formula feeding station. Mothlo required 15 to 20 litres per day of a much richer formula than Bwana's. To my great relief my previous supplier of fat-free milk powder could also supply 25 kilogram buckets of full-cream milk powder at a reasonable price. The full-cream milk needed to be further enriched with egg-yolk. I contributed greatly to what I'm sure was a boom-time for egg producers in the greater Vaalwater area. As a consequence of being left with all those egg-whites not needed for Mothlo's formula I discovered the limits of my husband's tolerance by serving at every possible occasion an ever-expanding range of experimental meringue recipes.

Mothlo's settling-in was surprisingly smooth. Her wounds healed and she was so sweet-natured that everyone adored her, although her astoundingly loud calls continued to frighten the unwary.

Long before she entered my life, on my first wilderness trail in the Lake St Lucia area, I'd been warned against hippo. It was late afternoon and we were canoeing to our overnight camp. We were told to keep quiet and get a move on; it was neither the time nor the place to encounter hippos either on foot or on water – not if you wanted to survive to complete your trail.

At Doornleegte I bottle-fed a member of this notorious species, her big eyes fixed on mine, tiny hairy ears moving constantly. It was difficult to reconcile the chubby, trusting little creature who so loved having her soft blubbery belly rubbed with the reality of a massive mammal, weighing between 1.5 and 3 tonnes, capable of killing people. I also didn't like knowing that, on the IUCN Red Data List, the conservation status of hippos was given as Vulnerable.

Waterberg winters have something of my childhood memories of Europe. At first light a field can shimmer and sparkle as if with snow. But it's frost coating the bleached dry-season grass and the countless spiderwebs criss-crossing and spiralling, trembling in each exhalation of crisp air. Bushes droop with dew-drips turned to icicles. Shallow ponds ice up. But overhead stretches a sky which is pure Africa: all possible shades from gold, green and red in the east to the aquamarines and blues of the kingfishers nesting along the Palala.

On such mornings the laundry door used to bear the brunt of Mothlo's impatience. But she'd have to wait while we laboured with buckets of hot water to get her pool ice-free and up to an acceptable temperature for her first plunge of the morning. Much as she had to be protected from overheating, she also had to be protected from the opposite extreme.

That pool created a lot of extra work. With Bwana doing so well after his early health crises I suppose we might have become just the slightest bit complacent about the horrors of stress-related illnesses assailing us again. We were not to remain complacent for long. It was the dreaded diarrhoea attacks again – not so severe as those suffered by Bwana, but serious enough to necessitate another round of hyper-vigilant checking and re-checking of our hygiene systems. As before, the cause didn't lie there. Nevertheless, until we were 100% sure and she had lost that heart-rending look of a helpless, sick infant, the location of her ablutions – her pool – had to be emptied out every day, thoroughly sanitised and refilled. At least the garden benefitted from the regular, copious applications of hippo-fertilised water.

Three weeks after Mothlo's arrival I had to leave Doornleegte for what I hoped would be just a few hours. It was Wednesday 27 April 1994 – election day. I was by no means a political animal, but it was important to me to make my own small gesture that day. My vote would not have made the slightest difference to the outcome of the first truly democratic election in South Africa. But this was the election that was to finally loosen the suffocating grip in which apartheid had held the destiny of all the peoples of this country. I'd been brought up to look forward to that day.

My father was born in West Africa. His family owned a chain of bookstores, and one of them was on the Gulf of Guinea, in Lomé, the capital of Togo. At that time Togo was under German rule and Lomé, with around 5000 inhabitants, the kind of place that promoted a comfortable blending of the cultures of Africa and its colonial rulers. When my father succumbed to the tropical infections rife there at the time and was sent back to Germany for treatment and for his schooling, his deep love of Africa went with him.

Fortunately Walther Hermann Renning Hagens did not rebel against life in Europe – his education continued within the family traditions of music, theatre and concerts. He excelled at his studies and, like his sisters, was a gifted and accomplished performing musician. They lived in a large beautiful house in East Berlin, the venue for some of their receptions and soirées. This was Berlin in its Weimar era – he had a life of elegance and sophistication. When it came to deciding on a profession, however, he chose Africa. He returned, not as the manager of a successful Hagens bookstore, but as a missionary in the employ of the Berlin Missionary Society. He learnt to speak Sotho, and in due course so did his children. When WWII sent him and us back to Germany, he kept on speaking Sotho to me, so I shouldn't forget the language of the people to whom we would one day return.

It was a circuitous route back.

In early 1945 all civilian radio communications in East Berlin had been blocked. But somehow disturbing news of the advancing Russian Army filtered through. One morning in early March I was told to choose a favourite toy – nothing heavy or too large to be carried in one hand. Without benefit of luggage we had to wear all the clothes we couldn't afford to leave behind. Many heavy layers that made our journey to the station hot and awkward. I remember my grandmother and great-grandmother, tears running down their cheeks and ours as everyone clung together. Suddenly the time was up, we were on a train, and through the small window I saw them waving and growing smaller. They were not to survive the cold and hunger of that bitter winter of 1945.

We'd escaped, but we were homeless refugees. We were taken in by a farming family in Oldendorf near the town of Schnega. In that period my father became the mayor of Schnega, his skill with languages – fluent in eight – being highly sought after in discussions between Europeans and Americans. I went to school for the first time. I was seven, but due to the education my parents managed to give us during the preceding war months, I was ready for the third grade.

As all parents must under such circumstances, they worked hard at keeping some semblance of normality going. The topic of discussions with their children was not the war or its legacy of suffering. They spoke about our opportunity to learn and absorb as much of Europe as we could, and of their work waiting for them in Africa.

Strange as it may seem, my memories are overwhelmingly of happy times, also when we moved to Clenze in the Hanover district, where my father was called to serve the large, spread-out church community. It was now our turn to provide shelter for refugees. Two Polish families moved in with us and I remember being taught to turn whatever meagre ingredients could be obtained with our post-war ration coupons into delicious Polish dishes. My parents, tending to post-war trauma and dysfunction in homes and schools, must have had a much less enjoyable time of it. Through the wet summers and icy winters my father cycled on his rounds from one small village to the next and on to the next. After two years, exhausted and suffering from debilitating asthma attacks, he requested a transfer back to Africa.

There was a last farewell. We travelled to Stuttgart to meet again the only other members of our extended family to have survived the war. When we fled Berlin my two younger aunts, both with fiancés on the battle front, had stayed behind to take care as best they could of their mother and grandmother. In Stuttgart I heard the stories of the family members we had lost, of the fiancé who had died in action, and of the terrible fear of the approaching Red Army that had caused the two young women to also flee, just in time.

I don't remember that my aunts tried to persuade my parents to remain in Europe, or that my parents tried to motivate them to accompany us to Africa. While the war undoubtedly strengthened such bonds of blood or friendship as had survived, perhaps it also resulted in a kind of acceptance of the impermanent nature of things – nothing is guaranteed, least of all life itself. Loved ones leave. The opportunity to live as fully as possible is not infinite. Do everything you can while you can. Perhaps that is something that went way down deep for a young girl and has remained into adulthood. What may now appear to outsiders to be a grownup's responsible sense of doing her duty may in large part simply be the response of that child who had learnt very early on that every day counts and that, at the end, there would have been too few of them.

That year drew to its close with another wrenching goodbye,

another long ocean voyage, another arrival on the shores of another continent, and then it was Christmas 1949. We were back in Africa.

It was not to be a resumption of the life we had had before the war. From the mission station at Heidelberg near Johannesburg I entered a world I did not know. Boarding school, the language of the Afrikaans people, the kindness of their children who shared their food and treats with us newcomers who, after the privations of life in Germany during and after the war, were unused to and unprepared for such largesse. I saved up half of all their gifts to take back to the mission station for my little sister.

There were surprises for my parents too. On Christmas Eve 1951 my father and a black lay preacher were sharing a communion service in our mission church. They were not allowed to complete the service. A group of black people stormed into the church and amidst the shocked and screaming congregation dragged my father from the pulpit and the lay preacher from the altar, and made their displeasure at white and black sharing their devotions absolutely clear. I learnt that these angry, violent people were called activists, and that their cause – though one might disagree with the way they fought for it – was a just one.

The Nationalist government that had unseated South Africa's war-time president, General Jan Smuts, in 1948, implemented a system of what they called "Separate Development" to the advantage of white people and the considerable disadvantage of all others. Apartheid. If you did not have a white skin, you did not have the vote and your rights – socially, economically, legally – were determined by those who did have white skins.

That church service in 1951 registered, as on a seismograph, the escalating stirrings of black anger at the oppression of the majority of South Africans by the minority. My father, and by extension his family, had once again been drawn into someone else's war.

His next posting was further north, in the land of the legendary Rain Queen, Modjadji, the matrilineal ruler of the Lobedu people. It was amusing to me that the little house a Lutheran minister was allocated as a base from which to befriend and serve both black and white – to do God's work – was in the tiny village of Duiwelskloof (Devil's Gorge).

My father's linguistic abilities, which had served him so well in Lobethal in Sekhukhuneland and in northern Germany, now smoothed his way with Modjadji and they got on very well. It was no surprise at all to our family that they should have developed a mutually respectful friendship which allowed them to share so much of their very different cultures. His work among lesser mortals, both black and white – Sesotho, German, Afrikaans and English – also prospered. His children grew up accepting the ease with which he moved among cultures as normal. We were expected to do the same. It was normal too, but less easy to accept, being sent off to boarding school.

I wonder now about the distress my parents might have hidden from us as they said goodbye. Wartime had cemented such a close bond, it must have been as difficult for them as it was for me. I now recall not just the encouraging words and little moral precepts my father tried to instil in me as we prepared to leave, I remember also the way he said it. A man who had already experienced so much, looking into the eyes of his daughter who had yet to meet her own allocation of life lessons. The words were the good and sensible wisdoms that all parents try to impart to their children at such times. As a parent myself now I understand that behind the words there was more.

I didn't enjoy school. I don't recall that I excelled particularly at anything. But I was a trier. Whatever was on offer in addition to the academic studies, I was there on the starting line. Athletics, basketball, drama, music, religious studies. The report cards I took back to Duiwelskloof paint the picture of an earnest child, gamely trying her best: I was praised for full attendance and diligence.

During mid-term breaks my report cards were of far less interest to me than what was going on at the mission station. In addition to their normal work, my parents provided a home base for young German missionaries who were sent there for a year's study of the Sotho language and culture. My father revelled in this work. The big enclosed verandah became the venue for the most interesting debates, especially some years later when he was asked to oversee the translation of the Bible into North-Sotho. For a child those gatherings were a multi-lingual, multi-coloured, multi-cultural feast.

The much-vaunted Rainbow Nation of later years already existed right there in Duiwelskloof, among the teacups and my mother's hand-embroidered trousseau-linen. But not in many other places. I certainly didn't see much of it at school, or out of it. Age-old resentments and entitlements were fracturing South Africa along the fault-lines of race: black against white, white against black. With every passing year the country moved closer to what seemed like the inevitable outcome of so much fear and hatred: civil war. In 1980, sadly, that was the image of South Africa that my father took to his grave.

When Clive and I first came to the Waterberg, racial tensions and the government's strategies for dealing with them came uncomfortably close. The fact that Clive was taking black as well as white children into a wilderness area, they said, ostensibly to teach them about the natural environment, had to mean just one thing: he was collaborating with the Black Resistance. The wilderness school had to be a cover for his activities as a spy or an arms smuggler or something else equally treasonous.

I got upset. Clive didn't. The hounding and interrogation by the security police meant as little to him as the unwelcoming attitude of some Waterberg neighbours for whom he was "that damned Englishman". Those neighbours have long since become close friends and allies, and on that Wednesday 27 April 1994, as I drove out through the gates of the reserve, it was the turn of the South African nation as a whole to change course.

At every polling station voters lined up in the longest, happiest, most optimistic queues this country had ever seen. More than the length of the queues, it is the degree of hope that has stayed with me. It was a new beginning. We honestly believed, I think, all of us, that the dark days of personal lives mangled in the machinery of politics would be behind us.

In 1994, however, it *was* the actual length of the queue at the polling station that was uppermost in my mind. I wrestled with a mathematical calculation: so many minutes per person filing to and through the Vaalwater school hall, multiplied by so many people still waiting to get to the front. Whichever way I tried it, it didn't come out at anything that would appease a hungry baby animal waiting for her foster mother 80 kilometres away.

There was a shout and a message was relayed along the queue: Mrs Walker was wanted on the phone. It was Clive. Something was wrong with Mothlo. She seemed weak and listless and was staggering and falling around in the heat of the day. She hadn't eaten. She was obviously dehydrated but refused to take her water or milk and if anyone tried to approach closely enough to hose her down, her distress would instantly become aggressive.

A dear, compassionate woman who'd probably been in that voting queue since much earlier that morning and was now virtually at the front, pulled me in. I cast my vote and rushed off.

Clive was waiting in the driveway. He had no patience with my desire to first change into work clothes, but hurried me up to the enclosures where Rosina was waiting. She held out Mothlo's bottles, and then gestured to everyone else to back away.

Mothlo struggled to get up. I was appalled at the drastic change in the happy, healthy animal I had said goodbye to just a few hours earlier. I knelt down. As I put my arms around her chubby neck she managed a weak grunt. She snuggled up against me, the one person she trusted absolutely. While I whispered and grunted my version of hippo language close to her face, she took her bottle of water and then her bottle of milk and allowed herself to be gentled into a more comfortable state.

There was no mystery to her behaviour. She'd bonded to me as her mother. In order to survive, that was exactly what she had had to do initially. But it was clear that we'd have to begin immediately to teach her to accept, as Bwana did, my assistants as surrogates. This was the moment for Fred.

Fred Baloyi was Rosina's husband, considerably older than his wife and also of a very different calibre. They both lived in the staff quarters at Doornleegte, but on his off-days Fred would disappear to Sun City. In the Pilanesberg in Gauteng Province there is a famous pleasure resort, a playground for gamblers and glitterati, named Sun City. This was not the one patronised by our Fred. Lapalala's version, although it promised pleasures which were no less addictive than gambling and strip-shows, was merely the staff compound up on the plateau, named for the fact that the morning sun struck that area before it reached the old compound (Dark City) down in the Palala valley.

One Sunday afternoon Fred was cycling home from Sun City with a blood-alcohol level which must have been off the charts. This was not all that unusual, Fred being extremely partial to Sun City's potent home-brewed beer. On this occasion though it ended badly.

When the rangers returned from their weekend leave they found Fred lying halfway down the very steep descent into the valley. His bicycle was gone – it was later discovered in the ravine next to the road. Fred had gone head-first into rock-hard gravel. He had evidently been unconscious for some time. He was rushed to the nearest hospital, Modimolle (then Nylstroom), 120 kilometres away. It was two months before he could return to Doornleegte and it was clear that many responsibilities would now be beyond his capacity.

Fred helped out in the garden and with Bwana, but it was with Mothlo that he came into his own. She needed a fair amount of patient persuading, but once she understood that I wasn't abandoning her, she found in Fred an indulgent companion. His leisurely gait – as much an indication of his temperament as his age – allowed the two of them to stay comfortably close, promenading under their outsize umbrella or enjoying Fred's smoke breaks. These he would take in the shade under a tree or our garden umbrella, while Mothlo joined in the mood with her head on his outstretched legs.

This suited her perfectly. Hippo calves stay close to their mothers. In the water they maintain bodily contact by lying on the mother's ample back or floating against her belly. Mothlo, programmed for such closeness, made sure that she stayed with Fred when he took care of his only other responsibility, pumping the water. No matter how tired or sleepy she was, she would follow on his heels: 100 metres to the pump, 100 metres back. And then both of them would again retire to the shade for a well-deserved rest.

In Mothlo's case, as in Bwana's, human foster parents could only be a temporary solution. I'd heard enough cautionary tales of hand-reared wild animals, including hippo, who start out cute and grow up to become not only a nuisance but a danger, with tragic outcomes for all concerned. I was determined to begin preparing her for re-wilding as soon as possible.

FIVE

Palala

THE DOORNLEEGTE FLOODPLAIN was always a good place to spot game. Impala, zebra, blue wildebeest, kudu, duiker, nyala, warthog, giraffe, vervet monkeys and on 1 September 1994, hippo. One small baby hippo. One small recalcitrant baby hippo.

"Get in," I said. "Go on, it's water. You like water. So get in."

I cajoled, I pleaded, I commanded. The rock pool was mere inches away but it might as well have been kilometres for all the interest Mothlo had in it. I tried pushing. She was as solid and immovable as the black rock on which we were standing. I leant down and with rapidly chilling hands scooped water over her, informing her that she liked it and would like it even better if she were to get in.

She was having none of it. She'd been happy to join me on the stroll from her enclosure up at the house. She'd paid perfunctory attention to everything over which I enthused – the glossy starlings, the little family of wattled plovers, the flock of blue waxbills, dung beetles working their way through the ample supply of animal droppings. My joyful exclamations at arriving at the river caused her to look at me, not the river. The pool with its smooth rocky sides that so delighted me got a blank, uncomprehending stare.

Lead by example. I got in. I splashed and shivered and yodelled, and submerged as much of myself as I could bear to in the frigid water. It was only when she noticed that I was getting a bit further away from her than she liked that she took the plunge. Figuratively speaking, that is – it was by no means an enthusiastic leap into the unknown. She loved her pool at Doornleegte, but didn't seem to make the connection until the moment her whole fat little body was actually *in* the water, and then suddenly, instantly, she was a hippo in her natural environment. She dived and bobbed and rolled, disappeared here and popped up there, bumped and sprayed at me and then it was head-first down and out of sight again to appear a few seconds later on my other side.

I laughed and cried and hugged her in that freezing Palala.

As I sat, teeth chattering, drying off on the shiny black rocks, I did what all mothers do: I dreamt ahead. When my eldest son tried to turn the pages of a book when he was barely six months old, it seemed to me that his nature and gifts would one day take him in an academic direction. That is exactly what happened. My younger son seemed to have an engineering bent. He would sit with the disassembled parts of a toy and with the utmost patience and concentration put the whole thing together perfectly. Twenty-five to 30 years later, he was a wildlife manager, working to understand and fix the parts of disassembled, broken ecosystems.

In Mothlo's behaviour that day I could so easily see the potential for her life as a free wild animal, something I desperately wanted for both my orphans. Bwana was already exhibiting the behaviours he'd need as a re-wilded black rhino living as he was meant to among Lapalala's rocks and thickets. Mothlo could be accepted by a resident pod and live out her days in the waters and on the banks of the Palala.

It would most likely be the Palala, I thought, rather than the Blocklands where she was born, given the location of Doornleegte. Her re-introduction would start right here – the rock pool was ideal.

Close enough to the house, secluded enough although it meant a scramble through dense riverine vegetation to get there, and safe enough surrounded by its high, water-smoothed rock walls. When she was ready, she'd venture further up- or downstream, where there were plenty of other pools to explore. Protected within the Lapalala Wilderness Reserve there were 88 kilometres of this river.

The Palala gets its name from "Lephalale", the North-Sotho word for "barrier". It's an apt name. Its meandering course, incised deep into the Palala Plateau, created access challenges for pioneers and sculpted a dramatic landscape. There are dark gorges, hemmed in by sandstone cliffs with overhangs where indigenous peoples sheltered and left their paintings – elephant, rhino, red hartebeest, shamanic trance states and finally the covered wagons of the next wave of Waterberg inhabitants. There are white-water rapids through broken basalt sheets and boulders with exposed conglomerate layers. There are wide, placid stretches, secluded pools covered in waterlilies, sandy beaches where crocodiles lie basking in the sun.

Dale Parker used to tell Clive that the river had to be their most important focus and he was proven right. Today, almost unique in Southern Africa, the Palala's waters are pure. It shelters 34 species of indigenous fish, two of them endangered. In its riverine vegetation – an ecosystem which is itself rare and endangered – you'll find a dazzling collection of wildlife that includes a veritable Red Data showcase: African python, narina trogon, little bittern, pygmy goose, bat-hawk, white-breasted cuckoo-shrike, African finfoot, pennant-winged nightjar, white-backed night heron.

And we so nearly lost it all. Right at the beginning, in Lapalala's infancy, a threat had been stewing all around us without us being any the wiser until one day Clive was called on the radio. A helicopter had landed at the reserve entrance gates. On board was a delegation from the Department of Water Affairs. They were conducting investigations in connection with a proposed dam site. As a courtesy they were requesting access in order to examine the upper reaches of the Palala. It was a red flag in front of a very annoyed bull – Clive flatly refused.

It was 1983. Lapalala was as yet barely more than a cosseted dream shared by Dale and Clive. It consisted of only the first two farms. Our wilderness school was also still no more than an intention. Clive had hardly begun with the long process of natural restoration in which he believed so passionately, and now there was a bunch of officious civil servants wanting to ruin it all. He phoned Dale, got the expected echo of his own outrage, and set about investigating the matter – Know Thine Enemy. The first thing he discovered was that he had already broken the law by refusing to allow the Water Affairs investigation. I got a fright. This was the Nationalist government – I didn't want my husband to land in their cross-hairs. But Clive was spoiling for a fight, because the second thing he had discovered was the planned location of "that damned dam". The western wall would be on Landmanslust, the second half, with Dubbelwater being the first, of Lapalala. Clive had motivated the purchase of Landmanslust to Dale because of the biodiverse integrity of that tract of land. It was pristine wilderness. He referred to it as "the Empty Quarter". Put a dam there and it was all over.

They needed a strategy beyond obdurate resistance. The planned eastern wall of the dam would be on Moerdyk, a farm on the opposite side of the river. Dale wanted to know who owned it, but without Clive letting on who was showing an interest. The moment a potential seller discovered that the enquiry came from a wealthy businessman the price was guaranteed to skyrocket. Clive contacted the owner, Isabel Vorster. She was not averse to the idea of selling her land, but she was not going to give it away. She rejected Dale's offer to purchase. A strategic pause, and a second offer was on the table. Rejected. Clive was biting his nails because as far as the opposition was concerned, the clock was ticking. The opposition was not only Water Affairs, they were backed by the surrounding Waterberg farmers. But not for nothing had Clive been a game ranger – he knew a *spoor* when he saw one. He followed it through rumours and gossip, old correspondence and newspaper cuttings, and his suspicions were confirmed. This push for a dam in the area was not new. Every time a national election loomed and the ruling party wanted to make sure of the Waterberg vote, they resurrected the promise of a dam to serve the Waterberg's agricultural and community needs. The farmers were all for it and not thrilled to find Clive in their way. He was threatened with civil action. I was in a complete state by this time and preached caution, but without any hope of being attended to since Dale and Clive had stated quite openly that the dam-builders would first have to bury them both in concrete before they'd give up the fight.

They weren't joking. There was one dreadful day when I was sure Clive would get himself arrested. In a militant mood he drove to Pretoria, confronted the Deputy-Director of Water Affairs in his office and informed him that he had a fight on his hands. It would be a fight in the courts and in the media. Especially in the media since, as the director of the Endangered Wildlife Trust, he intended to hold up to public scrutiny this unconscionable plan to destroy a sensitive natural area in order to make political gain out of the construction of what was nothing more than an "election dam".

Instead of calling the police, the Deputy Director actually listened, Clive said, because he was reluctant to risk the bad publicity. Besides, he knew he was on shaky ground. That Moerdyk site had not had an ecological survey done, or an environmental impact assessment. It was, moreover, only one of five possible sites for the dam, and not the most appropriate one to serve the needs of the community most in need of the water. This plan had neither science nor sense behind it.

The saga dragged on for the two years it took for a full ecological survey to be conducted by the University of Cape Town. The people tasked with the survey were accommodated in our bush camps. They held our fate in their hands, which put me on the defensive, but they *were* my guests. So I welcomed them and helped whenever I could. In any case they were not the villains of the piece, they were just there to do their job. But their presence in Lapalala taught me to be wary of the power wielded by scientists and other consultants. The word of such experts, backed by their degrees and sometimes obscure fields of specialisation which impress us ordinary people perhaps more than it should, can make or break. They can work *for* truth, if they're good and worthy of one's respect as most of them are, but they can also work *against* truth, if they're swayed by anything other than their scientific integrity or by something as ordinary and deadly as incompetence, laziness or graft.

Fortunately the UCT scientists were not of the latter breed and indeed, as it turned out, they were on the side of the angels. The Moerdyk site was *not* deemed the most suitable. The science backed what common sense had predicted years before: a dam sited in the lowlands beyond the northern edge of the Waterberg where a homeland community was desperately in need of just such an intervention.

When it was all over Dale had added the Moerdyk farm to the rest of Lapalala. Clive was standing amidst heaps of farming debris on the site that was eventually to become the Lapalala Wilderness School. And, to Dale's immense satisfaction, the Palala was left to run free.

So today it is still a living river. On sun-baked rocks you'll see skinks with green throats and electric blue tails, or striped backs and tails the colour of a Bombay curry. There'll be delicate flutterings of some of the area's 128 species of butterfly settling and lifting and settling again on damp sand or muddy patches. In the fine washed gravel of a mid-stream bank you'll see the water slowly seeping into fresh spoor – rhino or eland or buffalo. You'll see a reed swaying and dipping under the weight of a tightly packed row of swallow-tailed bee-eaters; in an earthen bank above the waterline, the nesting-holes of southern carmine bee-eaters. When high summer draws its migrants to the Waterberg, there'll be the iridescent purple flashes of plum-coloured starlings in the reedbed where the Blocklands joins with the Palala. And everywhere, wherever there is access to the water, you'll see *spoor*. The hoof prints, paw prints, claw, foot- and handprints of the countless lives that depend on the Palala.

I wanted that to be Mothlo's world. She'd be an adult, close to five metres in length and 1.5 metres high at the shoulder; perhaps with offspring of her own, diving and tumbling in the river as she was doing on that first morning of her first September, when at first I struggled to get her in and then struggled a good deal more to get her out.

"Time to go," I said brightly. She didn't agree. I begged, I ordered, I used sign language. She ignored me. I threatened to leave without her – she sank below the surface. I walked away – she called my bluff. Every time I was almost out of her sight and looked back over my shoulder, she was unconcernedly drifting, awaiting my guaranteed return. But when I really did disappear from her view, she hastily scrambled out, crashed through the vegetation to the chattering alarm of vervet monkeys, and trotted after me.

On the way back over the floodplain I became aware of the light changing, dulling to that eerie, leaden purple which was as much a visceral sense as it was a visual one. I looked up: smoke. It was that time of year. Soon after we came to the Waterberg I learnt to dread it.

We're told that the year has four seasons, of more or less equal duration. In Lapalala my year split into more seasons of varying duration, and not according to the Gregorian calendar which puts our annual beginning in January.

For me it began in October if it was a good year or as late as December if it wasn't – the rainy season. The Doornleegte floodplain turned green, braided with tracks of slick, sticky red mud. A sky that earlier promised nothing but blinding heat could, with a swiftness which never ceased to amaze me, deliver a terrific thunderstorm that lashed the trees and the animals hunkered down below them with driving, punishing rain. Within hours it would be gone, the valley again sweltering under a hot blue sky. Or there'd be a steady brooding build-up over days until a deafening release, with lightning that knocked out our communications and electricity. En route to check on bush camps I'd stop to watch the sodden grass fields with blue wildebeest or buffalo, hunched and darkly glistening, lowered heads turned to the storm.

There was a different rain too. A gentle sifting down, a tender green muting of the world. I can hear it now: dripping, dripping under the quiet trees.

The Palala would run faster and louder and I'd be preparing for as German a family Christmas as I could manage in the heat. We'd warn children and workers to watch out for snakes – at least 30 different kinds in Lapalala, from the harmless yellow-bellied sandsnake to the justifiably feared black mamba.

In a really good rainy season the rivers would flood like the year Clive, on a tractor tyre's inner-tube, took our younger son through the raging gorges of the Palala, running the gauntlet of oversized, hungry crocodiles. I made him swear to never ever do that again, not if he wanted the mother of his children to survive to old age, or to allow him to do so.

Then would come Doornleegte's main flowering season: the umbrella thorns now pale ivory mounds and the air heavy, sweet and yeasty, vibrating with the sound of bees.

After the rains: roadworks to repair flood damage to bridges and gravel access roads. The swallows would swarm and gather before leaving us. At the confluence of the Blocklands and the Palala the plum-coloured starlings would be gone from the reedbed, having begun their trek north to Zambia or Angola or even further to Sudan and Ethiopia. Around Doornleegte there'd be loud snorts and grunts and clashing of horns: the rutting season for impala, kudu and blue wildebeest.

As the days cooled down and trees lost their foliage it would be the time for game counts and game capture. Peak hunting season in the Waterberg. Vaalwater would be abuzz with talk of rifles and scopes and trophies, and I would drive back home wanting to escape not only their voices, but also my own, arguing over and over again the pros and cons of hunting, its role in conservation, its moral position, and arriving as usual at no other conclusion than that it felt like a season for vultures.

June-July would be dry, the veld crisp, thorny and scratchy. Flaming on rock-shelves and ridges there'd be flowering aloes. Unless a cold spell blew a clammy grey cloud-cover up from the Cape, far south of us, our chilly early mornings would warm up to the kind of mellow day that required coffee and the putting up of feet on a verandah. Rare moments of relaxation given Clive's temperament and responsibilities, unless Dale Parker was also on the verandah and then they'd be plotting. It was the season for game auctions, for "just going to have a look…".

Apart from the prevailing easterly breeze, hardly disturbing us down in the Palala valley, the days would be still. But come August there'd be a restlessness in the air. A dusty, gritty wind grabbing at your shirt and your temper and ushering in my least favourite time of the year, the burning season.

Whereas in areas like the Orange Free State farmers set fire to their stubbled wheat- or cornfields, or to bleached grasslands in order to encourage a new season's grazing, in the Waterberg they don't. Nevertheless, fires do occur. A lightning strike could spark a flame which in no time at all becomes a conflagration. It could be an accident: a barbecue fire which goes out of control. It could be arson: fires deliberately set for no other reason than to cause destruction. They're hot, fast fires. With a strong wind behind them, especially later in the season when the wind itself becomes hot, they're extremely dangerous. A fire raging out of control, devastating farmland and bush country, threatening lives, leaving charred carcasses and maimed animals in its wake is a terrible thing to experience. At the first sign of trouble therefore the alert goes out and everyone rallies around. Unless contained, your neighbour's fire is your problem too.

On that September morning on the way back from the river, Mothlo trailing at my heels, I was concerned about the dirty-brown stain bleeding into the sky. Fortunately it wasn't a particularly windy day and the source seemed to be outside of the reserve, but I hoped someone was watching. Such fires do not stop for fences. All over Lapalala there'd be heavily pregnant impala ewes, like the ones watching us, without alarm, as we strolled past. Their peak lambing season would begin soon, in October, just after the first rains which is the real beginning, I always think, of Lapalala's natural calendar.

As it happened the next crisis to hit was not a fire and it didn't come from outside. It began at my home. Perhaps even on the verandah, that pre-eminent place for plans and plotting. I was away, dealing with business and family in Johannesburg. So I don't know who said what first to whom, but given the pecking order of the reserve's management, the reserve manager sits where X Marks The Spot. In his defence, though, it appeared that he had had the support of the top brass, Dale Parker and Clive Walker. I can imagine that the decision that it would be best *not* to tell Conita had been unanimous.

I returned to Doornleegte to find that Bwana was gone. His enclosure was just the way it was when I left except that the gate was open. No, he hadn't been taken away because he was sick. He was fine. Where is he then? Out there, in the reserve somewhere. No, he didn't break out, the gate was left open. He walked out by himself. He is now a black rhino roaming free in the wilderness as he's supposed to. There we are, see? Re-wilded. Done.

Gradually, more emerged. On his first exploratory ramble Bwana set off south-east down the Palala valley until many kilometres away he happened upon the airstrip. A light aircraft was parked there. According to the evidence, he made vigorous use of its nose as a rubbing post, and then proceeded to push the now badly scratched and dented plane around in a 360-degree circle. When the fascination of that novel exercise wore off he found an electricity junction box which he demolished, by some miracle avoiding electrocution. His trail of everything that he encountered for the first time and had to investigate eventually led to a bush camp where visitors were staying in tents. By the grace of God they remained calm and after he'd nosed around through the camp as much as he wanted, he ambled off without injuring anyone. Or killing anyone, which, given the fact that this was a well-grown black rhino bull, might have been a very likely outcome.

I listened to the prepared speech in defence of the Lapalala males' formula for re-wilding a dangerous animal: Instant, one-step like a new patent bleach or floor-polish, or quick-mix batter for microwaved cakes. Then I heard that word again: "molly-coddling". With that I understood the Why of what they did. They thought I was on the wrong path with Bwana: too soft, too cautious, too much mothering. It was an animal after all, not a child. A wild animal, not a pet. It was time for a man's hand.

They made a good case. No harm seemed to have befallen Bwana or anyone else; most early mornings he'd return to Doornleegte and once lured into a corner of his enclosure with the aid of game-feed pellets and lucerne, he'd allow the gate to be locked again. When the gate was re-opened he'd set off, sniffing and nibbling, and disappear among the trees.

Perhaps they were right, I thought, we certainly had reason to be hopeful. I admired their ability to take tough decisions. I envied their confidence. All my concerns about re-introducing a black rhino bull into the wild would be answered by that one bold step that they were strong enough to take.

The first signs of trouble weren't long in coming. The fenced perimeter of Bwana's enclosure now marked an ineffectual boundary between him and the freedom he'd tasted. It was an equally ineffectual boundary between him and any free-roaming wild black rhino bulls who might have picked up his scent and tracked him as a rival. They could break in as easily as he could and did break out, again and again.

One night I was woken up by loud barking noises and the sound of heavy objects clashing. I rushed to the back door. It was a moonlit night and I could see all too clearly as, 20 metres away, my worst nightmare played out. Bwana was on the receiving end of a furious attack by another black rhino bull. I managed to get onto a high post of his enclosure, but there was nothing I could do except watch in horror as heads and horns smashed together. Then they were crashing through bushes, rocks rolling down the slope as they charged up the hill and disappeared from sight. The sounds of the chase grew faint and then it was quiet. I stayed there and waited for a long time. Bwana didn't return.

Soon after daybreak I contacted the reserve manager; he sent field rangers to help with the search. Perhaps I was being German again, but I would not accept their giving up. Dead or alive, he had to be *somewhere*. Eventually they found him, collapsed at the bottom of a ditch. He was alive, but injured. Their calls and prodding elicited no response. There was no way on earth they could get him out of that ditch; exhausted and in pain as he was he'd have to do it himself. They resorted to provoking him, trying to make him angry. It took a long time, but finally they managed to goad him into struggling to his feet and dragging himself out of the ditch.

It was a slow, dejected little procession that returned to his enclosure: Bwana limping behind his keeper, young Titus, and around them the field rangers who had found him. I stayed with him for the rest of the day, feeding him game pellets and bits of his favourite browse. Pain-killers seemed to give him some relief. There was no remedy for what I was feeling.

The men got busy with constructing a 20-hectare fenced area behind the house – a protective zone between Bwana and the wild black rhino bulls. As far as I was concerned the labour and expense of driving strong wooden poles into rocky terrain was justified.

Shortly after that I had to go to Johannesburg again, partly in order to obtain medication with which to relieve the muscle spasms from which Bwana was suffering. That night Clive phoned from Lapalala and urged me to come home as soon as possible. He'd been watching over Bwana for hours. I listened as he described to me, who already knew it so well, how it felt to sit helplessly by while an animal, too ill or in too much pain to be able to move, just lay there moaning softly. All I could advise was to stay close to Bwana and try to entice him to drink a bottle of his long-forgotten milk formula.

As I put down the phone I knew and I'm sure so did Clive, keeping his vigil at Doornleegte, that our life with Bwana had arrived at a crossroads.

SIX

The hopeful species

THE NEXT MORNING, less than two hours out of smog-choked Johannesburg, I crossed a river and was immediately surrounded by settler history. Legend has it that in the mid-19th century a group of Voortrekker believers, the Jerusalem Trekkers, on their quest to find the Holy Land, came across this water-course in the wasteland. Perhaps it had been summer and the river swollen with floodwaters, for when they consulted the maps in the back of their Bibles it seemed possible that the river (north-flowing at that point) could be the Nile. The previous few days, en route to this riverbank, they'd watched a striking landmark slowly passing on their right as their ox-wagons pulled north – was it a high cliff-crowned hill, or a ruined pyramid? The trek from the Cape had been so hard and so long, the possibility that they had at long last reached the neighbourhood, as it were, of their destination – the Holy Land – seemed reasonable. They forded their Nile (Nyl) River, found good grazing, outspanned to rest for a while, and stayed. It became a settlement, Nylstroom. From miles around pioneer settlers came to trade, and to worship at the monthly Nachtmaal. Their large silver-roofed church, in gracious Cape Gothic style, is a national monument now, Africa's earliest Dutch Reformed Church to have been built north of Pretoria.

Exactly like the first time I saw it from the passenger seat in Clive's little Volkswagen Beetle, way back in the 1960s, the steeple glinted up ahead as, just after sunrise, I drove into the quiet town. Garages were open for business, but not much else. With my flask of breakfast tea and the worries that had kept me up half the night I sat down to while away the time until the banks opened. The sun lifted above the trees and I watched as it lit, one after the other, the graves of 544 women and children who had died in the Nylstroom concentration camp. I wondered if anyone, apart from Anglo-Boer War historians, still visited this place. How many people came searching down these rows of simple stone-packed rectangles with their numbered markers? There were few headstones. Most just had the small green metal plate with its white number. 23, 47, 284 ... Were there still family members who bothered to cross-reference number and name in a file in an office somewhere, and then came here because they remembered the stories that had passed down from generation to generation and now to them?

There are fewer and fewer people who remember, or want to. It's the way of much of the modern world. It's not the way of Africa though. Kranskop, that "ruined pyramid" of the Jerusalem Trekkers, had already been known long before to generations of Tswana speakers as Modimo o lle – "the forefather's spirit has eaten". There they offered food to the ancestors, and cast their enemies off the cliffs to plunge to their death at the foot of Kranskop/Modimolle.

In 2002, by government decree, Nylstroom would officially become Modimolle, in honour of this ancient tradition of remembering and honouring one's forefathers.

It was still Nylstroom, though, on the morning when I walked away from the concentration camp cemetery strangely comforted by its atmosphere of ... I didn't quite know what. Other lives, other crises greater than mine, perhaps. Or maybe the stillness was enough, the sounds of the waking town and distant traffic more remote than the sense of repose around me. I'd visited other such graves with Clive – he could never understand why some people thought it a morbid occupation. Together we'd searched out settler graves, both black and white, on farms in the Melkrivier area and those of British pioneers in the grounds of the beautiful sandstone church of St John the Baptist at 24 Rivers. We visited Voortrekker graves at Moorddrift and wartime graves in KwaZulu-Natal. We revisited others I'd first seen as a missionary's teenage daughter in the tribal lands of Queen Modjadji.

En route back to my bakkie I walked past a memorial, erected by the M.O.T.H.S., to honour Nylstroom's fallen soldiers. On the plaque I read: "When you go home, tell them of us and say, for your tomorrow we gave our today." Not so very different from the Tswana injunction to honour the ancestors.

I dealt with the bank and set off for home, my mind still on that wartime memorial. The regrets of war, the hopes of war. Why did millions of people go into combat, to frontlines and into trenches and to death, if not for some hope? They fight and sacrifice for some outcome which they may not see themselves, but which they nevertheless rate higher than their comfort and safety, even their lives. While the battle rages, and victory is yet uncertain, the hope itself has to serve as reward.

Of course it isn't only when we go to war that we discover our capacity, and need, for hope. We're born hoping. No child needs to be taught to hope – it's who we are, the hopeful species. More than 60 years earlier I toddled around the Lobethal mission station and discovered the world through that optimistic lens. Never a doubt that promises would be kept and that hopes would deliver. Never a doubt that a need would be met, an illness healed, a family split by the war reunited. My parents spoke of Faith. I was far too young to fully understand or examine for myself matters of religion, but I grew up trusting life in this, that one doesn't hope in vain.

As a child during WWII I saw it all around me. Even when our horizons were limited to survival of that day, that hour or that minute, there was the stubborn flicker of hope to cling to. I felt the dark bomb shelter shuddering under the impact of bombs mercilessly aimed at destroying what remained of Berlin and us with it, but I was held close and told: "*Du brauchst keine Angst haben.*" Don't be afraid, this will be over soon. The war will end. We shall have peace, just you wait and see. I believed it, and I did see.

But then, hard on the heels of WWII, there followed the Cold War, slicing the world and most visibly Berlin in two. A different kind of war, and in some ways no less poisonous and destructive than the one which had finally ended with a handful of signatures in Berlin just before midnight on 8 May 1945. Still there remained something which would not give up. Peace, freedom, democracy – on both sides of that abominable Wall, people kept hoping.

In early September 1989 that hope enflamed protests in East Germany. The first of the Monday demonstrations began in Leipzig, and spread. In November 1989 the Berlin Wall fell. Five years later, in September 1994, almost half a century after the US Army had begun its role there in post-war occupation and administration, it closed its headquarters in Berlin. A signal, it seemed, that the hope of a unified, free and democratic Germany had finally delivered.

In South Africa the national election of April 1994 was such a signal. People were dancing in the streets, calling it Liberation. The hope that had sustained generations of disenfranchised South Africans had delivered. Under the wise and benevolent rule of their new president, Nelson Mandela, South Africans would be united in a free and democratic society.

Regrettably, inevitably, peace did not mean the instant cessation of all wars. Some battles continued. As day after day millions of people still woke up every morning to the reality of impoverished circumstances, frustration grew at what they experienced as an unjust extension of that companion requirement of hope: waiting. In a groundswell of discontent, hopes became specific and insistent, demanding a deadline.

In September 1994 the *Review of African Political Economy* published its 61st issue: "Land and Freedom in South Africa." It made the case for what was to become the Land Reform policies of the ANC-led government's Reconstruction and Development

Programme and the creation of a Land Claims Court. Land Claims became the Holy Grail. Millions of people, disenchanted with their New South Africa, found a renewed focus for their hope, and a rallying cry: Land.

That same September saw Clive at Onderstepoort attending a symposium on the future of rhino conservation. He delivered papers on rhinos in Africa and black rhino on private land. A Chinese delegate spoke about measures to curtail trade in rhino products; the South African Police's Endangered Species Protection Unit detailed their role in combatting rhino poaching and the smuggling of rhino horn; conservationists and scientists proposed and analysed strategies for ensuring the long-term survival of rhino: increased armed protection within national parks, ranching, de-horning, utilisation as a commercial commodity, the scientific management of captive rhino.

The unstated but unmistakable theme of the symposium was that enduring hope, the credo of conservationists everywhere: If we do enough, the species will survive. Better days will come. This war will be won. It was not a new hope and not a new war. The competing interests of human development and political aspirations on the one side, and biodiversity conservation and the preservation of wilderness on the other, were age-old adversaries. But the stakes were growing ever higher and in Southern Africa the board was set for an endgame. The prize: Land.

All the while, far from the debates and the chessboard moves of politics, I was at Doornleegte, taking my more modest hopes on daily walks between the house and the river. Mothlo had accepted the Palala rock pool as her playground. After a lot of coaching she'd learnt to eat grass in addition to the lucerne and game feed pellets with which we amplified her diet. I felt cautiously optimistic about the steps towards setting her free in the wild.

It was time for her next lesson, and this one confused her thoroughly. After the fuss I'd made about her having to follow me home after her daily dip in the river, I was now telling her to stay there while I left. This clearly made no sense to her. She got out of the rock pool and followed me, obediently as she'd been taught. I said, No, and led her back to the river. Once she was in the water I told her to stay and walked away. She got out and followed. I stopped, took her back to the water and tried to make her understand that I was leaving, but she had to stay. For long seconds she just looked at me. A human child could not have made a more heart-rending appeal: Please don't … Look at me, I'm still small …

I swallowed the lump in my throat and repeated the procedure, telling myself it was not cruelty. It was the small price for the big reward. This step was crucial. She had to learn to spend her whole day in the river and on its banks, and then in the evenings she could return to her old home and to me for all the food and attention she needed.

We made it to 10 metres, then 20, 50, 100 before she'd hurry out of the river and after me. At last she got it. She stayed while I took my worries and mixed feelings across the floodplain. We followed this routine for many days. Sometimes it took a dozen returns to the river while the morning warmed up and the vervet monkeys moved further away on their daily forage upstream.

At dusk Mothlo would wander up to the house and find me waiting for her at the railing of the verandah. Before Mothlo we hadn't needed a railing; soon after her arrival, however, she had discovered what seemed to be her mission: transporting as much mud as possible up the stairs and into the house. She went about it with stealth and surprising agility. For us, the ones who had to clean all the rooms into which she had dodged, the floors, walls and furniture that bore the muddy smears of her passage, the amusement wore off very quickly. I insisted on a sturdy railing that would keep her well away from the front door. In time we had to extend the barricading beyond the verandah: doors and windows were no match for her inquisitiveness and determination. We also learnt that it was a really bad and expensive idea to allow her to get into the garage or anywhere near a visitor's car. Vehicles were toys to be bashed and shoved around with her impressive bulk while she grunted her pleasure and resisted all efforts to interrupt her fun. As the third largest land mammal by weight (after the elephant and the white rhino) she was already well on her way to her adult load of 1.5 tonnes, with strength to match. If for no other reason, her excellent physical progress – resulting in Doornleegte becoming an ever less suitable environment for her – made her re-wilding imperative.

I began to delay setting off with her in the mornings. She had become so completely used to our regular morning stroll down to the river, she'd find the wait unusual and I hoped unwelcome. After one particularly extended delay she stomped and shuffled about impatiently, and then started walking. I watched from the lounge window. Mothlo's portly behind disappeared among the umbrella thorns as she sauntered off on her stumpy legs, independently, to the river which was to be her natural habitat. It was a beautiful sight.

For a while we stayed with this schedule. She'd accept her feed in the morning, enjoying being close to me, opening her mouth wide so I could tickle her tongue; then she'd leave for her day at the river until it was time for her to return to overnight at her old home. I was waiting for the next step, but this was one which she would have to take on her own.

It would be dishonest to pretend that I had no concerns for her safety. Crocodiles were at the top of the list. But I wanted her to live free with others of her kind, and that meant sharing their world, crocodiles and all. An adult hippo would usually be able to defend itself against even as canny and dangerous an attacker as a grown Nile crocodile, especially if assisted by other members of its pod. But this would be a young, hand-reared hippo on her own, pitted against razor-toothed jaws that can bite down with a force of 5000 pounds per square inch – 30 times the strength of a spotted hyena's bite, 75 times that of a great white shark.

One morning I was getting ready to leave Doornleegte for a few days – a trip I'd been looking forward to immensely. A friend from Europe was visiting Africa. Lore and I had met as children in post-war Germany, and over more than 40 years our long-distance friendship had matured into something I valued greatly.

The last time we had seen each other was in 1949, when my family left Germany to return to Africa. Now she was waiting for me in Pretoria.

Having packed and left notes and instructions, I was saying my goodbyes when something made me go out to the verandah. I don't know why, I hadn't heard anything. But there was Mothlo at a time when I was not expecting to see her, and obviously in pain. I dropped everything and ran down the steps. Her tail was hanging in tattered, bleeding strips. Crocodile? I couldn't be sure, but it seemed likely.

I sprayed disinfectant on her wounds and made arrangements with my assistants for her care. And then I left. I drove away from an animal that seemed to be pleading for my help. Anyone who thinks that that was easy is grossly mistaken. My Pretoria trip did enable me to consult with a supplier of veterinary medicine on the best way to treat Mothlo's injury and that was some small consolation.

Back at Doornleegte Mothlo surprised me. Her injury was painful, but she stayed with her daily routine: down to the river, and then back to us for the night. She'd come past our bedroom window and hint at her desire for some attention. She hinted strongly: one after the other the window panes cracked and broke. Then one evening I noticed a change. There seemed to be such urgency in her wanting to get to me that I began to wonder if there was something more to it, some threat disturbing or frightening her, something I had not detected. Another hippo perhaps?

My hopes for her soared.

All along I had assumed, with good reason, that the re-wilding of a hippo would be a very different matter to that of animals that are essentially solitary, such as black rhino. Mothlo's chances were even more favourable. A male would have had to contend with territorial bulls defending their turf – their stretch of river – and their pods; as a female the interest she'd attract from a territorial bull would be of a very different nature.

By the time she was two years old Mothlo was roaming as she wished. We still left out her night-time ration of lucerne and pellets, but often when I'd check early in the morning I'd find that she had already left or was just setting off. Occasionally I received reports from the wilderness school, several kilometres downstream, that she'd been seen there. The school was situated virtually on the banks of the Palala and the shallows where the river tumbled and eddied among black rock sheets was a favourite place for fun and water-based projects. Now it was also a place for observing Mothlo. She would be attracted by the children's voices and approach to investigate. Although she was used to humans, curious rather than aggressive, the teachers wisely always made the children calm down and retreat to a safe distance.

I made a point of keeping well clear of her day-time activities. Sometimes, when I'd come across her spoor and then spotted her, I'd allow myself to watch from a distance. But she was a hippo on her own terms now, and apart from the contact she initiated during her night-time visits I felt I no longer had the right to a role in her life.

Some time later, on my way back from inspecting camps and needing a few quiet moments by myself, I pulled off the road and parked in the shade of a massive weeping boerboon. I switched off the engine, closed my eyes and waited for the silence to come alive again: high, sharp twitterings and the whirring wings of sunbirds feeding on the scarlet blossoms. I got out to watch: white-bellied sunbirds, their iridescent heads and napes flashing cobalt, gold and green in the sun. As is always the case around mature trees there was ample evidence of life: the neat hoof prints of antelope, the touchingly child-like handprints of vervet monkeys and a little further away to accommodate the reach of their necks, the spoor of giraffe.

There was also something else: large, four-toed prints of an animal heavy enough to have pressed deeper into the soil than the other animals. Hippo – more than one. I wanted to believe that something seemed familiar, but in the loose sandy soil I couldn't be sure. The tracks went past the tree and down to the river, 30 metres away. White and velvety brown butterflies flitted around my legs as I balanced awkwardly on grass tussocks to avoid stepping on spoor in what was evidently a hippo path. There were many of these along the Palala, highways between the water and the hippos' night-time grazing grounds. The path became a tunnel through tall grass and reeds, and then a muddy gouge down to the water. On the far side of a long pool stretching away to my left and around a bend were water lilies and a solid fringe of bulrushes. On the nearside was a narrow muddy bank and there was my proof. I bent down for a closer look. There was no doubt: Mothlo, and she had company.

The pool was quiet. No sign of hippo or crocodile. A pied kingfisher torpedoed down, splashed into the water and, having missed, immediately rose again to its hovering position. I was tempted to stay and watch it at its fishing. If I kept quiet enough for long enough, there'd be a lot more happening. A cryptically coloured bittern suddenly visible among the reeds and bulrushes; herons and moorhens, a jacana stalking across the lily-pads; the snap and rustle of vegetation as an animal comes down to drink; the warm musky smell of it. Where I now saw only dragonflies and the reflection of clouds and sky, there might be a pinkish-grey mound rising to break the surface of the water, and the bubbly hiss and spray of expelled breath.

But I had vowed to let be, to let nature take its course; I had to accept that it would do so without my supervision or prying. I got up and left. By the time I was back at Doornleegte I knew it was useless. I was embarrassed enough at my lack of resolution not to want anyone to know about the lucerne I put out just beyond the perimeter of our garden. That night, with a clear line of sight from my observation post in the house, I got my confirmation: dim, distant glimpses of two hippos. But I wanted more.

The next day I waited until everyone was out of sight and then put out the lucerne at the carport. After dark I snuck out and hid in the car. It couldn't have been long, but it felt like hours before there was something moving on the far side of the garden, at the spot where the lucerne had been left the previous night. A hippo, and then another one. As they slowly came closer I could hear – amazingly clearly as one does at night – the ripping sounds as one or the other pulled and tore at a patch of long grass. Then they found my little offering of fresh lucerne. I watched as Mothlo and her companion – a wild hippo bull – mere metres away, contentedly nuzzling and fondling, fed together. My little orphan had grown up.

After a while they left. Quietly, as wild animals can do so well, they melted away in the dark. I crept back into the house. Clive pretended to be asleep. I pretended to wake him. He pretended to be surprised at my news. Of course he knew. He'd been watching me watching them, and was as delighted as I was at the evidence of what really began to seem like a successful re-introduction into the wild.

My dreams for Mothlo were coming true; my dreams for Bwana were not. He was well, recovered from his injuries, and within his expanded enclosure he was amply provided with all the care and natural black rhino browse he needed. But between him and the life that I'd wanted for him there was a stockade.

In the period immediately after that dreadful encounter with a wild black rhino bull, Bwana's recovery from his injuries was the concern we discussed. The bigger concern about his future was not yet something we could talk about. If people other than Clive or I had opinions about that, they didn't mention it to me. Nor did anyone voice the questions I'm sure plagued them as it did me. Where did we go wrong? Was it the way I had been rearing and gradually training him, or was it his precipitate release into the reserve while I was away? What if no one had done anything wrong? Black rhino bulls are about as tough a challenge for re-wilding as one can get. Perhaps we'd been over-ambitious; perhaps we'd been foolish; perhaps we'd just been unlucky.

I remembered the autumn of 1993 when Bwana first arrived at Doornleegte: the trepidation with which I prepared and waited, my insecurity about the responsibility of taking care of him; the months and years of getting to know his strong wild fighting spirit as well as his other sides – playful, inquisitive, naughty, intelligent, vulnerable.

A few weeks after my morning in Nylstroom's concentration camp cemetery I had still not mentioned to anyone the plan with which I'd driven back to the Waterberg that day. It wasn't something I could implement by myself, and I wasn't even sure whether it would be wise for me to moot it – better if it came from someone else. But everyone was being crippled by a tactful silence on the subject. Even Clive – despite all the openings I'd thought I'd given him – avoided the issue.

With the usual bucket of game pellets, I walked up to Bwana's enclosure. He was dangerous, but in truth he was at our mercy. Like all wild animals. We've removed their right to their own habitat. We make decisions on their behalf. If they are to survive, it has to be on our terms. All too often that means fences. Game reserves, game ranches, the illusion of roaming free among tarred roads and tourists, powerlines, hunters and poachers. They live with the dis-ease of instinct pulling against truncated territories, severed migration routes and dammed rivers. They submit to our notions of population management – birth control, relocation, culling. The sensory bombardment which is such an inescapable waste product of human activity interferes with their intricate communication systems via their senses. They have no choice but to adapt to the way we change their world.

Look at it from a particularly human perspective and our decisions make some sort of sense, albeit in the short term, given the distance we've travelled along the way of claiming every inch of this planet and everything inhabiting it as exploitable resource. Look at it from any other perspective, especially from that of the non-human – polar bears, riverine rabbits, old-growth forests, eagles, epiphytic orchids, frogs, tigers, chameleons, sea-horses – and it makes no sense at all. The innocent party is not the human.

Even when we try to help, with only the animal's welfare as our goal, it may still end up the loser. Like Bwana. We rescued and hand-reared him, and found ourselves with very few options. We were reluctant to risk another attempt at releasing him among the other black rhino bulls in the reserve. Translocation was not an attractive option either. Lapalala was his home, as it was ours. I hoped that I had found a way to make it work for all of us.

Bwana was waiting for me, leaning against the wooden poles of his enclosure railing, his head raised, mouth wide open in anticipation of the treat. I put my hand inside his mouth; his prehensile top lip curled under – firm, slightly moist on my hand – and he scooped up his pellets. As he chomped I talked to him as I always did, rubbed his head and checked him over. His nose was wet – a sign of good health – and on either side of his well-grown horns his small dark eyes were bright and alert, following my every move. There was a swollen tick low down on his flank, but that didn't worry me. In the early days I used to remove ticks and treat their bites, but I later discovered that his natural mechanism for dealing with irritating insects – mud and a rubbing-post – was equally effective, perhaps more so.

He strained against the railing and moo-ed his hints for more pellets, but before I could oblige I heard footsteps approaching. I waited for Clive to join me. For some reason I usually developed a rash when I'd had contact with Bwana's saliva, but Clive didn't, so I handed him the bucket. He scooped up a handful.

"I've been thinking," he said.

Finally, I thought, here it is. I'm going to be asked to do the very thing I've been wanting to do. I knew the signs. Ever since Clive was a young man with dark-brown hair and a rifle slung across his shoulders, all kinds of enterprises and adventures started this way: he'd been thinking. An organisation to train field guides, a new way to raise conservation funds or support a lone scientist-conservationist working in some remote wilderness; or it would be time to visit an old friend in Botswana's Savute, or join a colleague on a research trip to the Kgalagadi. If I wasn't invited along I knew it would involve dangerous exploits among predators or elephants – it was better if I didn't know. This was also the way he broached a subject when he had a favour to ask, or intended to persuade me into agreeing with a plan he'd hatched, "I've been thinking…"

"I'm listening," I said.

He started way out on the periphery of the matter: "… conservation … education … the need to reach young people …"

I curbed my impatience while he continued to circle: "… rhinos are misunderstood … you can't teach conservation from books … Bwana gives us an opportunity here…"

A hornet was aiming for my arm. I slapped and fussed while Clive beat around the bush some more. "We've got thousands of kids already coming to the school, you know. Guests at Kolobe Lodge, the bush camps…"

The hornet gone, I had to settle for rubbing a spot on my arm as if the hornet had in fact struck. I wasn't going to offer, I wanted to be *asked*.

Clive lowered his head to Bwana's. "You'd like it boy, wouldn't you?" He looked around to me. "So I thought we'll advertise. There's bound to be a conservation-minded youngster who'd be interested." He moo-ed back at Bwana and dug into the bucket for more pellets. "And then he can take Bwana off your hands."

Clive had the satisfaction of seeing my shocked face as I stared at him, utterly at a loss for words. He turned away and continued to feed Bwana while I fought with my pride. "Unless," he said over his shoulder, "you perhaps already know of someone who could do it?" I'd been out-manoeuvred. "Yes," I said. "I do. Me. Monday to Saturday. Three o'clock in the afternoon."

In order for Doornleegte to become an outdoor classroom, a place to encounter and learn about black rhino with me as the teacher, I was going to have to adjust to a much more public role than I'd ever imagined or desired. Clive was the one who was at home in the spotlight – accessible and approachable as he needed to be in order to effectively promote his conservation causes. On Dale Parker's insistence he was also the media face of Lapalala. I had been content in the shadows. Yet how often had I wished that other people too could share in my experiences? I wanted more people to see what I saw, and to really understand what it was that they were seeing. I wanted them to know Bwana for the splendid, rare creature he was. I wanted then to care about him and his kind.

By bringing people and children into close contact with such a flagship species, a greater good might be served for wildlife conservation. If our past experiences were anything to go by, a good number of the adults and especially children who met Bwana might go on to become supporters of efforts to save what is left of their natural world. What lay ahead of us then wasn't so much a new beginning as a new chapter in something Clive and I had begun many years before, first with the wilderness walking trails, then the wilderness school and the bush camps: expose people to the life of the wilderness, let nature do the rest.

It was an eventuality I hadn't foreseen on that long-ago first day with Bwana, but given that my greatest fear then was that I'd be responsible for killing him outright through my ignorance, what remained was still considerably better than a worst-case scenario.

Clive returned to the house to begin making the arrangements. Bwana and I walked up the rocky slope of his hill, close and relaxed as we'd done hundreds of times before. He sniffed and snuffled at everything, paused for a mouthful when we passed a favourite tree or shrub, or lingered at a rock to rub away some irritation. From the top of the hill I could see all the way across the floodplain to the dark green curving line of the Palala – Mothlo's domain. Further around to my right the rocky slopes climbed higher, the light picking out the massive candelabra of tree euphorbias among the mountain seringa and star chestnut and the many other trees that could have sheltered and fed Bwana. All around, as far as I could see, Lapalala stretched to the horizon. From where I was sitting I couldn't see a building or road or powerline, and all I heard were the sounds that naturally belonged on that hill – insects, birds, the dry rustle of late summer leaves, and a young black rhino bull contentedly exploring the world which rightly belonged to him as much as he belonged to it.

SEVEN

Munyane

IT WAS NOVEMBER BUT HOT enough for February. The weather had been building for days and I'd scheduled my Monday accordingly, with appointments in Nylstroom and Vaalwater as early as possible. By early afternoon I was already well on my way home. As the kilometres passed my eyes kept straying to the north-east. Cumulonimbus turrets and crowning them, a promising anvil, purple at its base. It could reach us in a couple of hours. I *willed* it closer.

The Waterberg, not as water-rich anymore as in centuries past, waited for the first rain of the season. I passed vineyards draped in acres of black netting. Table grapes, for the export market. The nets would fend off the birds, but would not stop hail. Should the rains arrive with too much force, the outcome for that farmer and his neighbours with their vineyards, citrus orchards and maize fields could be almost as bad as no rain at all. Farming, at the best of times, is a gamble. When it is dependent upon your ability to outsmart the weather, it could be a sure-fire recipe for bankruptcy.

No wonder so many farmers were turning to wildlife, trying

to make a living within the constraints of the prevailing climatic conditions, working *within* the natural ecosystem rather than against it. In more and more places farm fences had given way to game fences.

Once I was off the tarred road and trailing a cloud of red dust, evidence of agriculture had all but disappeared. On both sides of the road, behind the 2.5-metre-high fences, it was Waterberg bush. Trees grew higher, closer together, shaggily overhanging fences and signboards, until they sheltered the final sandy stretch to the Lapalala gate. Far ahead the boom across the road lifted. A tall figure waited with one arm held high.

I pulled up and let down the window. It was like opening an oven door. Andries Mokwena, in his neatly pressed olive-green uniform, had a sweat-shiny brow and a broad smile. As Lapalala's chief rhino tracker he infinitely preferred being out in the bush but even when co-opted for gate-duty I never saw him without a smile. A cattle-herder years ago in whom Clive had discovered a rare facility for intuitive observation, Andries had been groomed to become the head of Lapalala's game scouts with, as his special care, rhino. He became a master tracker and rhino monitor. It was unusual to find him anywhere except in the bush with his beloved rhinos.

He touched his forehead. "Magog!"

We exchanged news of our families and commiserated with each other about the clouds that were retreating yet again. He told me that Clive had driven through an hour or so before me – he'd probably be home by now.

He wasn't. A few kilometres on I rounded a bend and saw his Pajero parked by the roadside. His boot prints led down a game path which wound across a clearing where plumes of silky bushman grass stirred in the lightest of breezes. I felt the sweat-soaked back of my shirt cooling. The path headed for some rocks on the lip of a shallow green-treed gully. And there he was: light khaki trousers and shirt, the familiar bleached kerchief knotted around his neck. Rastunya, "he who carries the gun", the name Andries had given him. The two of them had spent countless hours together walking the Lapalala bush, each teaching the other and cementing a friendship. The gun had made way for sketching materials, but Rastunya stuck.

He was sitting with his back against a rock, his attention on the small family group of waterbuck grazing less than 30 metres away. I quietly sat down, my back against a rock of my own. This was my life. This man. This place. The smell of baked dust. The stillness not of things standing still, but of order. The natural order of the wilderness. I felt my body relax into the warmth of the rock and of that moment.

We were getting too busy. Moments for being still and just taking it all in were becoming too rare. My conscience wasn't helping: sitting still felt like slacking off, something lazy people did. I vowed, not for the first time, to strive for a little more balance.

The very next thing I did, seconds later, was to look at my watch. But I squashed the impulse to hiss at Clive, to hint that time was marching on. For once he'll finish sketching when he's ready, not when I tell him it's time to go.

The waterbuck moved off, their white-on-charcoal bulls-eye backsides gradually disappearing in the vegetation. Clive got up and walked over to me. He was surprised when I remained seated, and put out his hand to pull me up. "Shouldn't we be going?"

I made room for him next to me. "Not yet. Show me."

He sat down and flipped through his sketches. A lilac-breasted roller, a group of guineafowl, a flowering creeper, the waterbuck – one of them, a male with trophy horns, looking straight out of the page. As a non-artist I took it upon myself to have an opinion. As usual he took it in good part.

We stayed there for a while. I tried, and failed, to locate the crested barbet whose continuous alarm-clock *chirrrr*, together with the cicadas, was to remain the soundtrack to that memory. Yellow-billed hornbills cackled and foraged through the canopy of a wild fig tree. One took off and crashed into the deep green foliage of the next tree. Another one followed. I turned to look north – the clouds were further away. No rain for us that day. Clear, clean blue sky dissected by a vapour trail – people hurrying to get somewhere.

Another world.

Clive turned to me. "Regrets?"

I shook my head. "You?"

He smiled. "Never."

There was the sound of a vehicle on the road, slowing down where we'd parked, then speeding up and continuing on towards the gate. It was time to go.

As we strolled back Clive filled me in on the meeting which had taken up most of his day. All good news. Years earlier, soon after we came to Lapalala there had been another such meeting, much smaller, but as is the way of foundations, crucial. It would, in time, contribute to the reshaping of the entire management structure of conservation in the Waterberg.

Wildlife conservation is all about habitat, all about ecosystems. And since nature doesn't operate neatly within fenced title-deed grid-networks as landowners do, it is imperative that neighbours should cooperate. Well and good to implement wilderness principles within Lapalala, but what happens on the other side of the fence, the opposite bank of the river? How could it affect us, on this side?

Early in the '80s Clive had discovered that several farms on the other side of the Palala were owned by Mr Hennie Dercksen. Since he and Lapalala shared 25 kilometres of the same river it seemed like a good idea to cooperate on conservation matters. Mr Dercksen agreed. It was the beginning of a conservancy. By 1985 so many other farmers wanted to join that another meeting, a much larger one, was arranged to take place in the lodge of Mr Wynand du Toit on his farm Kliphoek. That night Clive came home and when I asked him how it had gone, he shook his head. It was the idea of a conservancy that had drawn people to the meeting in the first place, yet when it was fully explained to them, it wasn't welcomed.

For the next four years it must have felt like bashing his head against brick walls all the time. Discussions didn't lead to anything concrete; every so often a farm changed hands and then he had to start all over again with the new landowner.

Why was this so important? Because Lapalala was not an island. It was not isolated and therefore not protected from whatever happened outside its fences. Actions taken on neighbouring farms would impact what Dale and Clive wanted to achieve with Lapalala. Policies implemented in the greater Waterberg region would have an impact. Whatever happened in South African conservation, in South African politics, would have an impact. And if one did not have voting power let alone veto-ing power in matters that affected you, their outcome could not be guaranteed to be favourable to your goals.

For Lapalala to survive as a wilderness reserve, it had to have more muscle, a stronger voice within a wider system of policy support.

In autumn 1990 Clive found a sympathetic ear in Mr Rod Henwood of the Touchstone Game Ranch. Within months they, with a third member, Kwalata Private Nature Reserve, had established the Waterberg Nature Conservancy. They were on their way. Eventually the WNC would grow to 26 members, jointly protecting 150 000 hectares of the Waterberg, within which 100 kilometres of the Palala was safer than it had ever been before. In terms of Lapalala itself, the WNC was a first defence against threats from outside.

Almost six years later Clive was midway through his term as chairman of the WNC, and although it was going well, I was not at all surprised that even on a hot November afternoon, he needed a sketching break in the veld to soothe the stresses of the meeting.

We got back to the vehicles and he enquired about my trip. "I got fan-mail," I told him.

He laughed. It had become a welcome feature of my stop at the Vaalwater post office. On a weekly basis I had the pleasure of reading that I was a highlight. The best ever. "Awesome."

Of course it wasn't really me. It was Bwana.

Our sessions with the children were a delight. So much easier to hold the attention of children with a live black rhino as your teaching aid rather than books and a blackboard. Their excitement at meeting a dangerous wild animal, many times their size, was all the reward I needed. Bwana obligingly lingered at the feeding station in his enclosure until I had helped even the most timid child offer his or her tiny handful of pellets to be gently scooped up and contentedly chomped.

Amazingly it was sometimes the littlest ones that were most brave and insisted on being held up in a parent's arms, or in mine, to be able to reach Bwana's waiting, wide open mouth, and then finish their feeding turn by carefully patting his horn while he chewed. Bravest of all was probably Twana who, true to her lineage as the latest of the pioneering Waterberg Nels, did not have a timid hair on her cherub head. Overflowing with love for her new friend she leaned from her mother's arms and insisted on putting both her hands deep into Bwana's mouth. I watched in trepidation as his upper lip delicately manoeuvred around the little matchstick forearms and found his pellets in the small happy hands.

Children peppered me with questions, some of them so ingenious and unexpected that I had a hard time keeping a straight face and treating them with the serious consideration they deserved. On numerous occasions I saw fear or indifference turned to wonderment. And as young people, with all their vigour and appetite for life still un-jaded, do so easily they progressed to caring passionately. I received drawings and poems dedicated to Bwana. They wrote me letters to enquire about his wellbeing and to tell me about their own efforts to support conservation.

Once a teacher, always a teacher – this was work after my own heart. But I wasn't just sharing information about the behaviour of black rhino, their nature, their food and habitat requirements. I believe that an attempt to open someone's eyes to the wonders of the natural world is much more than teaching, or a recruitment drive for the cause of conservation. Volumes of feedback have strengthened my belief that a wider awareness of the natural world enhances our own life experience. Our need of the natural world is as great as its need of our care and protection. If we have no access to wilderness we are, in a deep and profound sense, homeless.

This was the theme of Clive's 1982 publication, *Twilight of the Giants*. He documented what he'd seen in northern Namibia, Botswana, and Tongaland: free-roaming herds of elephants were making a last stand, and so were the people who for centuries had lived with them. For the Ovahimba, the Bayé and the Tonga, the life they used to know was passing. Rituals and routines of a life *with* the wild were no longer possible. Wisdoms, which had been passed on for generations, lost their frame of reference, and with it, their meaning and purpose. In a world of diminishing freedom and unravelling biodiverse integrity, the elephants were not the only losers. A fight for wildlife conservation is ultimately also a fight *for* people, not against them. We lose such fights at our peril.

More than 30 years later I have to wonder if it's too late now. Has too much been lost already? I don't know. There are people far more qualified than I to answer such questions. All I know is that I have seen many of the wild areas we still have left needing to become "managed" environments because natural regulating systems have been compromised.

In nature and game reserves we have to install artificial waterholes to counteract the depredations suffered by wildlife populations no longer able to follow ancient migration routes between water and food sources; we have to manage their population sizes according to the carrying capacity of the areas in which we allow them to exist; we have to inoculate and vaccinate to contain disease outbreaks. It becomes harder and harder to simply let nature take its course: we rescue injured and orphaned animals – like Bwana and Mothlo.

On Monday 12 February 1996 this was the discussion on our Doornleegte verandah: to rescue or to leave be. Dale and Elizabeth Parker were about to depart after staying with us for a few days and now, at the breakfast table, we'd all agreed that, even if for no other reason, the enormous amount of extra work generated by adopting a wild animal was sufficient argument against taking on anymore. Enough was enough. No more rescues, no more orphans.

I poured another round of coffee and tried to ignore the sounds of a radio call coming from inside the house. I could feel Clive looking at me, but refused to look up. I fussed with coffee cups and biscuits and thought: No more orphans, you all agreed – no more orphans.

Rangers had called in an emergency; the reserve manager was on his way to the scene. On the verandah all conversation ceased. I drank my coffee and wondered who was going to be the first one to say it. Dale and Elizabeth looked at each other: perhaps they should at least go and see for themselves. With that I accepted the inevitable. Elizabeth was a mother; Dale was Dale – if he could not have resisted fully grown rhino, what were the chances that he'd be able to steel his heart against a white rhino calf, a little female, attempting to suckle from her dead mother?

They left with Clive and I shouted out the back door for Titus. Rosina stared at me.

"We're getting another one, Rosina. *Tshukudu*. White rhino."

She rolled her eyes and started rummaging through the store cupboards for the leftovers of our milk powder supply. While I waited for Titus I heard the radio updates. The calf's predicament had actually been discovered the previous afternoon when the standby rangers, while checking all watering points as part of their weekend duties, saw the tracks of a rhino calf leading away from a waterhole. There was no sign of the mother's tracks and that was a cause for concern. They followed the tracks to the spot where the forlorn little calf was desperately trying to obtain nourishment from the decomposing carcass of a large rhino cow. Unfortunately, with the field rangers away on weekend leave, the standby rangers' report had to wait.

Early on Monday morning the field rangers were horrified at what they saw. The mother must have been dead for days. The cause of death they'd investigate later, but first they had to make a plan with the starving and traumatised calf. The plan was Conita at Doornleegte. So much for the resolve on the verandah that morning. Dale and Elizabeth had to be on their way. They wished me luck and left me to my search for something for which I'd never had the least need before, glucose.

The remainder of Bwana's fat-free milk powder was fortunately not yet expired, but the white rhino calf would need 100 grams of glucose added to every litre of that formula. I phoned Vaalwater. While I held on for the pharmacy to check on their supply I tried to keep an eye on what was going on outside. We had moved Bwana to his larger enclosure so that his sleeping quarters and feeding enclosure could be re-customised to accommodate the new arrival. We weren't quite sure what was coming. Beyond the fact that she was a hungry white rhino calf of undetermined age I had no idea what special preparations might be required. The basics, however, kept us busy enough: everything had to be thoroughly cleaned and scrubbed and a new mud pool created in record time. There was a lot of running and shouting, and as on all occasions when Magog was in a hurry, much hilarity.

The pharmacy came back on the line. They had a small quantity of glucose, but they never kept more than 500 grams in stock. My heart sank. That would not do for even a single feed. But there was no time for any more searching: the radio call had come through – they were on their way. It was Clive's voice on the radio and while I urged the workers to hurry up I was thinking about that voice. Clive isn't given to dramatising. If anything, he errs on the opposite side, making light of situations that might cause many others to fall down in a faint. He takes things in his stride.

"We're moving. 30 minutes." There were no jokes, none of the light mood of the morning.

At first all I saw was that the ranger's vehicle had an awful lot of people on the back. There were in fact ten of them. Ten strong men only just managing to hold onto a rhino calf, hip-height to them and obviously extremely powerful.

Clutching my bottle of unsweetened milk formula I scrambled up onto the vehicle and into that crush of sweating muscle and noise. Close to the calf it was clear that she was in a shocking state of exhaustion and distress. She was only a few months old, but she was already strong enough and at that moment out of control enough to do serious damage to anything or anybody within reach. In an attempt to reduce her anxiety a cloth had been put over her eyes. When it was removed her look of terror was pitiful.

Try as we might, we couldn't get any milk into her and all the commotion of our attempts to force open her mouth resulted in nothing except a worsening of the situation. I jumped down and told the rangers to get her into her new sleeping quarters. Easier said than done. Everyone had to pitch in, pick her up and carry her. She resisted, furiously, and didn't stop even after she'd been put down and the heavy steel-barred gate slammed shut between her and us. Her repeated aggressive charges into the walls and gate soon resulted in her little horn shearing off. Her mouth and horn-bed bled profusely. I thought it best to get everyone out of sight so that she could calm down.

Several phone calls later I was a little reassured. She could survive without milk and water, I was told, for a maximum of ten days. Plenty of time to settle and get to know me. I was hopeful of being able to get her to drink long before her life was in danger. I kept checking on her. Her aggression was not letting up. The moment she sensed my presence she instantly went into attack. As the day wore on, my confidence, fragile at best, was eroding. By sunset it was gone.

Dinner was a gloomy affair. I tried to be positive and told Clive about my ten-day window in which to win her over. He didn't look up from his food.

"She's already very dehydrated," he said.

"Still full of fight."

"Pure adrenaline, that's all."

"We have time."

He looked up. "When do you think that rhino cow died?"

"I don't know. You were there, you tell me."

"That calf has not had milk for many days. You *don't* have ten days any more. Nothing like it."

"So how much time..."

He shook his head and looked down. We finished our meal in silence. He got up to help me clear the table. "Munyane," he said. "The rangers named her Munyane – Little One."

Of all the things that happened in Lapalala and in the world outside that next week I remember only one: Munyane's struggle.

She fought for her life the only way she knew how and that was to fight against everything.

It was so different from my experience with Bwana. To some extent it was attributable to the fact that she had already spent a considerable amount of time with her natural mother in their natural environment. She'd already learnt something of being a wild rhino, with her instincts and behaviour attuned to her survival within that environment, not the one in which she found herself at Doornleegte. That was already a double trauma: the loss of her mother at far too young an age for independence, and the loss too of the only world she knew.

There was another factor. Black rhino calves grow up in black rhino habitat: typically, dense bush. When they find themselves in enclosed spaces, they calm down more easily than white rhino calves that had been raised in what was *their* natural habitat, open grasslands. Whereas a black rhino calf follows behind its mother, a white rhino calf goes in front, enabling the mother to keep an eye on her calf and on any threat that might be approaching. Such a calf is accustomed to feeling safe in open spaces, habituated to an infinitely wider horizon than that of a Doornleegte enclosure.

Munyane refused to drink. Bottle-feeding, even with the correct sweetened formula, was a lost cause and so was everything else I tried both in her sleeping quarters and in her feeding enclosure. A water trough, a variety of pots and basins, even the two heavy iron ploughshares I half-buried in an attempt to simulate a natural waterhole. Everything got flung around and the ploughshares kicked full of sand. Her dehydration was worrying, but even more so her continued aggression. She was losing blood and hurting herself with her unabated charges, but no matter how quietly I approached she immediately hurled herself at the gate between us. Her strength, even in a weakened state, was tremendous. On the other side of that buckling, lifting, steel-barred gate I stood my ground, but the power of her assault scared me.

In my desperation, I made a bad decision. At that point I felt that getting liquid into her was so urgent it was worth any price. I was haunted for days afterwards by the memory of the rangers whose help I'd enlisted forcing open her mouth so I could pour some milk into it. Her screams were ear-shattering. She was resisting as aggressively as ever, and in her eyes I only saw that same terror with which she had arrived. Some milk went down, perhaps not even enough to make a difference. It didn't seem worth the additional stress inflicted on her, further depleting her remaining reserves. The rangers left and I alone remained outside the gate to be charged over and over again by an animal that seemed beyond my help.

There was more stress coming for her. We called in a veterinarian. Munyane had now gone for seven days at Doornleegte without taking in any nourishment and the wounds on her face urgently needed to be treated. It took gritted teeth, a heavy table top and a great deal of patience, but at long last Titus and I managed to back her into a corner of her enclosure. Dr Walter Eschenburg had a tough time with his enraged patient but when he left Doornleegte, I took what comfort I could from the fact that Munyane's wounds had been treated and she'd been injected with a vitamin booster and a broad-spectrum antibiotic.

There was a Johannesburg trip waiting for Clive. When he couldn't put it off any longer I helped him pack and nagged him to get going. Usually a man of quick and decisive action, he now dawdled and debated reasons for trying to delay the trip even more.

"Why?" I asked.

"Because I know you. That's an extremely dangerous animal, but all you see is that she's a baby. You'll do something stupid."

I closed his overnight case and shoved it towards him. "I won't."

At the front door he stopped and glared at me. "You won't open her gate?"

"No."

At the garden gate: "You won't try to go in with her?"

"No."

"She can kill you. You have to promise."

"Yes, yes, I promise."

Through the driver's window with the engine running: "You'll get some rest? You can't go on like this. You need to sleep."

"As soon as you're out of sight I'll be in my deck chair."

I got a frown and a finger shaken at me. I waved him down the driveway and within half an hour was, as promised, in the deck chair, though not in the usual location on the verandah. Around me were my sleeping bag, a notebook, a novel, bottles of water and five litres of prepared milk formula. A few inches away the steel bars shuddered under Munyane's furious charges. I took a deep breath and started to talk to her.

I knew I was being sentimental and unscientific. I didn't care. We were at last resorts.

She kept charging, I kept talking. With my stomach in a knot I tried not to flinch as the gate protested, just talked and talked in as soft and calm a voice as I could manage, calling her name while she was storming at me.

I dipped into the novel, but against the intermittent shuddering and clanging of the gate it failed to grip. It got dark. Eventually the little rhino was so worn out that she had to rest. It was my opportunity to sneak away for a bathroom break and to refuel my flask for the next shift. No sooner was I back in the chair than the gate gave a little bit more as a solid body slammed into it. I moved my chair a fraction closer, "Munyane, Munyane ..."

It felt as if my entire world consisted of just the three of us: that raging young rhino, the gate, and me. I fervently hoped that the one to give in first wouldn't be the gate.

The night of 18 into 19 February was New Moon, the stars over Doornleegte glittering and glorious. A sky like a benediction.

There have been other such skies, none more spectacular than a night in February 1986.

It began when Clive walked in on our EWT Ladies' Committee meeting one morning, helped himself to tea and biscuits, and declared, "I've been thinking..." If he'd come prepared with arguments against our objections to what he had to propose, he didn't need them. More often than not the task of the Ladies' Committee is a thankless one, performed in urban exile far from the wild that is the focus of their efforts. So the chairman's offer to treat us to our own wilderness trail received a most enthusiastic response. The Ivory Trail was an EWE flagship product, drawing trailists from all over the world to experience the pristine wilderness of areas like Botswana's Mashatu Game Reserve. Base camp was on the banks of the Limpopo River – an ideal spot for post-trail dinners under the stars while listening to the sounds of the bush. This was prime elephant country, with lion and hyena around too, so when daylight faded one was particularly grateful for the perhaps illusory protection of a tented trails camp with its comforting campfire. On one occasion, though, we broke with tradition and drove out of camp after dinner. In the headlights we saw the jeep track winding through stands of acacia tortillis and heavily browsed mopani – evidence of a healthy presence of Clive's beloved Tuli elephants. I had reason to trust my husband's skill among elephants at night, but it's one thing to do so on my own behalf and quite another to trust it on behalf of the seven other women with us. However, they seemed to have no qualms and when we arrived at our destination, the crown of a prominent koppie near the Majale River, cheerfully shared out sleeping bags, blankets, pillows, torches, coffee and sherry. Mindful of the area's hyenas we bedded down in a closely spaced row in the lee of the vehicle, and watched our familiar southern stars – so bright in that deep African night – and right overhead, Halley's Comet.

None of us spoke, but there were sounds enough. Among the smaller and more distant calls of nocturnal wildlife, there were lions roaring; close-by – terrifyingly close-by – the tearing and snapping of branches marked the passage of feeding elephant. Most beautiful of all for me were the nightjars, more than one pair, calling all around our little encampment. Halley's sank below the horizon and Clive lit a fire to take the first watch. We took turns to watch until dawn and had our coffee as the light lifted that wide expanse of bush into the day.

Such a night deserved a fitting conclusion, so we set off on foot, down the hill and along the Majale for several hours until, in the thick croton bush, we tracked down the herd of elephants that had shared our night. It was a scene of such peace – great grey backs appearing here and there among the lush summer vegetation, magnificent heads lifting above the green as trunks reached for higher branches. Their leisurely feeding took them through a clearing and we could see the juveniles and little ones. We watched until the elephants' unhurried, silent footfalls had taken them back into the bush and then also took our silent leave of that magical place.

In my Doornleegte night I longed for that peace, and was grateful for the soothing sound of the Palala which, on the far side of the floodplain, ran at peak rainy-season levels. But suddenly, deep into the night, there was another sound which instantly put me back on that solitary hilltop above the Majale, looking up at a comet in a field of stars; and even further back still to another Tuli campfire decades earlier, when beyond the crickets and frogs, beyond the sounds of something splashing into the Limpopo, beyond the stories my new husband was telling me, fiery-necked nightjars had been calling. The intervening years disappeared and, beyond Munyane's ragged breathing and the other sounds of my Waterberg night, there they were again: *koo-Weeu, koo-Wiriri, koo-Weeu, koo-Wiriri …* I guessed that they were where I'd so often seen them, at the Doornleegte turn-off, their invisibility betrayed by the ruby shine of their eyes in my headlights until, at the very last moment, there was that confident rise and flight into the darkness. I hear them still: Lapalala's nightjars calling the hours with me.

I risked a hand on the gate; later, in between the bars of the gate; still later a fleeting touch on Munyane's head, a micro-second only before she exploded again, but I kept my movements slow and gentle, talking to her and calling her name through hour after hour. I thought of the rangers who had found her and brought her to me: big strong black men who had had to wrestle her away from a stinking carcass, fight to contain her violence and knew very well that they were dealing with a highly dangerous animal. Yet they called her "Little One", an endearment which in North-Sotho lent itself to that night's chanting: "Munyane, Munyane."

I watched the stars fade and thought of Clive, how his artist's eye would have delighted in that day's beginning. I told Munyane about that. I told her many things. There was no one else, just us, and I spoke to her about everything that one sometimes needs to talk about and doesn't.

It was morning before she let me touch her forehead. When I stretched to reach as far as possible with slow light strokes along her body, she still flinched and jerked away but I thought her movements were less violent than before.

I became aware of stealthy sounds nearby. Still murmuring to Munyane and resting my hand on her head, I slowly turned to look. The workers had arrived and were going about their tasks in an uncharacteristic hush. It was touching.

Titus hovered until I beckoned to him. He approached with the usual respectful greeting, but with a wary eye on the rhino who had an equally wary eye on him. I gestured to him that he could get going with the morning's jobs. He nodded a couple of times, but remained standing a few metres away, shifting his weight from one foot to the other. I pointed to the gate which, battered but still holding, ensured that while Munyane was in her sleeping quarters she couldn't get to me on the outside. Yes, he said, with a doubtful look at the damage to the gate, that is a good gate. Can he see that there's an equally strong gate between her sleeping quarters and her feeding enclosure? Yes, he can see that gate too. Can he see that it is securely closed? He squinted at the gate: Yes, it is closed. Does he think he can open the outside gate into her feeding enclosure, knowing that there was that closed gate between him and any danger from her? He beamed at me: Yes, he can do that. I waited. Titus didn't budge. I tried again, reigning in my impatience so as not to spook Munyane. We did another round of the gates. Yes, he understands everything perfectly. So is he going to do it? Oh yes, certainly! What is it that Magog wants him to do? My sign language, hampered by one hand needing to remain on Munyane's head, must have been unclear, but suddenly the light dawned: Oh, Magog wanted him to actually go *in* there? Yes, indeed Magog did.

Titus, bless his heart, went in and meticulously as he did all tasks emptied out the ploughshares of their unused contents, scrubbed them clean, reburied and refilled them – fresh water in the one, freshly mixed milk formula in the other. I kept up my low-voiced schizophrenic conversation, instructing Titus while reassuring Munyane.

She didn't like him being there, but once he was gone she became calmer again. After a while she went down on her knees, then slumped down heavily as if wanting to sleep. With an old, heavy army coat wrapped tightly around myself I crawled into my sleeping bag and lay down right up against the gate. She seemed to be falling into a deep sleep with occasional grunts that I found oddly reassuring. I desperately needed to sleep myself and with my hand on her and still calling her name, I drifted in and out of a doze.

Two hours later she woke up, apparently calmer. I weighed up the risks of leaving her for a while and having to recover lost ground when I returned. The lure of a hot drink became irresistible and I also wanted to phone – Clive would want to know how Munyane was doing. But when his first enquiry was about her, not about me, it wasn't what I needed to hear. Lack of sleep, I thought, and swallowed hard.

"She hasn't drunk," I said.

"You mustn't take it personally."

"No."

"Win some, lose some. One has to be realistic about these things."

"Yes."

A brief silence. Then, carefully. "Conit, you all right?"

"Of course. If anything happens I'll phone Anton."

"You do that. He'll know what to do."

I was back in the kitchen busy preparing fresh milk formula before I realised that he'd been commiserating with me about what he regarded as a certainty: the inevitable, imminent loss of Munyane.

When I returned she stood at the gate and I had to admit to myself she still presented a picture of real physical threat. I approached slowly, calling her name, talking to her as I'd been doing all night. She moved away abruptly and snorted. I got right up to the gate. She stomped around and snorted again, but didn't charge. She watched as I cleaned and refilled the ploughshares and settled again at the gate for however much longer it might take.

It took hours. I became hoarse but kept whispering to her, watching for the least sign of progress. I held my breath when she sniffed at the water trough and after a long pause took a first sip. It was a day of small exhausted steps for both of us. By early afternoon I was able to stroke her body without triggering a startled or aggressive reaction. By late afternoon I reached now-or-never. My instinct told me it would be fine; my fear told me it could be suicidal. Misjudging a strategy with Munyane could leave me severely injured, perhaps worse. In all honesty by this time I was a mess, so over-tired that I was unsure if I could trust my own instincts, and after more than a week of witnessing Munyane's impact on a heavy steel-barred gate there was sufficient reason for some trepidation.

I unlocked the gate and eased it open. She retreated. While talking to her I tried not to imagine another one of her charges without a barrier between us. I stayed at that two-metre distance for a while. She snorted a few times. I saw signs of stress and nervousness, but not aggression, I thought, and inched forward, still talking. Many minutes later, my heart pounding in my ears, I was running my hand over her head, then along her back. More minutes, more stroking and talking, and I walked her out into her feeding enclosure. We got to the ploughshares. She lowered her head, then pulled away. I sat down next to her, kept up my monologue. From down there she seemed so much bigger – I had to reach up to stroke her. Her head went down again. She sniffed, blowing bubbles on the milky surface, and began to drink.

At sunset the ploughshares were empty and I was weeping, my forehead pressed against the dusty shoulder of a white rhino calf.

The next day Clive returned. He was used to being welcomed home: he would usually see me as he drove up. Not this time. I was sitting comfortably, my back against the nearest support: Munyane, slurping noisily from her ploughshares. I heard Clive's call, Rosina's answer. He appeared around the corner of the house and stopped dead. Munyane's head jerked up, splattering milk formula in my face. Prepared as I was, the change in her, in those shoulder muscles under my hand, was unnerving. I kept talking, stroking, and tried to keep my breathing steady. Many long seconds later there was a wet muzzle butting my cheek, a small messy snort and then her head lowered to her milk.

Clive stayed with us for a long time, leaning with his arms crossed on the top pole of the railing.

EIGHT

New beginnings

ON 15 APRIL 1996 I turned on the radio and forced myself to listen. A dispassionate voice reeled off names and statistics, as calmly as if she were reciting prices on a commodities market. But she wasn't. Other voices, anything but dispassionate, followed. They were telling stories which I, and millions like me, were hearing for the first time.

It was the beginning of formal hearings by the Truth and Reconciliation Commission, a milestone in South Africa's stumbling progress towards post-apartheid democracy. The TRC was not a military tribunal, although many, intent on retribution, had been calling for a clone of the Nuremberg Trials. But faced with the challenge of forming a nation out of a wounded and fractured citizenry, the new Government of National Unity determined that the overarching goal had to be reconciliation.

The TRC provided a platform for victims of human rights violations under the apartheid regime to tell their stories. Perpetrators of such violations could come to tell *their* stories, and apply for amnesty. The TRC sessions were harrowing, but it was the surgeon's knife cutting to where the wounds were deepest. An individual could stand up in front of the world and say: This was done to me; this was done to my people. The time for unwitnessed injustice was past.

For all its failings, the TRC offered something that had never before been available to the succession of peoples inhabiting the sub-continent.

Thousands of years ago this part of the world was home to a people who called themselves the First People – the San. In many places in the Waterberg, in rock-shelters, on hidden sandstone canvasses such as those above the Blocklands, they had left their paintings – a record by and of a people which, whichever way you interpret it, says one thing most clearly: We were here once.

Their cosmology did not include a sense of ownership, but it included a sense of home. They belonged to the landscape more than the landscape belonged to them. Earth, wind, moon and stars, water and wildlife: these were the coordinates that defined not only their geographical but also their spiritual home. We don't need to ask where they've gone and how that happened: archaeologists have unravelled that tragic history. The unbounded horizons of the San narrowed as settlers – black from the north, white from the south – arrived. They were hounded, hunted, assimilated and all but exterminated.

I doubt if anyone can stand in those painted rock shelters and not feel a deep sadness for the San. If they hadn't left their own poignant records we wouldn't even have known they were ever in those places. There were few witnesses to their lives other than those who came to kill them. And at the time no TRC where their own voices could be heard. We who came after express our sorrow, our remorse. We declare "never again". But our efforts at redress are too little, too late. Attempts at preserving fragments of bushman heritage only succeed in reminding us of how much they've lost, and how comprehensively we've all lost as a result of it. That world is gone, and what remains of it is also going.

Stand, as you can do in the Waterberg, in front of a rock painting of a rhino: the artist is gone, the subject very nearly so. Stand there, feel the world changing around you, and accept that we are moving inexorably closer to the point where those paintings could say of the rhino too: They were here once. There has never been and will never be anything like a TRC for the wild; they're voiceless and expendable. At this point in my life I have to recognise that our protests – those of us who care about such things – may have been too little, too late. Anyone who has worked with rhino as I'd done so intimately, knows how it feels to work within that narrow margin between extant and extinct. It lends a painful edge to your experience.

Every day I spent with Bwana and Munyane, and indeed with Mothlo too, was a privilege. A responsibility, a worry, a relentless treadmill of tasks, but a privilege nonetheless. In learning about them I learnt a great deal more about myself.

In the attempt to prove to myself as much as to others that I could be an adequate caretaker of rescued wild animals, I harvested as much as possible of the knowledge and training I didn't have from experts who were kind enough to help me. I needed to understand, to *know,* everything. But in the midst of the big crises when all the knowledge in the world seemed to fail us I defaulted to something far more primal. My need for approval was gone. It was motherhood – fierce, aching and uncompromising.

That surprised me. I had regarded myself as such a rational being. Sensible, practical, sentimental only insofar as it concerned my family and friends. Certainly I cared very deeply about the natural world and about the preservation of wilderness, but I'd always thought of myself as a people person. Love was for the people in my life. In Lapalala I discovered that perhaps that wasn't the whole truth.

Bwana had prepared the way, I suppose, being so small and endangered – his appeal went straight to the heart. With Mothlo too one simply had no defence against her pudgy baby vulnerability. Munyane arrived and it was war. An outsider would have observed what he might have thought was a wild animal fighting against me. She was wild, yes, but we were fighting on the same side. If we'd lost she would've died. The extent to which that mattered to me was love.

If I had been asked years earlier if I'd be able to find the time in my day, let alone my heart, to care for a wild orphan I would have been doubtful. Two orphans: No. Three orphans: Impossible. Perhaps it is just as well that our lives don't seek our permission before they send us such challenges.

With Munyane, even more than with Bwana and Mothlo, I could forget about clinging to such shreds as had remained of my dignity. There are women who can somehow manage to appear chic and delicately feminine even under the most trying of circumstances. I'm not one of them. My wild charges taught me to value practicality above all, even when it meant sweat, mud and letting visitors discover me in unflattering poses with my nails broken and hair in disarray.

After that first breakthrough, Munyane allowed us a brief honeymoon period. She became calmer and progressed from accepting me to also accepting Titus. She was growing rapidly in size, strength and appetite. She still flatly rejected the notion of bottle-feeding, but adored her very large quantities of milk formula and didn't take kindly to having that reduced even slightly as a start to the weaning process.

But she was a white rhino, a grazer – she needed to learn that grass was food, so our regular walks had a specific focus. She was content to trot along to and through grassy areas, but showed absolutely no inclination to graze. We played in the grass a little – at least that's what she seemed to think. I wasn't playing. I was on my hands and knees, my head right down to the grass, "grazing" as a white rhino would do. She looked puzzled and lowered her head closer to mine. I manoeuvred a clump of tall succulent grass right up to her mouth. Her lips clamped shut the way they always did at the first sight of a feeding bottle. Munyane was not one to take a hint. It took patience and muddy knees, but mercifully she got the message before I had to resort to actually biting off and chewing the grass myself.

Then came the day when the honeymoon was well and truly

over. I would not have been surprised if she'd presented with an upset stomach at the change in her feeding pattern, but Munyane was not going to do anything by half-measures. She got acutely ill. It seemed to be the same situation as we'd had with both Bwana and Mothlo: severe diarrhoea, difficult to arrest, without an identifiable cause or source of infection. I wouldn't have thought it was possible for it to be worse than we had with Bwana, but it was. It seemed as if we were fighting for her life all over again.

We removed all the topsoil in her enclosure and replaced it with fresh clean soil and sand. As a grazer a white rhino carries its head low to the ground – we needed to be sure that she couldn't pick up any pathogens that way. After every excretion we cleaned up meticulously. Our walks got shorter, then ceased. Her weight dropped alarmingly. We tried lucerne, but although she chewed willingly enough it caused her condition to worsen. She was only ten months old and I had to watch her collapse from weakness and exhaustion. I gave her smaller quantities of milk formula, increased quantities of sugar water every half an hour, and all the care and constant attention possible.

Almost as a last resort we tried the game-feed pellets, which we gave to Bwana and Mothlo but had not yet offered to Munyane. Game pellets are highly nutritious, consisting of maize, natural browse from trees, lucerne and several other good things unfamiliar to her. She sniffed at it, without much interest, and then, with a sort of dull obedience, took a small mouthful and began to crunch. Perhaps her illness had worn down her resistance and she just didn't have enough spirit left to refuse my pleading. Relieved not to have had to demonstrate the pleasures of the pellets by sampling it for myself, I sat with her and coaxed her through one small cautious meal after another. Within days even the most skeptical among us had to agree that she was better. Whether we could credit the turnaround to the pellets, or even partly to the pellets, I didn't know. But though it was much sooner than I'd have liked to have started her on such solid foods, with her health improving I wasn't about to argue. As long as she wanted her pellets, she got them.

As she got stronger she enjoyed her meals more, and I perhaps a little bit less. Bwana's pointed mouth and prehensile upper lip were very suited to his delicate way of scooping the pellets from your hand. Not so Munyane. She'd be just as eager for the pellets and like him wait with open mouth, but then she'd clamp those wide muscular lips like a vice over the pellets and the hand offering them, and pull. It was clear that for her these sessions became less about food than about her willingness to be entertained. Fortunately, since rhino don't have front teeth she didn't draw blood, but I wasn't sorry when she outgrew her mischievous insistence on tugs-of-war several times a day.

Her recovery proceeded without any further hitches and thereafter visitors to Doornleegte had the opportunity to come into close contact with white as well as black rhino. It was a bitter-sweet success. While I started to dream of a free life in the reserve for a re-wilded Munyane, I had stopped indulging such dreams for Bwana. Nevertheless he, like Mothlo and now Munyane too, was thriving. For that time I was content not to wish for too much more.

More came anyway. It started very quietly, but after 30 years of marriage I didn't need a banner headline to tell me something was brewing.

Clive had always been a generalist, a kind of life-ecologist: interested in everything and in the way each component connected to every other component. He had never lost a child's fascination with the world and enjoyed sharing that fascination with others. It was a most attractive quality to which people, adults and children alike, responded. I did myself. But there was a downside. He collected. Friends, stories, experiences, rhino skulls, grass seeds, bits of history, photographs, rocks…

When he started coming home with extra-long weathered wooden poles I suspected that it might be more than just the usual collector's mania. At the wilderness school and in some of the bush camps similar poles had been used to create striking rustic screening fences, but the poles kept coming. Not just any old poles: they seemed to be specially selected – poles with history and character. I refused to enquire. If he had another scheme, he was going to have to come right out and say so. For the longest time he didn't.

One day we were driving back from Vaalwater. About 40 kilometres out of town the route to Lapalala leaves the tarred road at a sign that says Melkrivier. You turn left and the gravel road takes you past several farms until you reach another Melkrivier sign. For Lapalala you keep left. The right takes you into the area named after the small river running through it. For most of the year this was hardly more than a "spruit", a stream. But when in flood it ran white with chalky sediment, hence Melkrivier – Milky River. As far as one could see from the road this didn't appear to be a particularly prosperous part of the Waterberg. Farmsteads tended to be modest. Here and there one would see derelict echoes of more successful times. Four kilometres from that second Melkrivier sign was one of them: an old school, fallen into disuse, for the children of pioneer families.

As we approached the junction I said something to the effect that it was a pity that no one had been able to find a use for the place – it was such a distressing reminder of time passing and of good effort going to waste. Instead of keeping left for Lapalala, Clive took the right-hand turn, and said, "Well, I've been thinking ..."

The old school environs were overgrown and strewn with garbage. A melancholy place. Clive filled me in on the history. In the early years of the 20th century, especially in such a remote area, building a school to serve a tough farming community was not a simple matter. This one had its genesis in the amalgamation of two smaller farm schools, but the negotiations over the new location became so delicate that it had to be settled by exact, witnessed measurements with a surveyor's chain. The precise mid-point between the two feeder schools lay just east of the Melkrivier.

For the first teachers' residence, corrugated iron had to be imported from England. The hostel required another import: Italian prisoners of war who built it out of cement bricks. The design was undoubtedly influenced by the conservative and careful parents of the pupils: boys one side, girls on the other side, the teachers' accommodation separating the two. Large black iron pots over an open fire served as the kitchen.

From those humble beginnings the Melkrivier Primary School expanded. More pupils, more teachers, more and improved buildings, a school bus, even street-lights. But in the 1980s its heyday was over. Pupil numbers dwindled and at the beginning of the '90s the school closed. By the time Clive and I saw it, what was still standing and left un-scavenged was already depressingly close to a ruin. We strolled through the remains of a garden. It had evidently been laid out with care; the well-grown trees, shrubs and aloes must have been given a really good start to have survived the years of neglect. There was something terribly forlorn about that unloved garden. It seemed such a shame.

But that was from the human perspective, of course. There were geckos sunning themselves on the cracked wall of what used to be a fishpond. There were spiders and beetles and busy lines of ants. Lots of birdlife too, and all the while we were there, the call of a Burchell's coucal – liquid burbles falling and falling again, over and over.

I found myself swept along with Clive's vision for the place. It really *was* a beautiful plan. He pointed out that it would also be an eminently practical plan, supported by the whole family: the prospect of having to inherit their father's 14 rhino skulls had become a running joke between our two sons. His Melkrivier plan would put a stop to that.

It was a lengthy process leading up to the purchase of the entire 100-hectare site and arriving at an integrated design and business plan with input from trustees and board members, but eventually in 1998 Clive's hoard of wooden poles became the handsome and characterful perimeter to the entrance of a cultural museum complex. The Waterberg Museum preserved artefacts from the Stone Age, the Iron Age and pre-industrial settlements up to the 1800s, as well as from the pioneer settler history of the Waterberg. The Rhino Museum – the first in Africa – focused on the natural history and conservation of rhino, and housed among many other objects of interest those 14 rhino skulls. The Eugène Marais Museum was dedicated to the famous poet and naturalist who chose the Waterberg as his refuge, as the study area to develop his ideas on Holism, and as the place to end his life. There was also an art gallery, a library, a tourist information centre serving the Waterberg Nature Conservancy, and a licensed restaurant, Walker's Wayside.

Closer to the little river, well away from the other buildings and busy-ness, there rose a small 12-seater chapel, open to anyone who needed to find a quiet space for contemplation or a private ceremony, or a place for remembrance and thanksgiving.

In the years that followed, that day – the enthusiasm and freshness of our hopes, the scope of it – has stayed with me. Did Clive sense the approach of something? Did I? I don't remember that either of us said so, but then how often doesn't it happen that one becomes aware of something moving, beckoning from somewhere just out of sight, and you *don't* mention it to anyone? You just acknowledge to yourself that a particular course of action feels appealing, or necessary, even inevitable. I do remember that the enterprise had a sense of *rightness* about it, a sense of agreement that sustained us through the very demanding period of planning and restoration that lay ahead.

It was a demanding time on another front too. It began with a phone call. For us in the reserve in those days it was landline or nothing. Most of us didn't bother with cellphones, and those who did very often found themselves in a locality without a signal. So people phoned when they knew they'd have a reasonable chance of finding you at home. Early mornings, evenings or, as in this case, lunchtime.

It was sandwiches and salad on the verandah. We'd only just sat down. I hoped it wasn't going to be a long call. Even though Clive had been happy to do no more than grab a cup of tea and drink it standing up, I'd insisted on something a bit more substantial and a lot more relaxed. I needed it as much as I told him he did. Somehow we were always having to hurry on to the next thing that urgently needed doing. It had proven to be a hard habit to break.

I heard just enough of Clive's side of the conversation to gather that he was talking to someone in the offices of the Northern

Province (later to become Limpopo) provincial government. He came back out looking slightly stunned, and sat down. "That was Annemie de Klerk. You won't believe what she told me. Asked me, actually."

Annemie, from the Department of Environmental Affairs, had just returned from the USA where she'd been impressed with the UNESCO Man and Biosphere programme. She wondered if Clive would be prepared to present this idea – the Waterberg as a biosphere – to the members of the Waterberg Nature Conservancy.

"That's it," Clive said. "That's our next step."

As the first ratified biosphere in the savannah biome the Waterberg would be globally recognised, with biodiversity conservation and ecologically sustainable development balanced within an integrated management system. There'd be a core zone made up of areas of the highest conservation status: nature reserves such as Marakele, Masebe, Moepel, Wonderkop, Mokolo and the Nylsvlei wetland system. Around them there would be the buffer zone: mainly private farms with a conservation mandate, incorporating the Waterberg Nature Conservancy. Then the transitional zone where different forms of land use would be accommodated – economic activity, agriculture, the Waterberg's 26 rural villages – in a way which would not adversely affect conservation.

Lapalala, due to the fact that it represented high conservation value, supported by environmental education and eco-tourism, would lie in the buffer zone. Its importance in safeguarding the core zone would in turn safeguard and enhance its own intrinsic value.

Clive was fired up. This was about more than Lapalala, but Lapalala itself couldn't lose. In fact, without going this route, it stood to lose too much. The way the world was going the challenges for anyone engaged in the preservation of wilderness were ever mounting. Policymakers tended to not speak of wilderness and conservation; they spoke of resources and land use. Wildlife conservation was nothing more than one form of land use – there were others that to many decision makers seemed more important. There were rumblings hinting at insecurity around conservation priorities or support for such priorities in the longer term. Clive pointed out that, in a biosphere, the stakeholders of the Waterberg Nature Conservancy would find their voices joined and strengthened by that of the National Parks Board, the provincial government and the conservation agency of the United Nations, UNESCO.

"We've *got* to go for it," he said. "I'll call some people tonight. Dale first – he'll support it. And then the Babers… "

With that I knew that we were heading into a campaign, one that would probably take years. Consultations, meetings, documents, presentations, travelling, more meetings. The Waterberg Biosphere Reserve was something Clive could already see, something that he *wanted* to see.

My mind was racing. "Where will you find the time?"

For once my anxieties spilled over. What about this, what about that, what about a hundred other things.

It wasn't the response he needed. "Conit…"

He seemed to be searching for words. I waited, but after a moment he simply got up, walked down the steps, through the garden and out of sight. I heard the Pajero drive off. I knew he had only minutes to get to an appointment at the reserve office up on the plateau. He'd hardly eaten anything.

I had appeared ungenerous and didn't like that picture of myself. I felt tired. Tired of seeing everyone else's side of every issue and accommodating that, and of watching Clive do the same. Tired of seeing my husband wear himself out working for causes and issues, labouring on behalf of other people's interests. I was tired of worrying about him.

The wife's job description included this, I knew. You stood by. Not only by his side to share his dreams and successes, but as a witness too to the erosion of fatigue and of the world's unkindnesses. Your every protective instinct might rear up, but you'd be told, "Water under the bridge. Let it go." So you stood by and picked up the pieces.

There was the distant sound of a vehicle. Visitors driving out of the reserve after their stay in one of the bush camps, I thought. Later I'd find their comments and thanks in the visitors' book. Always glowing. Always sad to be leaving. Always promising to return. There'd be lists of the animals and birds they'd spotted. Something wonderful they'd witnessed described with rows of excited exclamation points. Some people left poems. Children left drawings of lopsided antelope or a smiling giraffe or a Thank You garlanded with hearts and stars.

I listened as the vehicle approached, then slowed down for the turn-off and realised they were coming to Doornleegte for a last rhino visit. They were early. But the bus with the children from the wilderness school wouldn't be far behind. By the time they arrived there had better be a smiling, professional woman to welcome them. One who had the answers to their questions and the tact and patience to help them overcome their ignorance or fear. A neat, self-assured woman who would pose for their pictures and let them stay for as long as they liked to admire the creatures she herself admired and loved so much.

I cleared the table and went to the bathroom to wash my face and apply a token lick of lipstick. In the mirror was a middle-aged woman with reddened green eyes. More grey in the blonde hair than she remembered noticing before. Her skin – a fair German skin after all – needed more protection against the murderous African sun. Her hands too could do with some pampering. Though, pamper as she might, they'd still be worker's hands.

Just as well, I thought. The elegantly manicured hands of women with elegant and manicured lives would not last through one day of Doornleegte's unfeminine work routine. My work boots didn't go with petticoats and lace. I didn't embroider or paint or pot. My work involved shovels and buckets and paying attention to animals' excretions. Sometimes, at the end of the day, I didn't smell nice. But would I have it any other way? I loved my life – all of it. Also, perhaps especially, those parts that required a bit of backbone and grit. The woman in the mirror had the grace to look ashamed. "*Zählen Sie Ihren Segen,*" (Count your blessings) I told her, and turned to face the rest of my day.

Shortly after the last of the visitors left, I heard the Pajero return. I finished up at the rhino enclosures, got cleaned up and then took a tea tray to Clive's studio. He was rummaging through his sketchbooks. He looked up and after a moment cleared a corner of the table. I put down the tray.

He pulled me over to the window. It was open, letting in the warm velvety air of the bush. In the late-afternoon light the trees glinted and shone: bronze, copper, jade, gold. Apart from the ever-present cicadas and birds, it was utterly quiet.

Clive leaned his head against mine. "Tell you what," he said. "When it's all over and done we'll leave them to it, and then these two old elephants will lumber off and have themselves a nice long holiday."

NINE
Home

WHILE THE MELKRIVIER DEVELOPMENT and the biosphere initiative ate into every spare moment we had, there was a young white rhino engaged in a battle of wills with her foster mother over the matter of weaning. I was attempting to shift the emphasis away from Munyane's supplementary feed – her beloved milk formula and game pellets – to grass. Every day we'd set off on our rambles to her grazing grounds, Munyane in a sunny temper, playful and cooperative enough to humour me with a perfunctory effort at grazing. But then she'd suddenly stop, her head up, large ears twisting, a snort and she'd be off: a headlong charge, red dust flying as she launched into a dogged, unrelenting attack until the enemy was lying pulverised at her stomping feet, and she'd be snorting and wheeling, bulging eyes searching for the next termite mound to vanquish.

It was impossible to be stern with her. Her antics were less amusing though when it wasn't a termite mound or a fallen branch in her sights, but the 12-seater bus which the field officers from the wilderness school had ill-advisedly left in the Doornleegte driveway. Just like Bwana and Mothlo, Munyane appreciated motorised transport, especially the kind that had mudguards and bumpers tailor-made for the sharpening of horns, and that most inspired refinement of the ordinary rubbing post, a sliding door. She was just as inquisitive as Bwana and more active during the day. This was to be expected: the open grasslands, the natural habitat of white rhino, offered good opportunities for vigorous play and exercise, while the black rhino's natural inclination was to remain sheltered and concealed in its preferred overgrown habitat until night time when it would be more active.

The first time the gate to Munyane's enclosure was left open for the night the Doornleegte kitchen received a spring-cleaning to end all spring-cleanings. Clive protested, but was told that, if he wasn't prepared to help, he should just go to bed and sleep, astonishing as it was to me that he could do so while an innocent and ignorant little rhino calf was wandering alone and unprotected in the wilderness, prey to a multitude of threats. He made the point that she was not a baby anymore and not all that ignorant either – her instincts were intact, and if I wasn't reassured about the extent to which she'd acquired proper rhino behaviour I wouldn't have opened her gate in the first place. Besides, this wasn't another Bwana scenario. Munyane was a female, and like all females she would know exactly what to do if a male were to cross her path. On the whole he rather thought his concern should be for the male.

I tackled the kitchen cupboards which had to be emptied, none too quietly, of all their contents and scrubbed and re-organised. Halfway through the night I discovered that Munyane was back, fast asleep in her sleeping quarters as if nothing unusual had happened. This became the pattern: if she felt like it she'd wander off in the evening and by morning we'd find her waking up after a good sleep in her old quarters. I was enormously heartened by her placid acceptance of her freedom, and grateful too. She was growing into a massive animal, her need for grass was growing exponentially – the rangers who cut Bwana's browse every day also brought fresh grass for her, but it was an unsustainable arrangement.

As time went on it was as if Munyane was taking charge of her own re-wilding, one step at a time. Her gate was open, there was food if she wanted it, but she was free to come and go. Sometimes she'd choose to hang around the house, often at the stairs leading up to the verandah. I noticed the ticks that she'd picked up while grazing, but was reassured to see how competently she took care of them. The red-billed oxpeckers that had been re-introduced into the reserve in the 1980s were a good first line of defence, each one able to account for 100 fully engorged female ticks or thousands of larvae per day. What the oxpeckers didn't get went the way of the mud-bath and a variety of rubbing posts. I never tired of watching from the verandah as Munyane parked herself against a tree or over a rock and proceeded to enjoy a blissful abrasive massage of those hard-to-reach corners.

Bwana, although he could roam to the extent of his 20-hectare enclosure, required the ongoing care that comes with wild animals in captivity, so the growing independence of my two other orphans came as a considerable relief. Mothlo had of course been free for quite a while and was seldom up at the house with us during the day. It was logical to assume that she was doing exactly what hippos are meant to do: spending her days at the river. After watching her feeding with a male companion one night I resisted the temptation to check up on her progress any further. I felt quite proud of my resolve and was determined to do the same with Munyane. I would trust that she could handle her own freedom.

On one of Dale's solo visits to us at Doornleegte, Clive invited me along on an inspection drive – they would see Munyane, he said, and surely I would enjoy watching her, free in the wild. But that was exactly why I couldn't go along. Those hours or days she chose to spend away from Doornleegte were hours or days she chose to spend away from me. I had to respect that. So I waved them off with a last entreaty not to approach her so closely that she'd know they were there – there was more at stake than the male urge to demonstrate how clever and tough they were. Nevertheless I was pleased that Dale would witness the outcome of something he and Elizabeth had started: they saw Munyane, a distraught little calf with her dead mother, before I did and persuaded me to undertake one more rescue. Her freedom was reward and vindication for all of us – a token of the joint leap of faith that had created Lapalala.

On another occasion I did accompany the men on a long drive up into the eastern section of the reserve. Our last stop was Lookout Camp – four safari-tents hidden among cliff-top vegetation right on the edge of a headland. The kind of place and the kind of moment best enjoyed in companionable silence. Dale stood gazing at the view, a breath-taking sweep to the horizon with flat-topped Malora etched against the sky. Without clouds to flame the sunset it was that still, muted blue of day's end. Suddenly he turned to Clive and me, and pulled us both into a hug.

"We've done it," he said. "We've *really* done it."

He tried to say more, but seemed uncharacteristically moved and couldn't. After all the notes and letters of thanks he'd written to us over the years, I thought I knew how much Lapalala and our role in it had meant to him. But in that moment there was an openness very seldom on display.

We lingered on, hoping for a glimpse of giraffe browsing the tree-tops far below. If we were lucky, although we might not realise it at that distance, they might be rather special giraffe.

Ten years earlier: a flurry of phone calls and cryptic messages, and I was summoned to a council of war. Dale wanted to celebrate his 50th birthday in style; the main attraction was to be Lapalala. They wondered if I might like to be involved.

Of course, how lovely, Dale is our friend. What did they have in mind? They had a lot in mind, and as we worked our way down the column of items (catering, provisioning, accommodation, transport, staff) a second column grew next to it. I was startled to find my name sprouting in several places. I began with the most crucial item when entertaining in the bush: how many mouths to feed how many times over how many days.

D-Day arrived and I discovered that one rather crucial item had slipped through the cracks: my wardrobe. This was not quite as frivolous a concern as it sounds. The birthday bash was to last a weekend. As the wife of the Managing Director of Lapalala and the Alternate Director myself, I had to look the part. Bush casual, I thought, though not too casual. And for the gala dinner: something rather less bush and decidedly less casual. I had nothing to wear.

Clive was no help at all. With typical male myopia he thought that as long as the guests were comfortably accommodated (in bush camps with well-stocked fridges and freezers) and well-fed (including a slap-up multi-course dinner at Kolobe Lodge) they wouldn't notice anything out of place. He was wrong, but there was no time for debate. He had worries of his own. This was the part of the festivities about which Dale knew nothing. I knew, but had been sworn to secrecy. On the whole I thought I'd rather have my own worries than those of anyone who had to coordinate the logistics of Dale's birthday surprise. While I was hurriedly trying on and discarding, trying on and discarding, I kept darting to the window to listen. Dale was flying his guests up from the Cape in two Dakotas, and their arrival at the airstrip would be my signal to get into position to welcome them.

"But how will I know when?" I asked Clive.

"You'll hear them. They're loud."

"But there could be other planes. How will I know it's *them*?"

He gave me the sort of look a man gives a woman when she displays her ignorance about something which every man is apparently born knowing.

"Because they're *DC3s*. That's why. They'll *sound* like *DC3s*!"

"But what's that *like*?" I wailed.

He looked non-plussed. Then he said, "Like old movies. They'll sound like old war movies."

They did. That memorable weekend began with the sound of the Allied Forces flying over my childhood Europe at the end of WWII.

Every single Lapalala-staffer got into the spirit of the occasion, from the manager, Clive Ravenhill, on down. Even our EWE office staff came up from Johannesburg to help with afternoon teas and the gala dinner, expertly managed by the lodge manageress. Dale had the pleasure of showing off his Waterberg treasure to his friends, and they in turn had the excitement of springing the surprise. This was planned with the precision of army manoeuvres.

To keep Dale occupied and out of the way a game drive had been organised, the route planned to take him and his guests out of view and out of ear-shot of the main access road. Eventually they wound up at the old reception area in the western section of the reserve where Dale discovered a boma that had been prepared in secret. Within it was his birthday gift: five giraffe (Lapalala's first), which had been off-loaded a bare minute before the game drive vehicles arrived. Dale was thrilled, but scarcely more so than the conspirators who'd pulled off the split-second operation.

It remains a lovely memory. And so does that afternoon, years later, on Lookout's wooden deck facing west when I realised as I hadn't before, that Dale's response to that patch of earth was very simple: he loved it.

A man of decided opinions, Dale's choices did not always jump with mine, but this bond we had in common. This dream for wilderness was stronger. I understood why Clive took the risk way back in 1981 of trusting someone on the basis of a dream and a handshake. I understood why the two of them did not have to compete with each other. Dale called Clive "Bwana" and was called "Bwana" in return – a tacit acceptance of equals working together for a greater purpose.

We stayed there on the edge of the cliff while the heat leached out of the day. Between us and faraway Malora with its ancient stone-walling and ghosts, the lowland was falling into shadow. A sudden clatter of hooves on loose stones among the trees at the foot of the cliff set off a commotion of screeching panic. This was deceptive: guineafowl don't panic. They shriek and squawk and whinge, peevishly broadcasting their exaggerated upset – they're Mother Nature's moaners. When we left they were still complaining.

Our way home passed through one of the few cellphone reception spots in the area, but none of us felt like phoning or checking for messages. We dropped down from the plateau into the deeper dusk of the Palala valley. Richer air, heady with the sweetly astringent fragrance of flowering *sekelbos*; more spoor, more stops to read them. By the time we got to the bridge over the Palala the light was virtually gone.

If there is a more soothing sound than that of a flowing river in a wild place I have yet to discover it. And somewhere in it, or grazing next to it, was Mothlo. I hadn't seen her for a long time. As far as I knew she was fully part of the wild, free life of Lapalala now. One of those extraordinary occasions when losing something or someone you love is a source of happiness rather than sorrow.

Dinner was the usual relaxed occasion. Stories, jokes, plans, silences when some wild sound reached us and we stopped to listen. Life at Doornleegte was simple. Unfussy food, the unglamorous routines of working with earth and animals. Yet Dale, a dedicated businessman, settled into it with relish.

In our far-from-grand lounge with its 1930s furniture, piles of books, art works by African and European artists, and on one wall, the skin of a lion which Dale himself had shot in Zimbabwe when it was still Rhodesia and he a much younger man, he leaned back and stretched out his legs. "Home from home," he said.

His words niggled at me the next morning as I drove to the Waterberg Museum at Melkrivier. What is home? Not necessarily the place where you live – ask any exile. It is not where your family is, or your furniture, or your books and clothes, or where you spend most of your time. It may not be the place you've bought or constructed with your own hands. It doesn't even have to be a built structure – ask a child who grows up in a refugee camp, who sleeps in a donated army tent among a dozen others who, like him, know only war and fleeing from war. Whatever home is, it isn't the same for everyone.

Ask an old man of Bushmen blood where his home is. He'll go quiet and look away somewhere into the distance, past the trappings and conveniences of the place where he with his remaining clan members had been resettled, and then he'll begin to tell you about the sky and about the wind and the stories that it used to bring to him. He'll tell you the distance between water sources, and the names of the stars that showed him the way. The place somebody died, or survived. In his memory he goes home.

Not everyone is content with that. History might have moved on, but they are not ready to. Among all the apparent injustices, the nastiness and cruelty that people perpetrate upon one another, there is one that is more suited to recourse than most of the others. If you have killed my child, I (with or without the law) can make you pay for that, but it will not bring my child back to life. Punish you as I might, he will live only in my memory. But if you have taken my home I, with the full support of the law, will demand adequate recompense. Give me back the place where my forefathers lived, where their graves are.

In this way thousands upon thousands of South Africans looked to the law pertaining to land claims to redress generations of humiliation and want. A compensatory gesture.

For a government beset on all sides by an array of legitimate causes for discontent among its voters, land claims had to serve as the panacea. In September 1999 the Chief Land Claims Commissioner was called to report to the government's Agriculture and Land Affairs Committee. He was challenged on the apparent slow pace of delivery. In his defence he stated that to date 600 380 land claims had been settled in favour of the claimants. He promised that in another six months, by March 2000, he would have settled 3000 more. And in each subsequent year he would rule in favour of land claimants in at least twice, perhaps even three times, that number of cases.

Well-intentioned as that sounded I had to wonder about its practicability, and the likelihood that the process would be able to confer not just land on the claimants, but what everyone hoped would be the deeper rewards of healing. A successful legal challenge to land ownership is a transaction. A legitimate or in some cases a legitimised redistribution of land. Look beyond the paperwork and the court's proclamation and the question remains: what qualifies a particular place for a particular person, in his heart of hearts, as his home? Is it roots – some deep ancestral memory that binds him to that specific configuration of landscape? A unique composition of geology and seasons and memory, of growing up and growing old? No doubt.

But what then of those instances where ancestry plays no role? At least not in the obvious nationalistic sense. Take Kuki Gallmann, Italian born and bred. But no one can doubt that for her, "home" in the fullest, most complete sense of being the place where you belong, is Ol Ari Nyiro on the Laikipia highlands in Kenya. She lost both her husband and her son in Kenya – the one in a car accident, the other, most tragically, after a puff-adder bite. But she stayed.

I remember sitting on the Doornleegte verandah listening to her as she spoke about Ol Ari Nyiro and her work there – conservation, social engagement, education. That was in 1991, the first time she visited us at Lapalala. Around us it was the Waterberg, but in her telling – so passionate and evocative – I was there with her, on the edge of Africa's Great Rift Valley. What she was talking about was not just the work, her house, or the 100 000-acre ranch, splendid as it was, but the depth of her commitment, her love of it. Her enduring bond with the land. Home. An Italian, yet African. There are many like her. "Colonialists" some would say and not intend it as a compliment. In my view they would be wrong. Europeans in Africa are not always a curse. They may find great pain, like Kuki who held her dying son in her arms, but they cannot leave. Africa had taken them captive.

What of us, the Walkers? Clive with his British forebears, I with my German roots – where did we belong?

I turned in through the museum gates. Whose was that bit of the Waterberg before the first of the pioneers who had sold it to the first of the Nels, the ancestor of the generation of Nels who sold it on to us? Despite all the research we had done prior to purchase, we hadn't been able to discover such an original owner. No doubt the earliest inhabitants, the San, moved through the area en route to those places where we had evidence that they remained for a while. It was only appropriate, I thought, to site a museum honouring the Waterberg's pre-history at what was then, as it remained up to our day, a crossroads – a meeting point of people and history.

The restaurant, Walker's Wayside, was doing brisk trade in coffees and late breakfasts. A school group was trailing into the building on the right. I trailed in after them. Eavesdropping on visitors gives much more accurate information about the success or otherwise of your enterprise than any number of tactfully or carelessly filled-in questionnaires. This teacher had done her homework and fortunately it seemed that there was enough of interest for her to be able to hold the attention of her students. As expected the rhino exhibits got the best response – foetuses in formaldehyde bottles, the collection of rhino skulls, and backed by outsize posters of rhino in full charge, the complete skeleton of a white rhino.

That was Rocky, Clive's pride and joy. In 1982 he had bought him for 1200 rand to add to Lapalala's white rhino numbers, and to benefit the gene pool of the resident population. Rocky did extremely well until the day, a decade later, when a devastating veld fire swept through Lapalala. In his terror Rocky fled into an eroded riverbed, but his burns were too severe and he died there. It wasn't until a survey team spotted his remains from the air that his fate became known and Clive could retrieve the skeleton.

The school group moved on to a section devoted to the Save the Rhino Trust, and there I stopped listening, my thoughts going to the courage and commitment of the woman in the large photograph facing the door. Blythe Loutit. As well known as Dr Ian Player's name is in the story of the white rhino in South Africa, just as well known should Blythe's be in the story of the survival of black rhino in Namibia. Through SRT she had mobilised everyone from news media to mining organisations, government officials to tribal chiefs and geological prospectors and managed to halt the relentless butchering of rhino and elephant she'd seen in that country. Rhino conservation has its own Hall of Fame – she had richly deserved her place in it.

I left the students to the rest of their tour and got stuck into the task that had brought me there. The old Melkrivier headmaster's house was not required for museum business, and although the basic renovation was well underway, it was not yet habitable. I'd come equipped with a generous supply of putty and other materials for sealing gaps and holes and cracks where tiny field mice tried to gain access to their former homes and nesting sites.

That's the bush: so much vigour that if left alone it will quickly overtake our efforts at "taming" it. All over Lapalala I'd seen how evidence of the former agricultural use of the land disappeared under pioneer plants, albeit in this instance with human help encouraging the process. Season after season more life returned as the wilderness reasserted its own, prior, claim to the land.

In many places we'd come across heavy grinding stones, sometimes perfectly preserved as if they'd been used to grind corn only that morning, sometimes cracked by centuries of sun and frost. The users of those stones would have been women taking care of the domestic round as I was doing with my trowel and packets of putty. They would have fetched water from the rivers and there they would have seen the rock paintings left by people who'd lived there long before they did. Did they wonder about them? Did they care? Did they think the remaining traces of that long lost culture worth preserving? Ancient oral cultures, like our modern literate ones, had an acute sense of history – at what point did it begin to stretch beyond their own? We can guess, but we don't know. Museums are a more modern invention. And in any case, a museum only preserves what remains – the kind of cultural artefacts housed in the Waterberg Museum. Grinding stones, pottery shards, a weathered Bible, hand-printed schoolbooks, faded photographs – evidence of many generations of people who each, at some point in the long history of the Waterberg, called it home. Who's to say who was right or wrong to do so?

With the headmaster's house sealed against anything that might want to burrow, crawl, tunnel or slither its way in, I was ready to go. I roused my assistant. She had earlier got the message that her efforts were not valued and had retired to a corner in what looked like a sulk. At the first signs of what she recognised as packing up, however, she bounded up with as much exuberance as she'd shown earlier in scrabbling after mice and worrying packets of putty, and raced around my ankles, tripping me up at every opportunity until we were out of the door.

Button was mostly fox terrier and wholly personality. As a six-week-old puppy she had turned up at the Melkrivier Museum one morning, a disconsolate little bundle at the end of a wire tied to the chain of a bicycle. Also at the museum that morning was my animal-lover daughter-in-law, René. The outcome was inevitable. The owner of the bicycle, socialising with museum staff, found himself confronted by a petite blonde on the warpath. He was clearly not fit to be in charge of a baby animal. What would it take for him to remove that wicked wire around the poor animal's neck? It took 30 rand.

Clive was presented with a perky and perfectly groomed puppy as a gift, a much appreciated consolation for our beloved Staffordshire terrier that had died shortly before. Button adopted both of us and became fiercely protective. In the shortest space of time we couldn't imagine Doornleegte without her feisty energy. She seemed to have no sense at all of her limitations as a small dog. Mothlo and Munyane were playmates she could outrun. Bwana, at full speed, was too fast for her but she kept on trying, dashing underneath his belly, sprinting within inches of his thumping feet. On one occasion she miscalculated. Bwana's one foot came down squarely on her hip. I feared the worst as she clearly was in great pain. But miraculously there was no break. She recovered and was back to her fearless self.

While I locked up the headmaster's house, Button raced ahead, taking a short cut through the restaurant's outdoor seating area en route to her ride home. I followed in her wake, with apologies for my dog threading between chairs and table legs. I heard foreign accents – tourists from Europe and America. As a young girl I'd also dreamt of travelling the world, a dream that came true during my flight-attendant years when it was my job to see all those alluring faraway places. Some of my compatriots discovered localities on other continents where they felt more at home than in Africa. I didn't. Home was the place I returned to. Once Bwana had entered my life, that was Doornleegte.

Twelve kilometres from the museum there was someone at the reserve gates who knew me and my family as well as I knew him and his. A brief conversation, and in my rear-view mirror I saw him still smiling and waving after me. I was on a road of which I could describe every twist and turn. Didn't that feel like home? The Palala flowing past Doornleegte also flowed past Lepotedi and Munadu and the reed beds of Tambuti. The paperbark albizias with their peeling, flesh-coloured sheets, the sandstone cliff throwing the night's frog chorus up to the camp at Umdoni ... Maybe home was more than just that rustically comfortable farmhouse with its rhino enclosures among the umbrella thorns. Maybe home was all of Lapalala.

But what of those moments when, standing alone among broken, lichen-covered stone walls on top of Malora, I felt overwhelmed to the point of tears by 360-degree views of such peace and beauty, of the charcoal-green bush-clad bones and sinews of the land all the way to the edge of sight? There, scarcely real in the shimmering haze where the Waterberg gives way before the hills of Botswana, lay the northern extreme of Makuldubane, End Mountain. Maybe my borders were drawn more generously. Maybe home was the Waterberg.

TEN

Waterberg rain

NO ONE LIKES A BACK-SEAT DRIVER. I don't myself. But on the night of 31 December 1999 I subjected poor Clive to a full range of instructions, cautions and squeaks of alarm. Luckily the ferocious rain made all except my loudest protests inaudible. The windscreen wipers were all but useless. In the headlights we had intermittent, flickering glimpses of the flooded world outside. Torrents of muddy water where there used to be bridges, stretches of washed-away road which transformed our route home into something that for me became virtually unrecognisable and felt never-ending.

We had considered turning back, but Clive thought we'd get through. He'd been in worse. In fact so had I, but that was when I was still young enough to believe that fortune favoured the terminally optimistic. As we crawled beyond the point where turning back was an option, it seemed that Clive still believed that high spirits conquered all. "Good rains!" he bellowed above the din.

We reached the hair-raising descent from the plateau, the road gouged now by rushing streams carrying stones and red soil to the valley floor. A few more slithery kilometres further along what was left of the access road we guessed at our turn-off, the familiar landmarks lost in volumes of water that bucketed straight down. At last the headlights revealed the farm gate with its uniquely drunken list – an early encounter with a strapping young hippo, Mothlo. Clive volunteered to get out and open it, but I was already on my way. Drenched in seconds I waved him through, dragged the gate shut and squelched to the back door. The homely comforts of Doornleegte had never been more welcoming than on that night of severe flooding in Limpopo Province.

The weather seemed appropriately apocalyptic. If the media were to be believed the world as we knew it was about to end. The year 2000 heralded Something. The dawn of a new era, the final flowering of the Age of Aquarius, or according to the doomsayers, Armageddon. At the stroke of midnight the Millennium Bug would strike in a global electronic meltdown: computers would malfunction and satellites plunge to earth, banks wouldn't be able to operate, planes wouldn't be able to fly, things that shouldn't would blow up. Only those with well-stocked bunkers would survive.

But on the whole, even for the doomsayers, it was party time. In front of television screens in millions of sitting rooms like ours at Doornleegte, in pubs, town squares and closed-off streets around the world, people watched as nations, longitude after longitude, counted down the seconds to the New Millennium.

Outside, the storm was gathering strength. Telephone communications were already down; a power cut wasn't far off. But we had candles and champagne. Clive raised his glass: "To you, Grandma!"

It was true: we were grandparents. Our nightmare drive back that night was the return from a New Year's Eve celebration with our children and not-quite-two-months-old Ayden.

Our family now spanned four generations. Clive's mother was over 80 and as independently spirited as ever. But with every subsequent visit to us in Lapalala I noticed bigger changes. Her short walks to Bwana's enclosure became slower, the time she spent there to watch him or me working with him became shorter. She wouldn't admit to pain. For her children a difficult decision was suddenly made easier when we found a kinder alternative to the frail care options in Johannesburg for which she simply wasn't ready: we'd bring her to live with us at Doornleegte. If all went well, she'd be there with us long before the next New Year's Eve.

Clive, philosophically inclined as he was, yet found the frailty of the only parent he ever really knew hard to witness. The fact of our mortality hit him young, with his father's death when he was only eight. After that he was never able to take life for granted to the same degree as so many other young people did and still do.

I looked at him, sitting across from me in his comfortable old easy chair. Thirty-two years earlier I did the same. We were living in Johannesburg then, we'd been married for just over a year and he was holding our one-month-old firstborn son on *his* first New Year's Eve. Now we were what could politely be termed "mature". His hair and beard were streaked with grey; his eyes, like mine, needed glasses. The South Africa we were living in would have been unrecognisable to that young couple in the 1960s.

Apartheid had gone and so – at least from the political arena – had the most famous post-apartheid icon, Nelson Mandela. With the 1999 national elections he was as good as his word and did not stand for re-election as president. His successor, Thabo Mbeki, was facing fearsome tests on all fronts. The initial euphoria of the new freedom had worn off. Too many South Africans were becoming impatient with the non-delivery of too many election promises; health and social services and educational institutions were buckling under over-idealistic reforms; every so often a member of the new ruling elite was found to be considerably less noble than his or her Struggle persona. The Reverend Alan Boesak, a shining beacon in the fight against apartheid, was found guilty and jailed for defrauding European donors through his Foundation for Peace and Justice. Winnie Madikizela-Mandela – though she was ultimately untouchable – had to stand trial for, among other crimes, murder. We reluctantly had to give up on the naïve mythology of a shift in South Africa's socio-political order delivering also a morally impeccable governing authority.

However pragmatic a view one took of nations in transition, the facts were not reassuring. Crime was on the rise, significantly so even in a society where such things were known to be grossly under-reported. In 1999 violent crime was up by 22% since 1994. A third of all recorded crime was violent.

Still, elsewhere it was much worse. There was growing political and social instability in Robert Mugabe's Zimbabwe. News of land invasions, summary arrests and torture of journalists and political opponents began to reach us. There was a noticeable increase in refugee movements across the border. We were uncomfortably aware that the only thing preventing Zimbabwe's problems from becoming South Africa's was that porous border along the Limpopo, a scant few hours' drive north of our home-base in the Waterberg. Like a Waterberg veld fire, your neighbour's politics affected you too.

Our field of operations was not primarily political; we worked for a cause which we believed was greater than that. But under apartheid we'd learnt that in the end *everything* is political. Nothing is immune. The agendas that drive the politics of the day will draw borders between countries and between people. They will affect your life and work, no matter how high the moral ground on which you think you stand.

Conservationists would like to think that conservation priorities trump political ones. That is not always the case. In 1998 the South African Land Claims Court published a landmark ruling. It decided in favour of a claim by the Makuleke community. The claim comprised almost 20 000 hectares of pristine wilderness in South Africa's oldest and largest nature reserve, the Kruger National Park, run by a parastatal organisation, the South African Parks Board.

Protracted and difficult negotiations were undertaken in the hope that the claimants would support, to their own financial and social benefit, the continued utilisation of the land as conserved wilderness. It was match-making between politics and conservation. An agreement was reached: the Makuleke Contractual Park was formed and would continue to operate as part of the KNP. What seemed at first to have been an ominous sign turned into a favourable outcome for both the claimants and for a national conservation asset.

In the 1950s Clive's mother had taken her two small boys on trips to the old Kruger Park, and many years later as young parents ourselves it was our turn to do the same. Pafuri, the northern area around the Levuvhu River, including the triangle between the confluence of the Levuvhu and the Limpopo which was to be claimed by the Makuleke, seemed a paradise then. At the end of 1999 it was good to know that it was to remain so.

In that mysterious and deceptively comforting way one has of dealing with the passing years, we still felt like those same much younger people, as if all the changes were only in the world outside. But every so often life hands one a moment when, even by the light of candles – so much more merciful than electrical light – one has to quietly acknowledge to yourself that the years have left their mark on the one who is closest and most dear to you.

It could hardly be otherwise. The Waterberg Environmental Centre and Museum at Melkrivier were up and running; Clive was appointed to the Limpopo Province Tourism Board; a book, *Larger Carnivores of the African Savanna*, which he'd illustrated, got published and he'd begun writing a co-authored book, *African Elephants*. He still served on the African Rhino Specialist Group of the IUCN and was heavily involved in the campaign for the formation and ratification of the Waterberg Biosphere Reserve. All of this in addition to his responsibilities in Lapalala, his ongoing patronage and support of the Endangered Wildlife Trust and his chairmanship of the wilderness school. Whenever there was a spare moment he painted and donated his art works to raise funds for conservation.

It was the life he wanted and he went at it with the vigour of a young man. Sometimes with the agility of a young man too, as I reminded him when the evening and the champagne reached the stage where I was brave enough to risk mention of The Day of the Leguaan.

Clive's studio was situated about 15 metres from the house. In summer, when the Palala valley lay shimmering in the heat, he left the windows open to the surrounding bush and the occasional lazy stirring of heavy, perfumed air. The stable door was of unusual design; Mothlo's attentions and the necessity of effecting repairs that would keep her out while still allowing Clive in saw to that.

One morning he opened that stable door and realised that someone or something had managed to get in. Not Mothlo. For one thing the door was intact, and for another no hippo could have caused that smell. A silver beer mug, a 21st birthday gift from way-back-when, was lying on the floor surrounded by the collection of paint brushes normally stashed in it. Some of the animal skulls with which he cluttered up the place – decorated, he said – had been moved.

It might have been a squirrel or a vervet monkey. They were always around. But so were the black mambas – the hill behind Doornleegte was alive with them. From his collection of "knob-kieries" he selected as good a weapon as could be found in an artist's studio and starting poking around. He tracked the source of the smell to a generously-sized white, yellow and black deposit next to a large wooden architect's cabinet which housed his art paper and finished works. Leguaan, he thought.

The culprit had to be underneath the cabinet. He bent down to peer into the dark space, then carefully retreated and shouted for back-up. While he waited he ran through the number of options available in such a confined space. There weren't many. His back-up, Fred and Rosina, arrived and armed themselves with their pick of the knob-kieries. Then they retreated. In order to do their best work, they felt, they required lots of room, well away from the action, outside the studio.

Clive entered alone. The few centimetres of tail he could see sticking out was attached to something which filled up all available space under the cabinet. Not all reptiles are venomous, but most of them can bite, and almost all of them if grabbed by the tail will do the same thing: whip around with lightning speed and sink its teeth or fangs into you. If it had neither teeth nor fangs it could clamp bony jaws onto your hand or arm with enough force to draw blood. So you didn't do that, you went for the back of the head. If you couldn't, you grabbed what you could and trusted to speed.

The sight of Clive flying through the open door, trailing a 2.5-metre snake and then with adrenaline-fuelled strength sending it sailing over the grass, stunned Fred and Rosina into horrified inaction. As the large rock python made a bee-line for the undergrowth Fred was the first to recover. He was highly indignant. Didn't Clive realise what strong medicine could have been made from a snake that size? For probably the first time in his life Clive had absolutely no interest in indigenous culture and said so.

Much of our reminiscing that night involved wild animals. Naturally – they so often dictated the shape of our days. The duration if not the distance of a trip either within the reserve or to any destination beyond the reserve gates was determined by the truculent rhino blocking the road, or the herd of antelope refusing to be hurried out of the way. A sudden heart-stopping stampede of a group of eland could have you slamming on the brakes. A magnificent kudu bull might cross right in front of you and you'd find you simply had to wait to see its family materialise out of seemingly impenetrable bush, looking as poised and graceful as only kudu cows with their young can. Or a field ranger might radio in an emergency and all at once whatever plans you had had for the day would be scuppered. The rescue of a baby rhino, for example, sending your whole life veering in a direction you'd not foreseen.

Little did I know when I first agreed to become foster mother to a wild animal that I'd relinquished control over even the time I got up in the morning. As with a new baby in the home I knew that there'd be initial disruptions and discomforts, but I naïvely assumed that at some point we'd settle into a routine. In any case, I'd never been a late sleeper – I'd be up long before anyone else. Bwana took care of that illusion.

I have vivid memories of Clive and me scrambling out of bed and like a well-coordinated if bleary-eyed team sprinting to our allocated stations: I to get my hands on a bucket of game pellets, he to open the gate to Bwana's enclosure. Once in position we'd proceed to phase two: attracting the attention of the black rhino bull busy sharpening his horn on that long-suffering studio door. This was Bwana during his carefree days of roaming the Lapalala wilderness. In the dim, uncertain light of dawn he appeared colossal and every bit as dangerous as he was, especially when viewed by people in their pyjamas. I would call out to him and with the aid of the pellets lure him along the verandah, manoeuvring to a point where he could catch sight of Clive who, now poised at the entrance to the garden, was semaphore-ing to initiate phase 3. From that point on timing was everything.

Bwana spots Clive and gives chase; Clive bolts into the enclosure and, with Bwana's charge a heartbeat from his fleeing heels, heads for the highest fence pole; I race after Bwana, frantically rattling the pellet bucket; at the last moment Bwana, unable to resist a racket that implies food, wheels around and comes for me; I stop breathing, pole barrier and bribe-bucket between Bwana and myself; Clive shinnies down his pole, vaults the fence, gallops around the outside, slams the gate and triumphantly locks it.

We'd always end up laughing and, still out-of-breath over coffee, assure each other that of course he wouldn't have hurt us. But the next time it happened it would be as nerve-wracking as before. After the night when Bwana was attacked by another rhino bull it was the end of his freedom. I know now that I'd have been willing to endure any number of his uniquely fraught wake-up calls if he could have remained free.

Inevitably, that New Year's Eve also became a stock-taking of our life's work. All was not well with conservation in South Africa. If one looked hard enough you could find hopeful signs but on the whole it wasn't a matter of advancing nature's cause, more a case of fighting to slow the retreat. Biodiversity conservation made for good green slogans, but was in reality slipping ever lower on the political agenda. Organisations in charge of natural areas – botanical gardens, provincial nature reserves which were in fact national assets – were warned that they'd have to survive on greatly reduced subsidies, or on no subsidy at all. Places of refuge for wildlife and lovers of wildlife had to become commercially viable. Only if it pays, it stays. Biodiversity conservation would be determined by the marketplace, dictated by the whims and vagaries of consumers. I wished I had more faith in the wisdom of consumers.

My faith in the wisdom of governmental structures was already rather threadbare. Very good at talking, they'd make a statement, call a meeting, form a task group, launch a consultative process. But far too often an unacceptable situation would only improve if a private individual stepped in. And that wasn't only true for conservation.

In the early 1990s I had discovered that there was no school nearby where Lapalala's 70 staff members could send their children. For a teacher like myself that was an unacceptable state of affairs. My appeals to the relevant authorities resulted in a lot of forms to be filled in, not much more.

Finally, frustrated with the wait-and-see attitude of the Department of Education, I phoned a farmer, Louis Nel. "Come over," he said.

He showed me a piece of land, right on the boundary he shared with Lapalala. "Will this do?" he asked. I assured him it would. His ready cooperation shouldn't have surprised me, and perhaps it didn't. Louis, like so many other farmers I'd come to know, came from pioneer stock – farm schools were simply an accepted part of the farming landscape. His wife, Ansa, promised to teach the first two grades.

I drove the 120 kilometres to Nylstroom (Modimolle), withdrew my personal savings and sent a message to Klaas Mashasha, a builder who worked at Lapalala. On 18 February 1994, a crowd of well-wishers and prospective pupils joined the Nels, Klaas and me for the school's opening. Glowing red facebrick, proper ablution facilities, a playground with jungle gyms and swings and various other opportunities for exercising and strengthening young limbs. We named the school Refihlile: We have arrived.

Almost six years on the school was thriving, the learners now on their Christmas break. All of them have also passed through the Lapalala Wilderness School, their education rounded out by learning about the environment that determined their own survival to an extent our rulers weren't ready to fully acknowledge, even when they were ready to fully understand it in the first place.

Clive got up to look out at the night. I joined him at the open door. The world had disappeared. There was only rain. Fragrant, blessed rain.

I wondered how Mothlo was faring in the fiercest storm she'd yet had to survive. I asked Clive whether we ought to be concerned about the level of the Palala. He refused to worry. If the water was over the bridge, or had already damaged the bridge, there was nothing to be done – no right-thinking person would be outside and trying to cross. As for Doornleegte itself, the Palala might burst its banks, but short of a flood of biblical immensity we'd be above the flood-line. In any case, he said, looking at me over his glasses, a shared bottle of champagne was nowhere near enough alcohol to make him go out in the middle of the night in the middle of a storm to go stare at a flooding river on the impossibly remote chance that he might be able to spot his wife's hippo.

With Doornleegte's candles burning low, the last of the champagne served to toast Ayden, the newest of the Walkers, too young to know that what he was hearing that night, just like his grandparents, was hard Waterberg rain on a tin roof. Where would his fate take him? He might grow up to live and work, like his parents and grandparents, in the Waterberg. Or he might leave one day to make a life elsewhere and discover that he is forever longing for the smell of Waterberg rain.

ELEVEN

Ayden's world

OUR NEW MILLENNIUM BEGAN much as the old one ended, wet and getting wetter. No sooner would we have cleared away the soggy lucerne and mud-trampled browse from Bwana's feeding area, and replaced it with freshly cut branches, than another ear-splitting salvo would roll down the valley and the heavens open once more. Bwana, untroubled by thunder and lightning, would waken from his doze under the trees, stretch, amble over to a favourite rubbing post and stand there rocking gently while the rain poured down his glistening flanks. Then, the last of his sleepiness washed out of him, he'd look around for entertainment. He'd find it. Titus and I had taken to placing the fresh browse on top of the enclosure railing, wedging it there within Bwana's reach but well clear of the mud. It was no use. Bwana didn't share my fears about contamination risks and in no time at all the branches would be yanked down and swung and shoved all over the place. It was playtime. Rain never failed to plunge him straight back into puberty. He'd jump up and down, splashing mud over himself, his food, over Titus and me. He'd race off to the furthest corner of his huge enclosure and then come charging back, blowing like a bellows in that glorious rain-fresh air and making me laugh with his sheer delight in life.

This side of his nature showed very early on, during his first rainy season at Doornleegte. He was just over a year old. We were halfway up our hill on an exploratory ramble when the rain started spitting. As the first heavy drops steamed away off his back and off the rocks around us there was that unmistakable sense of charged air with the smells of the bush intensifying. Within minutes we were in a drizzle and Bwana's dusty shoulders darkly streaked. The hard rain arrived, so loud I could no longer hear Bwana's rapturous sniffing at every wet bush or branch. I was drenched and wouldn't have minded a rapid retreat down the hill, but he had other ideas. He clearly loved being out in the rain, pushing through the sodden vegetation, taking sips from small puddles, and smelling, smelling everything. I didn't have the heart to cut short his excursion. I squelched up and around and eventually down that hill back home, soaked and shivering with my contented little rhino by my side.

His love affair with rain and mud continued. As an adult bull he still revelled in trampling every patch of water-softened soil into a mini mud-bath and then trying to get as much of his bulk as possible into it. When the high heat of summer forced most creatures into the shade he'd spend a lot of time lying in his water hole, getting out from time to time to scrape in more mud from the perimeter and then wallowing in that richer, stickier bath. That whole water-logged 1999–2000 season, whenever I passed his enclosure or glanced out through the kitchen window, there he was: an enormous adult black rhino bull endeavouring still with the single-minded enjoyment he'd shown in his first years to coat every inch of himself with Doornleegte's thick rust-red mud. It's an indelible memory in which my summers are anchored.

Since heavier rains made heavier work I have memories too of that season's weariness, of power cuts and clothes that wouldn't dry out; of my old Toyota's grinding, slithering progress from one bush camp to the next; of getting out in the pouring rain to first test river-crossings on foot before low-gearing into the rushing, swirling waters. For a brief time the Waterberg was living up to its name in a way it hadn't done for many decades. Everywhere there was the sound of water: thundering in foam-fringed rapids, trickling in rills across and in between rocks, dripping from the thatched eaves of a bush camp.

There was one morning... Before the start of the school year, I was at the wilderness school campus with my perennial list of items to be checked or repaired or improved. A red-chested cuckoo was calling – three liquid notes endlessly falling in counterpoint to the river which tumbled and roared less than 100 metres away. Hoping to spot the cuckoo somewhere in the canopy, I rounded a corner and stopped in my tracks. Under a stand of monkey thorns, covered in golden flower spikes and abuzz with bees and insects, a nyala ram had its head down, nibbling at the carpet of flowers and the previous season's split seed pods. Saffron-tipped horns with their elegant twist, dark charcoal-brown coat, cinnamon shanks against the cream of the fissured and flaking tree trunks. I remembered the planting of those monkey thorns 15 years before – slender saplings to mark our hopes for the school. Now they towered into the summer-blue sky. The nyala moved off down to the thicker vegetation of the river bank. I stayed under the fragrant trees mesmerised by the play of refracted light in drops suspended from recurved thorns and feathered leaves. Each one, falling, flashed purple or crimson or gold. Little jewels to be shown to an infant grandson.

Lapalala that season was an Aladdin's cave of treasures that I looked forward to sharing with Ayden. Nursery groups of baby impala staring at me with wide un-afraid eyes, a blue-headed tree agama in its breeding livery, garishly bright on a tree trunk at Kolobe Lodge. I tried to see again with the fresh perception of a small child. The delicious surprise of everything discovered for the first time, when you're free to marvel without needing to understand any of it. When you still have permission to be awe-struck, to see wonders everywhere. Mysteries and miracles. When you can give your heart so unreservedly, without calculation.

My grandson, by the extraordinary everyday miracle of his

birth, brought me this gift. I looked at my world anew, and gave myself full permission to express the joy it gave me. I'd been entrusted with a wondrous life, and I allowed myself to be openly in love with it. So what if South Africa had problems? There was still a future full of possibilities. What of the many conservation battles that still had to be fought? If we were still fighting it meant that we hadn't lost yet. If we were still fighting it meant that we still had the conviction that it was worth the fight. One look into Bwana's eyes, and I had all the conviction I needed. Here was a cause worth fighting for. Wildlife conservation was so much bigger than any of us, too big for individual agendas, I thought, too big and too important to allow for the possibility of failure. With all of the Waterberg around me bursting with new life I felt up to the fight, whatever it took. So what if mine was a rosy-hued perspective, sentimental, unrealistically optimistic? I didn't care who knew it. I was older; I felt younger.

Every day, several times a day, I pulled on my mud-stained no-longer-white rubber boots and splashed through the puddles to Bwana's enclosure. Every day the railing creaked as he leaned towards me and moo-ed his welcome. Most days I pushed back the hood of my waterproof coat and lifted my face to the rain. I was happy.

That same rainy season that brought such loveliness to us in the Waterberg, brought misery to others. Night after night I stared at the television screen and felt undeservedly protected. I also realised – ever the teacher I suppose – that if one wanted a perfect illustration of the fact that nothing stood apart from everything else, you need only look at the weather. Our nail-biting drive home through torrential rain on New Year's Eve was due to a weather system that had formed thousands of kilometres away – south of a mid-ocean coral atoll, Diego Garcia – just before Christmas. Storms brewing off Diego Garcia were hardly unusual: we were mid-way through the South-West Indian Ocean cyclone season when meteorologists were always tracking such things. But this one, Severe Tropical Storm Astride, was the harbinger of terrible news headlines. In the early hours of the first day of the new year, as Clive and I stood at Doornleegte's verandah door, the strong rain we saw was but the furthest fringe of Astride's reach. At that very moment its centre was pounding the northern tip of Madagascar, and edging into the Mozambique Channel.

At midnight on 3 January Astride made landfall near Mogincual in Mozambique, causing heavy downpours. Subsistence farmers in the area probably wouldn't have been unduly concerned – it was after all the appropriate season for heavy rains. Perhaps, like us, they were just grateful to have escaped that dreadful African scourge, drought.

But they would not have known that the seas off Diego Garcia were spawning another disturbance, Tropical Cyclone Babiola, also aiming for the coast of Africa. A few days later a tropical depression had settled over the Mozambique Channel, and farmers on either side of that 1600-kilometre-long passage between Madagascar and the Mozambican coast might well have been thinking that they'd had enough rain now. But there was no let-up. Two weeks later Intense Tropical Cyclone Connie appeared on the meteorologists' watch list. She hovered north-north-west of Mauritius for three days and then turned her 190-kilometre-per-hour winds south-west on course for the African coast which, like a magnet, seemed to be drawing one storm system after another. While still hundreds of kilometres away Connie was increasing the rainfall on Mozambique's already saturated soil. In low-lying areas farmers' shambas were under water. In Nampula Province the Zambezi was steadily rising. Further south, in Gaza Province, the Limpopo surged against the supports of road and railway crossings. The rains continued.

Within days storm watchers were once more looking south-east of Diego Garcia. A low pressure system there was rapidly building into a tropical storm. This was Damienne. But two days later, of more concern, came a warning from the Cyclone Warning Centre in Perth, Australia: a storm was strengthening off Christmas Island, and moving west-south-west. Tropical Cyclone Leon, which merited a second warning from the Joint Typhoon Warning

Centre. On 5 February Leon reached hurricane strength and bore west, honing in on that magnetic African coast. Three days later Leon passed from the Perth meteorologists' watch to that of the Mauritius Meteorological Service, and was renamed Eline. The Mozambique Channel countries already had had enough to contend with, but this was the name they would remember.

With Eline still on her approach Southern Africa was dealing with widespread flooding. We heard from our friends in Botswana that in just three days they'd had three-quarters of their annual rainfall. I could clearly picture the run-off into the water courses of Clive's old stomping grounds. Many times I'd seen those streams turned into rivers and rivers into raging torrents. Water as unstoppable as fire. There was news from further south-east: South Africa's Kruger National Park. There also large volumes of water made river crossings impassable. Having seen the Kruger in all its moods we were not at all surprised to hear that the military had had to be called in to airlift people stranded by floodwaters.

From the comfort of our armchairs it was safe to speculate on the possible benefits to Kruger and Tuli, to their other-than-human inhabitants at least, of such a scouring of their water courses. Mother Nature has her own way of spring-cleaning. Face to face with her in that guise, man is very small indeed: already 26 dead in South Africa. That number would rise.

Further west, we had a much milder time of it. In breaks between rain squalls the Lapalala maintenance teams got started on the most urgent bridge and road repairs. From the wilderness school I heard their vehicles grunting up the incline on the further side of the Palala valley. As I slipped and slid down an animal track the throb of the engines receded and so did the call of the red-chested cuckoo. The nyala's spoor led to the river bank and then angled into vegetation too thornily formidable for me. I climbed onto a slick black rock that was only just above the foaming rapids. To my right the waters, freed from the rocky chute below the school, spread out into a wide pool grown into a small lake. From my vantage point it seemed to be stretching across the floodplain almost to the foot of Malora. I wondered if more than just the usual flood debris had washed downstream to come to rest here among the reed fringes. Where was Mothlo? Had this powerful Palala surge been a danger to her, or a liberator, forcibly freeing her from her safe and familiar growing-up territory? There was no way of knowing.

I clambered down and walked out of the noise of the rapids, back to the school and to that cuckoo call that heralds our every spring. From somewhere up north in Africa they migrate down, timing their breeding to the abundance of food in our rainy season – one of nature's countless perfectly synchronised rhythms that we shared with the children who passed through the wilderness school.

On the whole they tended to come from two very different frames of reference. There were the ones we sponsored and brought in from impoverished communities; some of them had never encountered wildlife, and had little awareness of the world beyond their rural villages. Others came from greater privilege with a frame of reference significantly enlarged by their access, through travel and media, to global realities and made much more complex because of it. They posed as much of a challenge to us as those who had never been in a position to view an animal as anything other than either food or vermin. How could our conservation message compete with everything else clamouring for their attention and their support? How could I tell them that, even in a world with millions of destitute people and dying children, the survival of a wildlife species mattered?

They came to visit Bwana and as I held out the bucket of game-feed pellets for the hands – brown, black, white – to dip in and then offer to Bwana a small portion of his favourite treat, I tried to puzzle out who these young people were. I was out of step with their generation. For all I knew they were ill-equipped to care about the things that mattered to me, desensitised on the one hand by greater survival needs, and on the other by an oversupply of distractions and crisis-news from around the world. How could my dedication to an animal like Bwana make sense to them? And how on earth could I, an old lady in their eyes, inspire in them a passion, to match my own, for the natural world?

I couldn't. All I could do was to meet a need where I saw it, and for the rest keep doing what Clive and I had always done: facilitate their exposure to the natural environment. Mother Nature herself would do the rest. On that lovely riverside campus with its monkey thorns and wildlife she had as good a chance as we could manage. And the next intake of young people would meet her in her most generous, voluptuous guise.

But for Mozambique that same rich season was a nightmare. Roads and infrastructure, power supplies, health services and sanitation – it was all falling apart. The numbers of homeless people rose to hundreds of thousands. On 11 February the Limpopo, swollen by its many flooding tributaries, including our Palala, burst its banks, inundating the vast Limpopo basin. A natural disaster became a humanitarian crisis.

And all the while Intense Tropical Cyclone Eline was still advancing, closing in now on Mauritius, Reunion and Madagascar. She hit the islands as a Category 3 hurricane. She hit Mozambique as a Category 4, with winds of 260 kilometres per hour. It was devastation. And a month later, in a cruel stroke, Very Intense Tropical Cyclone Hudah arrived.

Madagascar was left reeling, its vanilla crop wiped out, its people facing floods, famine and a cholera epidemic. On the other side of the Mozambique Channel conditions were, if anything, worse. At least 113 000 of Mozambique's small-scale farmers lost everything, most had to flee for their lives, some into trees where they survived to be rescued, days later, by helicopter. From the air they looked down on their broken world, perhaps not yet realising that another horror would await their return: thousands of landmines – that deadly legacy of the civil war – dislodged by the floods, carried and deposited all over roads and tracks that had previously been cleared and pronounced safe.

At Doornleegte we took to having our suppers in front of the television set to watch the drama as it unfolded. Pictures of drowned landscapes, rescues of desperate people. Clive and I knew Mozambique, but not like this.

It wasn't the first time Mozambique had been crippled by

Conita Walker, née Hagens, and Joan Dobson, née Keyser, at Barcelona airport in front of Trek Airways' 'Super Star' Constellation 4 engine propeller-driven aircraft in 1965.

Clive and Conita at an Endangered Wildlife Trust function at the Johannesburg Zoo offices in 1980. Clive at the time was the trust's director.

Ladies' Committee members of the EWT. Front row, left to right: Val Whyte (Chair), Jill Morrison, Joy Cowan. Back row, left to right: Petra Mengel, Conita, Anne Deane and Wendy Farrant.

Dale Parker, owner of Lapalala Wilderness, visits the black rhino orphan Bwana at Karen Trendler's orphanage for the first time. Bwana was by then a month old.

Karen Trendler with the three-week-old black rhino orphan, Bwana

The Natal Parks Board transport vehicle, which was kindly made available to bring Bwana to the Walkers' home at Lapalala Wilderness.

Bwana being treated for polyarthritis in his knees by Karen Trendler while Conita gets his attention with a milk bottle.

Black rhino calves require large quantities of fat-free milk.

Karen Trendler's Jack Russell gives baby Bwana a friendly lick at her Pretoria rehabilitation centre.

Rosina Baloyi, Conita's right-hand assistant, feeds the now one-year-old black rhino with game pellets.

Bwana and Conita take time out on the veranda of her home, Doornleegte, at Lapalala. Note the swimming pool fencing to keep him off the verandah.

Mothlo the baby hippo orphan, badly scarred from hippo bites on the day she was found, receiving her first bottle from Conita.

It was not long after Mothlo was found that we built her a swimming pool in our back garden. Here she is taking a dip while her keeper, Fred Baloyi, splashes water over her.

A very different, contented hippo with Conita in the front garden. Mothlo grew to hate human males, other than Fred, which made life very difficult for any male visitors, including Clive.

Half asleep, a rapidly expanding, fully recovered Mothlo allows Conita to tickle her.

Conita and Mothlo on the one-kilometre walk to the Palala River for her daily swim.

Mothlo watched over by Conita in her favourite swimming hole in the Palala River to which she eventually returned permanently. Clive returned the first three wild hippo to the river system in 1985.

Around 3000 school children from our environmental school came to visit our orphans yearly with their teachers. For many this was a life-changing experience listening to Conita's stories of their histories.

On rare occasions we were able to slip away to one of Clive's favourite places – Savute. Old friends, Avril Shepherd, Conita, Lloyd and June Wilmot, David Shepherd and Clive here at Pump Pan.

Fred and a sleeping Mothlo in front of Bwana's enclosure, here being fed cubes by his keeper Titus.

Munyane the white rhino female orphan dozes next to the seated note-taking Conita in her driveway at Doornleegte.

Munyane's favourite toy was an old motor car tyre, used here as a pillow.

Munyane preferred to drink her milk from a ploughshare, rather than a plastic bottle.

Conita with her two boys, Renning, the eldest, and Anton enjoying sunbathing at her Glendower home in Edenvale.

Conita's human family in the Waterberg – Back row, left to right: Renning, our eldest son, Cynthia and Charlie Odendaal, Rene's parents. Middle, left to right: Enid Walker and Conita. Seated in front row, from left to right: René and Anton, and Ayden Walker seated on Clive's lap.

Conita with the now full-grown, magnificent black rhino Bwana in his enclosure adjacent to their home at Lapalala Wilderness

Daily lectures were given to children visiting the Wilderness School and members of the public. Nothing quite prepares you for standing up close in front of one of these animals. Since 2008 more than 6000 rhino have been killed in South Africa.

Munyane, the white rhino, brings her calf, Mokibelo, to her feeding station outside her garden. Munyane was by now a free, wild rhino.

Bush baby, Clive and Conita's granddaughter, Tristyn Amber Walker.

Conita in a moment of happy reflection.

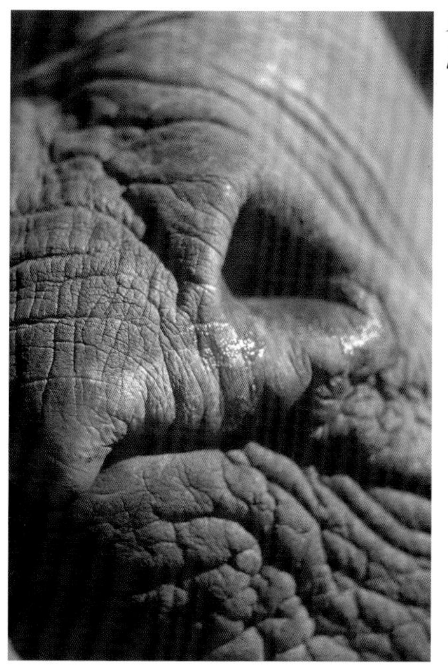

A close-up of the prehensile lip of a black rhino.

Conita spent many patient hours encouraging Bwana to eat wild plants, which she carefully noted. Rhino have their likes and dislikes, which can include poisonous plants.

Moêng, the black rhino female orphan whose terrible injuries came close to killing her only for her to be gunned down in her enclosure by persons unknown at the start of the South African rhino war in 2008

ruinous floods, but the previous times there weren't television cameras in the rescue helicopters hovering above the floodwaters, and the news commentators weren't speculating about increasing volatility in weather patterns that might or might not be the result of climate change. The previous times I wasn't looking out at the sodden landscape around Doornleegte with as comprehensive an understanding of our vulnerability to weather systems spawned half a world away. I felt that the planet had somehow become smaller. The troubles of other people in other places had come a whole lot closer.

Of course, and this is not wrong, it is the plight of the human population that got news coverage. As a conservationist I had to wonder, though, how this disaster might play out. More of the dwindling bush cleared for the re-settlement of so many people; further destruction of the remaining hardwood forests for the already damaging charcoal trade; funds desperately needed for conservation diverted to pressing social needs; subsistence farmers having to look to bushmeat to feed their families. When communities of people get hit by disaster, natural or man-made, the environment always pays a price.

Mozambique wasn't the only country to enter the new millennium on its knees. In January 2000 there were wars in Sierra Leone, Algeria, Somalia, Ethiopia, Chad, Eritrea, Liberia, Burundi, several in the Republic of the Congo. There were others: Nagaland in north-east India, Afghanistan, Nepal, East-Timor, Chechnya. By the end of January the Balkans, hardly at peace after Kosovo, again erupted with the Macedonian insurgency. Months later there were clashes on the Bangladesh-India border, and the never-yet-at-peace Middle-East flared once more into escalated Palestine-Israel hostilities – the Second Intifada.

And every one of those conflicts over territorial and resource rights. All of them, without exception, extremely costly to the bio-diverse environment as well as to the human population.

Such was the world my grandson was born into. Billions of people on a crowded planet battling against each other and against the forces regulating the natural systems of the earth. As a child of the internet age, Ayden would know of the world's crises virtually instantaneously, as they happened – in Japan, in Europe, in South America, in Africa. He'd know about the polar ice caps melting and the glaciers disappearing off Mount Kenya and Kilimanjaro. And he'd know that all of that, in one way or another, could impact his life. Childhood, it seemed to me, had been robbed of some of its innocence.

On the day Ayden was introduced to Bwana I stood back and watched as his parents, Anton and René, comforted his initial whimpers and later guided his tiny hands to touch Bwana's massive, prehistoric-looking head. A meeting of fates, I thought. The one in the hands of the other. If the highly endangered black rhino managed to avoid extinction for a few more years it would be up to my grandson's generation to help it avoid it for a few more.

If I could have poured all my hopes for Ayden into that scene, I would have done so. I didn't want him to grow up overwhelmed and weighed down by the immensity of challenges that we'd brewed up to bestow upon his generation. More than anything I wanted him to be a hopeful child. Even with a global perspective on humanity's troubles and misery, I wanted him to believe that there's good to be achieved through being alive during such times.

In his father's arms Ayden had cheered up and wriggled to be allowed closer to Clive who was feeding Bwana, answering each rhino vocalisation with one of his own. Before long we were all laughing and I thought: maybe there'd be an advantage to growing up in a conservationist family – if ever there was a resilient and hopeful bunch it's the conservationists of the world. No matter how chilling the odds, they don't give up. They take on governments, multinational corporations, the apathy of voters and the greed of those who get voted in. They tilt at windmills and risk ridicule. They don't win every battle, they may lose their life-savings and break their hearts. But they don't sit on their hands. If an opportunity offers, large or small, they'll muster their dreams and jump right in. Our elephants were a case in point.

When we first came to the Waterberg the only elephants to be seen in the region were the ones fading on rock walls. This despite the fact that the elephant was the totem animal of the Langa people in the Bakenberg community – the owners of the community-run Masebe Nature Reserve. There were beautiful San rock paintings in Masebe, in Lapalala and in other places, but live elephants had been gone for at least 150 years. With more and more Waterberg landowners converting to game farming and wildlife tourism, Clive thought it would only be a matter of time before someone was ready to undertake the first re-introduction of elephants – an enticing prospect for someone with his life-long fascination with the species.

In 1989 I was still living with one foot in Johannesburg and one evening, after the long trek north, I arrived at Lapalala to find my husband big with news. As he helped me off-load he said, "I've been thinking..."

A game dealer had three young semi-tame elephants for sale at (a princely sum for those days) 10 000 rand each. Dale Parker was attracted to the idea, but in the end shook his head and said if Clive wanted to go for it himself, he was welcome. Clive was sorely tempted. Truth to tell, so was I. We sat down to do our sums. The purchase price would not be the only cost. As item after item got added the total crept closer to the absolute ceiling we could set for ourselves. But when we went to bed that night the decision had been made.

In due course Rambo, Rogan and Rachel arrived. If all went well, we thought, it could turn out to be another step closer to that fully restored Waterberg ecosystem for which Dale and Clive were aiming.

It began well enough. During the day the young elephants roamed, in the evening they were lured back with the aid of lucerne to the old white rhino bomas near Rhino Camp and locked up for the night. This was not far from Doornleegte, and a fantastic area for elephant, with sufficient water and browse and a grassland plateau for their grazing.

Then, after six trouble-free months, we had a visitation from The Authorities.

So we had elephants: Fine. We wanted them to roam free: Not so fine. *Unless* their entire roaming area was electrically fenced. The Authorities had been Reliably Informed by A Source (our suspicions fingered a neighbour) that Appropriate Measures had not been taken to Securely Confine The Animals Under Consideration within The Area Under Consideration. We exhibited our permits, which clearly stated that we had permission for the enterprise, the only proviso being that the animals had to be Contained.

We argued that term: "Contained." They were in a fenced area in the middle of a huge well-managed wilderness reserve that was itself fenced, and at night they were more than contained, they were locked up. Surely that was enough?

They countered with the clincher: Were we aware of Paragraph 481 of The Law Pursuant to The Ownership and Confinement of Wild Animals which governs Liability under Roman Law, specifically the *actio de pastu*, the *edictum de ferris*, and most particularly the *actio lex aquilia* which states...

The Animals Under Consideration, by now happily adapted to their environment, roamed their corner of the Waterberg for a little longer while their fate hung in the balance. The then Transvaal Division of Nature Conservation could neither budge nor assist. Neither could Dale. The Walker finances could not stretch to the electrification of a 10 000-hectare enclosure. All the same, we had no wish to tangle with The Law Pursuant. Our three young elephants went back to the dealer.

To this day I wonder how that might have turned out. If our plans had succeeded there might in time have been a small herd and who knows, I might one day have found myself rearing an orphaned elephant calf, rather than or in addition to, hippo and rhino calves.

In an ideal world no wild animal would get orphaned and require the help of a human foster mother, but our world is not an ideal one and wild nature does not play by our sentimental rules. Neither do poachers. There will always be orphans.

At the time I did indulge in the occasional fantasy, inspired by television programmes in which adorable baby elephants were rescued and hand-reared by people like David and Daphne Sheldrick in Kenya. How I admired them! I remember lying awake one night, trying to picture myself in that kind of role and speculating about how I might have managed if I'd ever found myself with a large and potentially dangerous wild animal on my hands.

Life has a way of answering our questions: less than two years later Bwana was born.

Our three young elephants remain a slightly conflicted memory. There was disappointment initially, of course. But since then the conservation world has changed along with the socio-political landscape. Electrified fences have become a non-negotiable requirement of wildlife conservation. Not only are there now many more people living along the borders of wildlife preserves, it has also become impossible for landowners to keep poachable wildlife without allocating a sizeable slice of their budget to security, including armed personnel to patrol those electrified fences. And, as we know, even that is not enough.

There is also the matter of habitat loss. It is no news anymore that the land available to be set aside for wildlife is not increasing. Confine an elephant population to a fenced-in reserve, and you may well find that you're placing your botanical diversity under threat. This was a factor in Dale's reservations about introducing elephants into Lapalala.

Elephants, unable to migrate, will eat their favourite food until there is no more of it left. In the Waterberg, unless you have a vast wilderness at your disposal and the means to manage its utilisation by elephants, trees like the knobthorn, marula and kiepersol would be heavily browsed, so heavily that they might soon disappear altogether. The first to go could be the mountain syringa (*Kirkia acuminate*), the Tree of Heaven. And along with those losses the integrity of the entire ecological system that had evolved around them would be under threat.

Every conservation-minded landowner wrestles with such dilemmas. Solutions are not simple and don't come from shortcuts. Much though one might like to, you cannot bulldoze your way to your goal. In a socio-political context that seems hell-bent on destroying what remains of the natural world, all the easy tricks are on the side of your opposition. So you talk and listen, negotiate where you can, re-group where you can't, and then talk some more. Especially when your goal is a biosphere reserve extensive enough to accommodate all species and all interests. In the five years since Annemie de Klerk, representing the Limpopo provincial government, phoned to suggest that Clive, representing the Waterberg Nature Conservancy, should join her in spearheading the formation of a biosphere in the Waterberg, Clive had had to do a lot of talking. To his amusement he earned, and no wonder, the appellation of Walker the Talker.

It paid off. One afternoon in August 2001 I found myself sitting among more than 150 Waterbergers in the auction hall of a game capture and auctions outfit 30 kilometres from Vaalwater. As I glanced around the predominantly male audience, khaki much in evidence, I realised that the wonder was not that the establishment of a biosphere reserve could have taken five years, the wonder was that it hadn't taken longer. Represented there that day was the full spectrum of divergent opinions and agendas that had had to be brought on board – game rangers, hunters, farmers, community leaders, members of the South African Police Service, game dealers, representatives of municipal and governmental structures, of conservation organisations and tourism concessions. Every stakeholder an independent-minded operator who had to be convinced of the fact that this holistic model, holistically managed, would benefit him, on the ground, in real practical terms. In March 2001 the Waterberg Biosphere Reserve was ratified by UNESCO and five months later South Africa's Minister of Environmental Affairs and Tourism, Valli Moosa, joined us at Mpatamacha to launch the newest of our country's biosphere reserves, the first one in the savannah biome. A new beginning for the Waterberg.

The WBR logo featured, unsurprisingly since Clive had a hand in it, an elephant. The steering committee had agreed that as the totem animal of a Waterberg community the elephant would be an appropriate symbol. Clive submitted a design based on a San rock painting he'd seen in Masebe. The idea was good, the committee said, but the rock art image of an elephant didn't read well enough. Couldn't Clive just draw or sketch or paint, or whatever it is that he did, the thing himself?

In the studio at Doornleegte I saw it taking shape: a mature elephant bull striding across a Waterberg skyline. The colour brochure was familiar to me too: on the cover, waterbuck initially sketched on a hot November afternoon with the sound of cicadas and a crested barbet and the faraway drone of an airliner dragging its vapour trail across the sky.

At the WBR launch venue that day there was another waterbuck. A majestic animal that had had its trophy status accorded the tribute of being killed, stuffed and mounted. Like the others on the walls around us – buffalo, gemsbok, kudu, eland – it had outwitted, out-fought, and out-run every predator. Save one.

I was glad not to have been faced with a rhino in that setting. Could that day come? I'd heard all the arguments favouring rhino farming. Some of them, although uncomfortable to me, were not easy to counter. But I had great difficulty in seeing an animal like Bwana or Munyane as a commodity, a provider of harvestable rhino horn, or an earner of tourism dollars in the form of hunting licences. I simply couldn't picture Bwana's head on some trophy hunter's wall.

Such thoughts are personal and not politically correct – I'd learnt to keep them to myself. But I was reasonably sure that at least two people present on that occasion shared my sentiments. We didn't discuss it, but I'd seen Clive and Dale Parker with Lapalala's rhinos – I didn't need to be told that they infinitely preferred a live rhino to a dead one, regardless of the profit that might arise from such a death. The furthest thing from Dale's mind at that point would have been to see Lapalala as anything other than a safe and protected sanctuary for his rhinos. The formation of the WBR was, in his eyes as in Clive's, a little bit of additional insurance for Lapalala's future. He didn't want to miss an occasion that signified the successful conclusion to that particular phase of their efforts, so he'd opened up a few days in his schedule to fly up from the Cape and attend the launch.

With official proceedings concluded, Dale was itching to leave. The next day his brief Waterberg break would be over and he preferred to spend as much of his time as possible surrounded by the Lapalala bush. With Clive unable to get away so early, Dale and I said our goodbyes and set off. Our drive back was, as always for me, a shedding of the rest of the world. Once through the reserve gates, what we'd left behind seemed so much less real than what was around us – less real and less true.

A few kilometres in, at an extensive grass-field backed by a range of hills, we slowed down hoping to spot a white rhino bull that frequented the area. Dale had insisted on naming him Hatton, Clive's middle name chosen in remembrance of his grandfather, that 16-year-old soldier from London's Hatton Garden who'd brought this branch of the Walkers to Africa.

Dale braked, and pointed. There, less than 100 metres away, as impressive and as perfect for his setting as always, was Hatton. The heavy head lifted. Trophy horns where they belonged: on the rhino.

Tempting as it was to linger, I had responsibilities waiting at Doornleegte. Clive's mother had been with us for close on a year now and although she didn't make any demands, I didn't like leaving her on her own for too long. There was also Bwana, of course, and as soon as Clive arrived home, it would be time for supper, which I still had to prepare.

I asked Dale to drive on. I wish I hadn't done so.

TWELVE

Rapula

THE RAIN ARRIVED BEFORE daybreak that morning. No thunder, no lightning. None of the wild summer-storm drama to set your ears ringing and your heart racing. Still, long before I heard the first drops on the roof, I had felt it. Clive too had been wakened by the sense of distant, approaching weather – a primitive sense, like that of a wild animal, restored to humans by a lifetime in the bush. We were not the only ones in the Waterberg to lie awake waiting for the cool air to turn moist, or to get up and stand in front of an open window to breathe it in. But perhaps we were the only ones to realise that morning that for us something had shifted. Rain would never again arrive the way it used to. Much as our lives had always been tied to, indeed often been ruled by rain, from that point on the connection would be even more personal. With the rain would come a flood of memories of a man who'd borne the Sotho name Rapula, Giver of Rain.

Because of him every shower, every storm would be a commemoration. Renewal and loss, beginnings and endings all mixed up in the same memory. And that morning, the first time it rained again after he'd left, it hit home. Sixteen years ago now.

On the clearest of spring mornings, with Doornleegte's garden glowing in early sun, I was on the verandah. I might have looked up at the sky as I so often did and still do with some idle speculation about the day's weather, although I don't recall that particularly. The moment that remains etched in my memory came next, when I walked back indoors to answer the phone. It was Elizabeth Parker. First I and then Clive listened as she told us what she herself found impossible to believe. Dale was gone. The previous afternoon, following a tree-felling operation during which he'd over-exerted himself, he didn't feel well. She took him to hospital. Later that night he had a massive heart attack. He did not survive. On 7 September 2001, after just 61 years, his life was over.

There were phone calls to be made, people to be told. None of it seemed real. Later I walked out with Clive and watched as he went down the verandah steps and through the garden to his Pajero – he had a presentation to do at the wilderness school. All I could think about was that Elizabeth would never again have that: her husband's voice, his way of going about his day. I couldn't even begin to know what that meant, how one dealt with such a blow. Clive was five years older than Dale; they'd always joked about him going first, and I'd usually joined in with a wifely protest and some silly quip about women outliving their spouses. Now I smarted at the heedlessness of it.

After a while I went back inside. Mother, her wheelchair still pulled up to the breakfast table, looked up. Suddenly it struck me: widowed at 27, with two pre-teen boys. She knew. Whatever Elizabeth, also a mother of two, was going through, she knew. Quietly she wheeled herself out onto the verandah. With the pretext of clearing away breakfast I stayed behind and watched through the window until she'd settled at the railway sleeper table, her devoted little terrier at her feet.

I knew she wouldn't want me fussing over her. She never did – she expected me to get on with my work. For much of the day she remained there, alone with her thoughts, observing the life of the garden, the birds and the small wild creatures that visited it.

It was appropriate that there should have been someone at Doornleegte that day who was not caught up in the rush of life, who would go apart, who would be silent. It fell to Mother to do what, in a more respectful world, more of us would have done. I like to think she was there on the verandah on behalf of those of us who, for the whole of that day and long after, still kept hearing Dale's voice calling to Clive to hurry up and join him for a sundowner.

That evening we spoke of Dale's last day at Lapalala, just a few weeks before. On the day following the biosphere launch he and Clive had finished their inspection drives and taken whatever decisions needed to be taken about reserve business. As usual Clive was to take him to the airport and, as usual when departure time loomed, there was just one more thing they wanted to do, one more thing to see. On this occasion it was a spot about which our Anton, then already wildlife manager in Lapalala, had told Clive. Dale *had* to see it. I protested: it would take too long. It was in a particularly rugged part of the eastern section of the reserve and I was already anxious about the time. But deaf to my nagging, Clive grabbed his camera and they set off.

One month later almost to the day we looked through the pictures he took that August afternoon. And there it was, the last photograph: on a monumental cliff-top tumble of broken sandstone, surrounded by nothing but wilderness, nothing but Lapalala, was Dale.

He had found it difficult to leave, Clive said. His flight was due to depart from Johannesburg's OR Tambo airport in fewer hours than it seemed to Clive he needed to get him there. Dale refused to be hurried. Alone and without talking, he stood on those rocks, staring out for a very long time. Far below, flowing strongly that year even at the end of the dry season, was his beloved Palala.

Inevitably we were left with a heightened awareness of the fragility of life, of the precariousness of it all. Three days later it was 11 September. Planes crashed into New York's Twin Towers, and all at once the world was a different place. Modern history forever divided into Pre- and Post-9/11. Millions of people entered a season where they saw every day, every experience, every love in their lives for what it truly was, a meditation on mortality. Never again, we told each other, would we take anything for granted. Life was precious. It was brief. It was uncertain.

On Elizabeth's request, Clive flew down to the Cape to speak at the memorial service at the Parkers' home, the Zonnestraal Estate in Cape Town. But even that unambiguously final and witnessed farewell, he said, did not make Dale's absence any more believable.

As far as Lapalala visitors and most of the reserve personnel would have been able to see, things continued as before. Dale's wishes, insofar as they were known, guided whatever new decisions had to be taken. I have no doubt that his heart would have been gladdened by everyone's acceptance that the sanctuary that he and Clive had dreamt and sweated into being should continue. So business and work went on. The summer rains arrived, the hillsides turned fresh green, on the Doornleegte floodplain the umbrella thorns burst into flower.

The wilderness school trained another batch of environmental teachers and welcomed group after group of children. The bush camps kept running at full capacity. In the visitors' books there were messages of condolence from old-timers, personal tributes to a generous benefactor whom they'd never met but to whom they would always be indebted.

Suddenly it was less than a week before Christmas. I was standing at the fire-pit at Lepotedi, the Parker family's special camp. It was swept clean, the wood stacked ready for the next campfire. I looked up. Against the leaden cloud cover that had moved in that morning, two landmarks: to my right Malora, to my left the towering sandstone cliff where in 1981 Clive had brought Dale and Elizabeth for their first look at Lapalala.

Two decades on it still amazed me that a businessman could have chosen to seal this venture with something as un-businesslike as a handshake. I was less surprised at Clive's part in it. As an artist and conservationist his ability to function at all in a cynical world required a fair measure of idealism and a stubborn, some might say foolhardy, reliance on man's better nature. There was no contract. He gave his word, Dale gave his word. Unusually in this world of ours, it was enough. The enterprise would cost a great deal in hard currency, but an even greater deal in a scarcer commodity – trust.

The Lapalala Wilderness Reserve was 20 years old. Like my sons at that age, almost grown-up. But not quite. Not yet measured against the complications of the wider world. Its maturity lay ahead, further ahead than I could see.

I did my usual check-around. Lepotedi was ready for the visitors who would arrive the next day. Not the Parkers. It would be strangers, first-timers who in all likelihood wouldn't know much of the history of the place, and who certainly wouldn't know anything about the woman who'd finally stopped hurrying, who had taken the time to stand silently at the fire-pit before walking the few metres down to the Palala to join the man standing there.

Clive looked up. "Did I ever tell you about the time…" He shook his head. "Of course I did. You know all the stories."

"Never mind," I said. "Tell me again."

Two belligerent little Davids, Dale and Clive, facing the Goliath of the apartheid security forces in defence of black kids at the wilderness school. The two of them in another fight, even closer to Dale's heart, to stop the construction of a dam in the upper reaches of the Palala. One memory triggering another, and another.

I became aware of the chill breeze stirring my hair. Drops pitted the water in front of us, setting small silver circles racing across the dark surface. It got rapidly colder, the day's warmth fading with the light. Clive put his jacket around my shoulders. We turned and walked back up the bank, away from the river. We left Lepotedi to the hushed rustle of rained-on leaves.

The storm broke just as we emerged from the river valley onto the western flank of Malora. It was a big one – full-throated, powerful and urgent as life. Rain as far as I could see. No horizon. No limit to a landscape ancient and vast enough to contain all the lives that had known it, and had been known by it.

Today a lone massive slab of Waterberg sandstone lies 2000 kilometres to the south, on the Elandsberg Nature Reserve in the Cape. It marks the grave of Dale Parker. Rapula, Giver of Rain.

THIRTEEN

Rescues

THE WALKER FAMILY TRADITION was *Heiligabend* (Christmas Eve) at Clive and Conita's. From the first year of our marriage the spicy-sweet comforts of a German Advent kitchen have kept alive much more than just the recipes.

However much I resist the commercial exploitation which, from October onwards, has shiny made-in-China baubles and tinsel strings incongruously sprouting all over hot, humid, dusty Vaalwater, and "Frosty, the Snowman" accompanying me up and down supermarket aisles, come December I succumb. And with the preparations come the memories. My mother guiding my first attempts at the icing-sugar swirls and stars that seven decades on still decorate my *Weihnachtsplätzchen.* The plotting required to devise gifts and surprises on a missionary's budget. My father at the piano: *"Herbei, o ihr Gläubingen, Fröhlich triumphiernd."* The musical talent which could dazzle his listeners with Bach and Mozart made something unforgettable of the simple hymns and carols performed with his family clustered around him.

I count it as one of the great blessings of my life that Christmas time for me has always meant Family. Gifts, candles, my special-occasions-only crockery and crystal, the traditionally stuffed goose with enough side-dishes for several take-home freezer meals, and family. In 2001, as I sat with my grandson well past his bedtime wide awake on my lap, it struck me that all that was most precious to me in the entire world was in that room. And no guarantees for any one of those lives. The thought caught at my throat. Like the others I joked with Renning who was good-naturedly officiating as Father Christmas. I watched as he and Anton laughed over some shared childhood memories. My beloved sons. I needed to fix that moment in my mind. I'd have been willing to negotiate anything for guarantees of protection, for them, for René and Ayden and Clive and all the others. *Nehmen Sie mich, aber ersparen Sie ihnen.* (Take my life, but spare them.)

It was a glorious summer. At Bwana's enclosure festive season visitors told me they envied me – living in the bush, the opportunity to work with wildlife... It all seemed so wonderfully idyllic. I would nod and agree, of course. On my bush camp rounds I'd stop at river crossings to watch and listen to the rush of water; at Munadu swifts flew their slaloms around sandstone towers and scythed down to skim the surface of the dark waters below the camp; there were shrill calls of giant kingfishers echoing off the Umdoni cliffs, tinker barbets in the bush around the camp; at Molope and at Lepotedi woodland kingfishers were calling up- and downstream, hour after hour. Yes, it *was* idyllic. But there were other sides to the picture that the visitors didn't see.

In January I stood on the Doornleegte verandah and waved to Clive as he drove away. His responsibilities with SANParks needed him in Cape Town for a few days. This wasn't to be a lengthy trip, nor on the face of it a hazardous one, and we'd have daily phone contact. So why the feeling of uneasiness that I carried with me throughout that day? The next morning it was still there, and the next, until just before the week was out the phone rang around midnight. It was Anton. "Mom, I'm afraid we have a problem..."

David Bradfield, the chief rhino coordinator who was

responsible for all of Lapalala's field rangers had been seriously, perhaps fatally, injured by a black rhino bull. Bwana.

I phoned Clive in Cape Town to give him what information I had, which was little more than that Clive Ravenhill, the reserve manager, was rushing David to hospital. Then I called Titus. When Bwana, as he'd always done after a breakout, returned to Doornleegte I'd need help – this time he might be in a dangerous mood. After that there was nothing to do except sit down, with Button at my feet, and wait, all the time agonising over David's survival and wondering how on earth it had come to this.

It wasn't until a couple of weeks later that we were able to unravel the events of that night.

Bwana had wandered out of the Palala valley, up onto the plateau and found his way to Landmanslust, the home of the reserve manager. At around 9 pm Clive Ravenhill heard noises outside and spotted Bwana near the house. He had some bricks at hand and started throwing. Bwana melted away into the dark. A short distance away, at a spot overlooking the river valley, was Driemanslust, and that was where Bwana turned up at around 10 pm. David Bradfield and his partner, Andrea, had just said goodnight to their house-guest and gone to bed when there was a terrific noise outside: something like the clashing of metal drums and the frantic barking of David's little mongrel dog, Woogsy.

The dining room lights spilled out only far enough to illuminate the garden path, not the cause of the disturbance, so David grabbed a torch and cautiously went outside to investigate. Bwana was rubbing his horn on Andrea's car, a borrowed vehicle so this was not to be encouraged. When shooed away Bwana headed for the washing line where laundry had been left to dry overnight. Again David tried to intervene, but Bwana had had enough and charged. David was flipped high into the air and flung to land some distance behind Bwana. He knew rhinos and he also knew the wisdom of rhino specialist, Peter Hitchin's advice: Avoid the human instinct to curl up in a foetal position – you wouldn't be able to see the rhino, and he could horn you in your back or vital organs without you being able to do anything to protect yourself. No, make sure you get onto your back so you can keep an eye on him, keep swivelling to face him and push yourself away or shove your boots in his face.

But before David could get into position Bwana was already there, and flipped him a second time. David landed hard, tried to swivel, but again Bwana was too fast for him and kept on mauling him. With his front horn he got David pinned against a small tree; David heard and felt his ribs breaking. At this point Andrea was running between the house and David's Isuzu bakkie looking for his rifle, and shouting for their house-guest, Magnus, an ex-parks ranger, to come and help.

Finally, with a split-second to spare, David managed to turn onto his back, shoved his feet into Bwana's face and kept pushing until he somehow found himself able to slide in behind a bigger tree and haul himself into a standing position. Bwana hadn't given up. They dodged right and left around the tree trunk for a few seconds. David then feinted to one side and as Bwana followed he turned and sprinted for his life. He rounded the house, the charging rhino at his heels, and was pulled in through the front door by Andrea and Magnus just as Bwana was about to connect with him again. David, in shock, anger and frustration turned around, shouted and flung his heavy torch at Bwana. To everyone's immense relief, the enraged rhino bull finally turned away and trotted off.

Andrea, thankful that it was over, felt that David needed something for shock and left to fetch sugar water. She returned to find him sitting in a pool of blood which was rapidly spreading over their khaki-coloured couch cushions. David hadn't realised that he'd been gored, but now saw his green game-ranger's shorts in shreds and a deep wound pulsing blood in his lower back, just below his belt. Wrapped in crepe bandages, deathly pale and in intense pain he was collected by Clive Ravenhill who set about breaking all speed records to the hospital in Vaalwater. Upon arrival there the local doctor made short work of assessing the bigger wound at the back and a smaller one in front, and pronounced that he could clean 'em up, stitch 'em up and have David back on his feet the next day. Clive disagreed and insisted on more specialised care. An ambulance was summoned and David, by now in critical condition, was rushed to St Vincent's Catholic hospital in Warmbaths (Bela-Bela) 150 kilometres away. There, in the Intensive Care Unit, he was stabilised and the full extent of his injuries discovered. Seven fractured ribs, and a horn-stab which entered from the back, pierced the hipbone, and exited in the groin. David had been fortunate in two respects: he was extremely fit and strong, and Bwana's horn was unusually smooth – the rougher horns of most rhinos could have done considerably more internal damage and almost certainly would have torn the femoral artery.

Waiting at my kitchen table during the long pre-dawn hours of that January night I knew none of this. I kept hoping for a phone call that could tell me that David had survived the goring, but it didn't come. All I heard were the small sounds of a house at night. The creaks of something cooling as the temperature dropped; the hum of the fridge and freezer; Button's small twitches and snores. Many cups of tea later, just before sunrise, Button jerked awake, bristling, and I knew Bwana had at last come home. I shut the door on Button's frenzied yapping and went outside.

Even if I hadn't known about David, Bwana's mood would have told me that there'd been some sort of drama. I'd seen enough of his early-morning returns to know when he'd been involved in a scuffle with another black rhino bull, or had been aggressively attacked by one – invariably he'd come off second-best. This time was different, but he was still running on adrenaline – tense, agitated and wild. With as much quiet, calm confidence as we could muster, Titus and I slowly approached and followed the same procedure that Clive and I had perfected. When at last Bwana was securely locked into his enclosure I stayed behind to watch until he'd calmed down.

Bwana wasn't mine, he belonged to Lapalala Wilderness. I had taken him on because I'd been asked to. But I'd become so used to the responsibility of caring for him and working with him that it was difficult not to assume the responsibility also for his actions. Out there with just the railing between Bwana and me, I felt as if my rhino had gone and attacked a human being, perhaps killed him. I felt responsible, and without Clive there, very alone.

Every time Bwana had broken out and been attacked by Lapalala's free-roaming black rhino bulls I felt for him, what I imagined must have been his frustration and pent-up anger. I felt for his situation, trapped as he was somewhere between wild and tame, with no realistic prospect of living a free life. I don't mind admitting now that I had dreaded the prospect of him encountering a human on one of his walkabout nights. Of course one would pity the human, but I pitied Bwana too.

This was a dilemma the tourists did not see. They saw the cute baby rhino that had grown into a magnificent adult. They saw the fortunate woman who loved that animal; they did not see the one who agonised over his fate. Clive did, and when he returned from his Cape Town trip he was able to give me news of David whom he'd seen in hospital. A full recovery seemed miraculously, mercifully possible. And what he could tell me about David's state of mind astounded me – it seemed hardly credible, but turned out to be true.

As soon as he was well enough David came to Doornleegte. I watched him limp up to Bwana's substantially reinforced enclosure, and had to bite back my tears. He'd wanted to "make sure that there were no hard feelings" between him and Bwana. I admired the great-heartedness that could make him stand, without aggression or fear, within two feet of the animal that had so very nearly killed him such a short time before. As I watched them, man and rhino in some incomprehensible peaceable communion, I felt my burden of irrational guilt lifting. That was David's gift to me and I daresay to Clive too. His visit was balm for the soul.

As summer moved into autumn David was back tracking the Lapalala rhinos with Andries Mokwena and the other rangers, delighted to have found that his connection to rhinos and his passion for tracking them had remained unaffected.

For Christmas 2002 we again had the family at Doornleegte and I was grateful that this time Clive was not preparing for a trip away from home. Boxing Day arrived to find us still obeying the traditional seasonal imperative to take-it-easy. Light meals of

Christmas leftovers, time to begin reading a gift book. It wasn't to last beyond mid-morning. I was in the kitchen preparing Mother's tea-tray when I heard the radio: a field ranger calling the wildlife manager. A few seconds and I heard Anton responding. The ranger seemed excited: "Come and see the visitor." It sounded like good news. Anton had told us of their search for an elusive black rhino cow who'd been due to give birth some months earlier. The rangers had clearly succeeded and there was a new baby. He congratulated them on tracking down such a secretive animal in that remote, hilly corner of the 36 000-hectare reserve. The ranger interrupted: "How soon can you get here?" Anton began to answer, but was cut short. "Ae Morena, No! It must be now. Please."

I took the tea-tray to the verandah and told Mother that I suspected Anton might have a black rhino emergency on his hands, and so it proved. All day we eavesdropped on the drama. Every time I returned from some unavoidable task up at the rhino enclosures Mother filled me in on the episodes I had missed.

Anton arrived on the scene to find the field rangers in a stand-off with a highly aggressive black rhino cow. She had been trying to help her calf, perhaps six months old, to stand up. To no avail. It was injured, bleeding from its horn-bed, a gash on one side and a stab-wound to the upper left thigh. Worse: internal organs were bloodily protruding from its rear end. The sounds coming from the little one could only be described as screams. In between charges at the rangers, the mother kept returning to her frantic attempts to lift the calf with her horn.

Anton marshalled the rangers for another attempt to shoo the cow away from her calf, but she was more than a match for them. Anton had to bolt up a tree rather speedily.

Meanwhile, at Doornleegte, I fretted at my inability to do anything to help my son with the biggest crisis he had yet had to handle. I tried to imagine the scene. I knew the area, because we had explored it on foot – there was no road access. In such an emergency though the field rangers would have forced their Land Cruiser through the typical obstructions offered by that kind of rock-strewn open woodland: wild syringa, red bushwillow, peeling plane, *sekelbos* – every one of them designed to stab and scratch and effectively impede access. A stream further limited their options of approach.

I counted the difficulties: the remote location; extreme physical trauma to the calf; dangerously protective mother; the fact that it was a public holiday. If Anton wanted to attempt a rescue it would be a bold decision and would have to be a quick one.

Whatever you decide, I thought, get permission first. It was one of many occasions when I really felt the loss of Dale. A next generation of his favourite black rhinos – I felt sure I could have predicted his response. But it was a new era. All such decisions were now taken by the Parker family in Cape Town together with the man who had been appointed to the directorship of all the Parker land assets, including Lapalala. I didn't know Mike Gregor personally. I had no idea how much he might know of the Waterberg, of black rhinos or of what we'd been trying to achieve in the reserve.

The phone calls began. I kept busy, trying to quash my fears of someone opting for the most cost-effective solution, a bullet. After all, what was the worth of a single rhino? True, it's a member of an endangered species, and Anton had determined that it was a female, which makes it an even more valuable asset, but the kind of rescue required would be very costly. Factor in the absence of a guarantee that she would survive to breed successfully, and it becomes all too clear that her rescue could not be seen as a sound financial investment, at least not in the short term. The calculus of the marketplace is not helpful to a rhino calf that might be mere hours away from death – let nature take its course.

But no, that little one was to be given a chance. I heaped blessings on the heads of the decision makers.

A phone call to Mpatamacha Game Capture struck pure gold. Kutu Venter had a helicopter plus pilot on standby, and he not only knew of a wildlife veterinarian who happened to be holidaying within the Waterberg area, in the Marakele National Park, he would arrange to fetch him.

The hours dragged. Every subsequent walk up to the enclosures was hotter, every return to the house more of a relief. By lunchtime it was sweltering. From the verandah I watched a fiscal shrike, mercilessly nagged into repeated hunting forays by the screeching wing-shivering appetite of its chick, dart in and out of the red-flowered tangle of the bauhinia bush, flower-petals bleached and shrivelled by punishing light. More fortunate were the starlings, sparrows and bulbul that perched open-beaked in the shade of the plumbago. Button, spread-eagled on Clive's chair, could barely summon up the energy to snap at a horsefly. Not a breath of air to cool down the valley. Chances were that the rescue scene was no different. It would be sweaty and uncomfortable work as wildlife rescues always are; stinging and biting insects drawn by the smells of blood and pungent skin.

Anton's voice came back on air: they could hear the approach of a helicopter. And then: Yes, Dr André Uys was on board and he had his surgical kit with him. Yes, including the immobilising drug, M99. And wonder of wonders, Dr Uys just happened to be an expert on black rhino. Mother and I cheered.

Clive had lent ground-to-air communications equipment to the team. Heaven only knows how much more difficult that rescue would have been without it. From the air Dr Uys was able to do the first assessments and dart the calf. The mother, enraged as she was, remained a danger. Anton, having been charged one time too many, asked Kutu Venter to herd her out of the area so that the ground crew could move in. I'd watched such scenes before. I could picture the helicopter dropping lower, nose on a downward slant, the noise and flying dust, the big rhino cow trying a charge, then wheeling and running, turning again, blindly jerking her head at the threat which must have been deafening to her acute hearing.

It was frustrating not to be there myself. Not that I would have been able to do much beyond keeping out of the way, but I was rooting for the little calf. However dangerous and upsetting the scene, waiting at the radio for the odd snippet of news was surely more stressful. For no rational reason at all I'd adopted that animal's crisis as my own. Knowing full well that it was none of my business and that, with all the trauma to which she'd already been subjected, it might be more merciful not to prolong her agony, I found myself imploring her to pull through. While no one was looking Bwana got an extra few handfuls of pellets that afternoon and was told that another of his kin was in trouble.

I returned to the house and to the news that Dr Uys was busy operating: a major surgical procedure to repair and reposition the calf's internal organs. As soon as he'd finished with that and with stitching up her other wounds, all of which were serious, the patient was to be taken to the Animal Rehabilitation Centre at Onderstepoort – Karen Trendler had agreed to take charge of another of Lapalala's black rhino babies. This was the best news: if the calf survived the surgery she'd need expert nursing.

From then on both Mother and I stayed within earshot of the radio. I knew how much could still go wrong. At best Dr Uys's estimation of the calf's weight could only be an educated guess. M99 was a notoriously twitchy drug – get the ratio of dosage versus weight even slightly wrong, and you lose your patient. Given the extent of the calf's injuries and blood-loss and her panicked state, there would have been no margin for error. In any case, I wasn't sure that such a radical operation under make-shift conditions in the field could succeed.

It seemed to take forever, but then came Anton's voice: It's done, the calf still hanging on, but remains critical. He would take her to Onderstepoort himself.

Food, I thought, finally something that I could do to help. When Anton arrived he lifted an eyebrow at the size of his *padkos*, his ration for the road – a feast assembled out of the choicest of our Christmas Eve leftovers. I was burning to know more about the rescue, but there was no time. I assumed he'd stay over at ARC for the night and only return the next morning. But he shook his head. "I'm coming straight back." He gestured over his shoulder to the crate on the back. "Just as soon as we've settled Moêng."

The rangers had chosen the name, "Visitor" – she'd arrived only to leave again.

Throughout that late afternoon and evening our widely scattered circle of friends and family came to my rescue. There are benefits to being a dinosaur in a digital age. Pen-and-ink correspondence required sitting down at a desk, more time to reflect, to pick up threads, share and reconnect. A welcome distraction that day. I did not consider myself an anxious type of mother, but my son was rushing with an emergency through Boxing Day traffic, and assuming that all went well he would still be facing the return journey after dark. And Moêng? Terribly hurt and traumatised, disoriented, suddenly without her mother and without her natural environment – shock upon shock for such a young rhino.

Over supper Clive filled me in on what they thought might have caused her injuries. After giving birth the cow would have come into oestrus again. A bull must have tracked her and when the calf somehow got in the way, attacked it. The injuries seemed to suggest a violent head-butt to push the calf away, resulting in her bleeding horn-bed, then a horn-swipe from the side, causing that stab-wound in her upper leg, and then a full-on chase. The bull's horn would have stabbed into her rear and, as he flung her aside, hooked internal organs which got pulled out as she fell. It's a miracle she survived.

At bedtime there'd been no word from Anton. Long after bedtime, still nothing. I nagged Clive to phone. But he, annoyingly, was the voice of reason. The boy knew what he was doing. If there was something he wanted us to know, it would be for him to phone us. I had to wait until breakfast, but the news was worth the wait: Anton was fine, Moêng was in good hands. As soon as she was well, she would return to Lapalala.

It was only later that it struck me: Return to Lapalala – what did that mean? Several months away from her mother and from her natural environment, and then straight from ARC's nursing care back into the bush? Not very likely. There would have to be an intermediate stage, a process of re-introduction, possibly a lengthy one. But the new Lapalala regime would no doubt have thought of that. After all, with an eye to the future, they had gone to great lengths to save her. She's an investment. They would make a plan.

Two weeks later there was another life to be saved. If I'd thought

Moêng's was a narrow escape, this one was even narrower. And as with her rescue, I missed most of the drama.

It was 6 January. One of those deliciously drowsy Sunday afternoons. After 28 mm of rain earlier in the day the air was humid and heavy. We'd all taken refuge in the coolest spot, the lounge. Clive, who'd been drawing at the table, muttered something about a pen that needed refilling and wandered off to his office. Mother was dozing in her chair. I was at my desk nodding over my camp admin files, taking the occasional irritable swipe at a fly buzzing around. As flies manage to do so unerringly, it found those spots where it could be most annoying. Back of the neck, sweaty from the heat – I swatted and slapped. Earlobe – I slapped, missed again. It went south, settled on my toes – I wriggled, shifted my feet. Toes again – I stamped a foot.

It was not the fly.

That flattened copper head, flared throat – black-banded. Unmistakable: Mozambican spitting cobra. Its first blow struck, it was now rearing back and up and aiming for my eyes. I heard myself screaming. Clive came running along my blood-trail into the kitchen and took charge. I was told to keep still while he efficiently and speedily wound crepe bandages around my leg, from the ankle to well above the knee. Then, over his shoulder as he ran out, he issued commands to remain calm and stay put, to shut-up and get out of the way, to breathe slowly. Mother, Button and I collectively disobeyed as two shots rang out. Clive reappeared, brandishing his revolver: he'd killed the computer cables and wounded the snake.

I was trying to hang onto what sense I had. The pain was indescribable, radiating out from the bite on my left foot. I knew panic and agitation would only serve to increase Mother's alarm and speed up the spread of the poison. I *had* to slow down my breathing. Don't focus on the pain, focus on the counts: *ein, zwei* … I wanted to tell Clive to get hold of Anton, but he was in the lounge; I could hear him dialling numbers, dialling again and again. Then his voice: he was speaking to the reserve manager. More dialling, then the phone rang and Clive was talking. The phone calls ceased to matter, because the worst kind of thought had come crashing in, and stayed: Kuki Gallmann's son, a strong young man who didn't survive a puff-adder bite. At least this wasn't a puff-adder. But a cobra... My mind raced through what I knew of snake venom. Neurotoxin, cytotoxin, we were dealing with both. Among Africa's venomous snakes only the black mamba is considered more dangerous than the Mozambican spitting cobra. This bite was a serious one. I was in trouble.

Der Herr ist mein hirte – it must have been me, although I was still counting breaths – *mir wird nicht mangeln. Der Herr ist mein...*

Suddenly Clive was back and with him an angel in the shape of Madeleen van Schalkwyk, our school officer. That strong, no-nonsense, six-foot-something blonde put her arms around me, ignored my protests and lifted. "Come on then. Hospital."

Clive was driving, but he was going the wrong way. It wasn't the road to Vaalwater and beyond that to Nylstroom with its hospital. Instead we were heading deeper into the reserve, a shudderingly painful vibration of tyres on gravel. Through the rumble I strained to hear Madeleen's voice: she was explaining that we were heading *through* the reserve, north and then west to Lephalale. The reserve manager had ascertained that there were two doctors there who were experts on snakebite. "Just relax," she said, her arms holding me upright in my seat. "You'll be fine."

I tried to talk to Clive, but he ignored me. I shouted to him. What about Mother? How could he have made us leave without arranging for someone to stay with her? Why didn't he get hold of Anton? His eyes remained fixed straight ahead. Why wasn't he listening to me? I kept shouting. He was going too fast. Much too fast for that road, for the puddles of rainwater, for everything that loomed up right in front of us, then in the cab with us. Shadows were moving, like water, like snakes. Madeleen's arms around my chest were too tight. I couldn't breathe and Clive was going to kill us all and no one was listening to me.

The next thing I remember was my father's voice, or it might have been my mother's, or mine. *Auch wenn ich wanderte im Tale des Todesschattens ...* I was in Madeleen's arms again. *Fürchte ich nichts übles...* There were two voices: a crying child, a shouting man. A nightmare duet that wouldn't stop. I tried to see Clive and Madeleen, but couldn't. *Denn du bist bei mir...* I was lying down, sweating in unbearable heat. The nausea took over.

Then there came a moment of absolute clarity: this was a hospital, it ought to be cleaner. Nurses were lounging around, chatting and laughing. It was all too loud. Unprofessional. Long before I became a teacher I had wanted to be a nurse, and I should have done so: I would have put myself on a proper, cool and comfortable hospital bed, a *clean* one.

And then the tears came. All of it was my fault; I got myself bitten and everybody upset and now I was going to die.

I woke up to the dark. Someone was holding my hand. I knew, beyond a shadow of a doubt, that it was Clive. Comforted, I returned to my position next to the piano, watching my father's hands on the keyboard. His voice the deepest one among all of ours: *Du bist die ruh, Der Friede mild ...* You are peace, the gentle peace, You are longing and what stills it.

A week later I was again in the passenger seat of the Pajero. Clive was driving, slowly. He looked terrible. We left the outskirts of Lephalale. We were still on a tarred road, but bush had taken over from industry and shacklands. Bright blue wings of lilac-breasted rollers swooped in and away again. Too much light for my splitting headache. I closed my eyes.

It was the same road as the previous Sunday and between that journey and this one, Clive said, we had been through hell. After 100 kilometres at breakneck speed with the air-conditioning going full blast to slow my circulation, he and Madeleen had got me – hallucinating, slurring my words – to the Lephalale provincial hospital. No sign of any doctor. No sign of any interest at all in the patient who had arrived with a life-threatening emergency. Madeleen and Clive, fed up with the lack of cooperation, picked me up out of the Pajero, put me in the wheelchair they'd commandeered and got me into the emergency room. Still no sign of any snake-expert doctor, and the only activity that of an intern and a couple of nurses chattily removing stitches from a screaming child. The rest of the staff seemed to be indifferently hanging around in an indolent stupor. The air conditioning wasn't working, no one cared. The place was boiling. Clive lost his temper and eventually got some attention, but not much joy. He insisted that I should be given immediate help. They obliged by tipping me out of the wheelchair onto a gurney where I started to vomit. The intern sauntered over, ordered a drip to be put up and proceeded to ignore Clive. Without bothering to first check for adverse reactions he confidently began administering antivenom intravenously. Clive was beside himself, but faced with that most lethal of professional qualifications, Ignorance inflated by Attitude, he had to watch as the ampoules of antivenom went in. The result was anaphylactic shock. An antidote made no difference. At that point, mercifully, as Dr Attitude had run out of plans, Dr Bouwer arrived.

The receptionist, an Afrikaans girl spurred on in all likelihood by Madeleen's quietly forceful presence, had somehow managed to conjure up this wonderful man on his off-day. He marched in and immediately did two things which probably saved my life: he injected another drug and told Clive to get me out of there.

The discovery, amidst several sets of shrugged shoulders, that the ambulance seemed to have disappeared was the last straw for Madeleen. The next moment she had nurses running to assist her in rushing me from the emergency room, out through the casualty entrance to where Clive was waiting with the Pajero's engine running. It was another breakneck race through sluggish Sunday traffic, 20 kilometres to the Marapong Private Hospital, with me delirious on the back seat. At Marapong medical personnel were waiting at the emergency entrance. They rushed me, unconscious, into intensive care.

A woman spotted Clive in the driveway. He was on his knees next to the Pajero. She brought him a glass of sugar water. She was very kind, he said, and encouraging. Earlier that day she'd brought in her six-year old son with a black mamba bite. Marapong's emergency team had pulled him through – she was sure they would do the same for me. But she didn't know that, thanks to my first-stop medical help which had added a time delay as well as an antivenom overdose to the shock of the cobra bite, I'd gone into cardiac arrest. In the end, though, that professional team didn't disappoint. They managed to resuscitate me and once I was more or less stable, Clive was allowed in. He'd never prayed so hard in his life, he said, nor had he ever had as much cause to be grateful.

The death of Kuki Gallmann's son had haunted him, as had the fact that he blamed himself. A few days earlier Button had shown all the signs of having been spat at by, most likely, a Mozambican spitting cobra. But he had neglected to seek out the snake and kill or relocate it before it could harm me.

Of his drive home that night he didn't remember much, just his eventual arrival at Doornleegte and his overwhelming relief to find that Clive Ravenhill had finally managed to contact Anton, and that they were both there with Mother. He tried to thank Madeleen properly, but didn't manage. He'd broken down, he said. She just grinned and crushed him in a hearty embrace.

The next morning he roped in both Fred and our camp maintenance man, Fransie, and began the search. It took them a week to find that snake. Not a case of catch-and-release – it was dispatched and deposited in formaldehyde.

That was the second disagreement of my homecoming. I would not have objected if that particular reptile had been buried, never to be seen again. But Clive – out of consideration for my profession as a teacher, he said – thought I'd have wanted it to be preserved. A museum exhibit or a teaching aid. I wasn't at all sure about that, but he seemed so hurt by my lack of appreciation of his good intentions, I let it go.

Our first disagreement had been more serious, and I had refused to let it go. I was still in hospital, hooked up to monitors and drips, and wanted to go home. Too early, he said. The doctor, a diplomat, agreed with both of us. More bed-rest and monitoring would be beneficial, but if that meant fretting over the neglect of people and animals that depended on me, it might do more harm than good. I made all kinds of promises about rest and obeying Clive, and was allowed to be discharged.

It took no more than the first crutch-assisted hobble to Bwana's enclosure to convince me that Clive might have been right. There was no strength in me. Emotionally too I was a mess. Bwana's evident pleasure at seeing me again had me sobbing against the railing, then all over the bucket of game pellets and at last into Clive's shoulder. I was naturally pleased to find that Bwana, like everyone else at Doornleegte, was fine, but also dismayed that my absence had apparently been of so little consequence. Nobody needed me.

A good sleep took care of that momentary low and the next morning, with immense gratitude, I was able to resume most of my normal activities, albeit for a while on crutches and for a much longer while still in open sandals. The daily chore of dealing with dressings and the unattractive reality of a wound going septic as well as the apparently permanent loss of sensation in part of my foot, were nothing. My life had been spared.

Why? To what end?

All those stories about life-reviews in the face of death turned out to be true. The Marapong hospital bed had been a front-row seat: the events, the people, the assignments, the loves of my life. It was a courtroom too, and I both prosecutor and defendant. So much to do, so much still left undone; so much given, so little as yet given in return. So richly blessed.

I emerged with an invigorated sense of purpose. No challenge too big, no fear I couldn't face. If a mountain needed moving, I would move it. It got to a stage, one morning, when Clive felt he had to intervene. He reminded me of my hospital promises to rest. That did not go well. It went not-well all the way to the Melkrivier Museum. I'd insisted that he take me there – an inspection was overdue.

"It can wait," he said.

"*Katz' aus dem Haus, rührt sich die Maus,*" (When the cat's away, the mouse will play) I flung at him.

"Nonsense. We have good people there."

"*Ver van jou goed, naby jou skade.*" (Far from your own, close to your ruin.)

Poor man. He had learnt not to argue with a wife speaking in tongues. Besides, the truth of that old Afrikaans Boere proverb was indisputable, and in this case most apt. The Melkrivier complex was our personal investment, in finances, furnishings and, not least, faith in the future of the Waterberg. It was doing well, but I believed that it would only continue to do so with a committed hand on the reins. Clive and I had always tackled everything as a partnership, and in this enterprise too I was keen to do my fair share. His schedule of responsibilities was full to overflowing. On top of all the rest he had by now been appointed to the South African National Parks Board, the Green Trust, and the Limpopo Tourism Board. He had also co-founded the Clive Walker Foundation to support the museum.

And now, I silently admitted to myself, he had to make time for a wife's convalescence and ill-humour. As the Pajero climbed out of the valley I couldn't think of a single positive thing to say; cheeriness was beyond my resources for that day. An unfamiliar gloom had claimed me for its own. We emerged onto the Palala plateau to find it lying under a sullen horizon-to-horizon cloud-cover. I stared out at the passing bushveld, which in the dull light appeared dreary and unaccountably empty. A number of the metres-high mountain aloes we passed looked desperate and dying, their crowns blackened, their characteristic broad fleshy leaves thinned, drooping and broken. Even a majestic mature aloe can be decimated by a tiny invader, the aloe snout beetle that burrows into the plant's succulent heart to lay its eggs. By the time the damage shows on the outside there will be a swollen grub in the hollowed-out stem, voraciously consuming the plant's life to feed its own.

Leaving the scenery to Button who, as was her habit, had her head out of the window, I closed my eyes.

I woke up when the Pajero switched off. Clive smiled at me. "Fancy a cup of tea?" He nodded in the direction of the restaurant's patio which, in dappled shade, was looking quite charming. "They tell me this place is not too shabby; the boss has very high standards. Bit of a battle-axe. German I believe."

Walker's Wayside was buzzing. Many familiar faces. I matched greeting for greeting, smile for smile, and lied to everyone that I was perfectly fine again. We had our tea and around me conversations ebbed and flowed, while overhead a pair of paradise flycatchers ferried food to their nest. This was the third year I watched them in the massive Schotia (*huilboerboon*) which spread its generous, deep shade over the outdoor restaurant seating. The male, flamboyant in his breeding plumage, his bright chestnut tail streaming almost 20 centimetres behind his compact boldly dressed body. The pair's clear calls, loud enough to be heard all over the museum grounds, had become so familiar that hardly anyone bothered anymore to glance up at that free and wild life so busily, so magically, being lived right in their midst.

If my life had taken a different course I myself might have been oblivious to such things. But two decades of living in the Waterberg bush, and especially my experience with wild orphans, had taught me to marvel at what we call "wild" life. Perhaps it would be more accurate to speak of "free" rather than "wild" life. I'd spent hours pondering this while working with my animals. Is a rhino in a boma, or a lion in a zoo, still "wild"? It certainly isn't free to follow its natural, instinctual life. Bwana was by no means a tame animal, but he wasn't free. Many, many times we were up on his hill and I'd hear the cry of the Palala's fish eagles. I'd watch them soar, dive, rise again in their unbounded sky. Free. Truer to their wild nature than my rhino in his 20-hectare allocation.

Anyone who has taken care of orphaned wild animals, for years as I've done, will tell you that it is a singular, incredible experience. However calm the animal may appear to be with you, however much it trusts you, you always know that it is a trust that the animal *grants* you. You cannot force it; you can earn it but you are not entitled to it. It is an agreement between the two of you, and in my opinion it is quite different from the relationship you might form with a domesticated animal. When I looked into the eyes of my rhinos, I always found something unfathomable there, something beyond my reach, something not own-able by man. In that sense, its freedom – freedom from subjugation by man – is what defines it, and what defines it as "wild". We might keep it in captivity, but there remains some deep untameable essence that it holds in reserve, something which will never be "owned".

Even with the easiest of my charges, Mothlo, I had felt it. I cared for her, but it was with her consent. There was intelligence there, and not only the ability to choose but also the right to do so. Grow to love such an animal and more than anything you will want to see it go free. A lesson in letting go.

Mothlo was five-and-a-half years old when she disappeared. After the flood of New Year's Eve 1999 I knew there were only two possibilities: she'd died, or she'd survived and our re-wilding programme had been successful. Then one day – it must have been more than a year later – I was sitting in just about the same spot as on that gloomy post-snakebite morning, watching the paradise flycatchers at their nest, when someone brought news from Horizon Horse Safaris. A small pod of hippo had appeared, all of a sudden, in a dam in the Melkrivier system. No one knew how they got there, but the horse trailists have consistently reported seeing them, and one very large female – the matriarch they thought – behaved differently from the rest. She seemed to have no fear of people and didn't flee back to the water like the others. She stood her ground and in fact seemed to be rather inquisitive.

I knew immediately: Mothlo. It had to be. In time those first rumours were borne out by fact. It was indeed Mothlo. Everything I had dreamt of for her on those freezing mornings at the Palala rockpool had come true. She, now with a pod of her own, was living according to nature's design. She was free, and therefore according to my personal definition of the term, at last truly "wild" again. For that reason I had no intention of seeking her out. A chapter of her life and mine had closed, and had closed most happily.

To my delight Dale Parker had agreed to let her be. A lesser man might have wanted his property returned, but for Dale our re-wilding success was too good a thing to wish to spoil it.

With hindsight now I wonder if some of the emotions I was

feeling on that difficult day in late January 2003 weren't due to something similar, albeit less happy. Certainly the aftermath of the snakebite was no fun, but perhaps there was also a sense of finding myself in an open space between chapters. An insecure space. Dale's death had closed a chapter. With the Melkrivier Museum doing well, it seemed as if another chapter might be beginning, although as yet without allowing me any clues as to the meaning it might hold for me personally. What was clear though was that our timing had been good. 2002 had been a year for the conservation-minded. The UN had declared it the Year of Sustainable Development, International Year of Ecotourism, International Year of Mountains, and the Year for Cultural Heritage. And there was our museum, set up right from the beginning to promote sustainable development within the biosphere, ecotourism in the entire Waterberg region, and the preservation of the cultural heritage of all its peoples. Everything seemed poised for the next chapter to be a good one for both the Waterberg and for the Walkers.

FOURTEEN

Mokibelo

I WAS LEANING ON THE VERANDAH railing, staring at a white rhino cow. Like some dry-land whale beached in our garden, she'd been lying there all morning. A few pale golden pom-poms of the flowering fever trees had landed on her shoulders and broad rump. Decorative, but with her not moving, too funerary for my liking. I summoned Clive from his studio. "What's wrong with her? I've never seen her so lethargic."

"She's fat. If you were that size you'd also be disinclined to move."

Munyane was certainly substantial, well on her way to her adult weight of 2.5 tonnes. She'd been free to roam as she liked for about two years, but she still chose to spend some of her time around Doornleegte and often returned for the night. I was therefore able to keep a reasonably consistent check on her welfare. She seemed to be doing absolutely fine, although beginning in early 2002, her behaviour had occasionally given me cause for concern.

She'd come back from an excursion into the veld panting, as if she'd taken some unusually vigorous exercise. A couple of days without anything unusual, and then the next day, there she'd be again: out of breath. Then came another change. If she was around during the evening, I'd notice that she became unusually restless, more and more so into the night. One evening she abandoned her old quarters and took to sleeping very close to the verandah stairs. The next sign of something going on was alarming. I noticed a white secretion running from under her tail and down her back legs and immediately feared that she'd developed an infection. I checked the spot where she'd slept and found that the creamy fluid had dried to a chalk-like, flaky substance. Suddenly it dawned on me: Munyane had come into oestrus.

As with Mothlo I had vowed to let nature take its course; I would not interfere with Munyane's further progress. Observe yes, when I could, but the policy was strictly hands-off. It wasn't easy. One night, Clive, lured out of the house by loud noises, discovered not only the source of the noise, but also his wife watching from the verandah. A fully grown male white rhino was very interested in Munyane who was fighting back and barking loudly at him. If this was a courtship it was not a gentle one: the next morning she had bleeding scratches on her face from the aggressive horn-on-horn clashes of the previous night. This went on for a few nights and then came the morning I discovered Munyane lying in the front garden, looking decidedly like the morning after the night before. She seemed dejected and reluctant to move. The reason wasn't hard to find: under her tail bloody pieces of flesh were protruding from her vagina. Not the most tender initiation into adulthood, but nevertheless a significant positive step in Munyane's re-integration into life as a wild rhino.

There was no way I could know if that first contact with a male had been successful. No amount of careful observation, and I did plenty of that, gave me any indication whether she was pregnant or not. Taking a hopeful view, I marked off the 18-month gestation period of a white rhino on my calendar.

She began to stay away at night and sometimes we wouldn't see her for days on end. I tried not to worry. Every time she returned to Doornleegte she seemed to be as calm and friendly as ever. By now her size was impressive: at least two metres in length, 1.5 metres high at the shoulder, and very heavy. But in the absence of any confirming evidence I couldn't with any certainty ascribe her bulk to a pregnancy – as a white rhino she was meant to be huge. In October 2003, when 17 calendar months had been crossed off on my calendar, it was clear to me that for some reason Munyane was needing to rest a great deal. We were approaching the end of the 18th month when I discovered her lying, bedecked with golden blossoms, and called Clive for a second opinion.

He refused to commit to a diagnosis purely on the basis of minor changes in her behaviour, which might or might not be the fruits of his wife's fond imaginings. But a few days later I called him again and handed him the binoculars: "Have a look at my imagination."

Even without the aid of binoculars he could see that Munyane's mammary glands had begun to swell. "Congratulations, Grandma," he said. "That makes three."

In February, to our great joy, Anton and René's daughter, Tristyn, had been born. With her brother Ayden she provided us with the brightest and happiest moments in a year not noted for undiluted good news, neither in Africa nor in the rest of the world.

The end of February saw the beginning of an ethnic war in Western Sudan as rebel forces took up arms against the Sudanese government, an escalating horror that would become known as the Darfur Genocide. In March American and British-led coalition forces invaded Iraq and set the agenda for a renewed global debate on the morality of war. As in Darfur, and in Afghanistan and most other conflict-ridden areas, it was, understandably, a human-centred debate. The cost to the biodiversity of these regions received barely a mention in the corridors of power.

In July another international debate, one which did include biodiversity conservation, ended in defeat for all parties except the all-powerful Chinese government. Waters started pouring into the newly constructed Three Gorges Dam; 1.3 million people were displaced; archaeological and cultural sites lost; and thousands of already endangered plant species (57% of the more than 6000 in the area) doomed to an even more tenuous hold on life. The dam was bad news too for 27% of China's endangered freshwater fish species and for the remaining critically endangered Siberian cranes which lost their over-wintering wetlands. Most threatened of all: the Chinese river dolphin, which occurred only in the Yangtze River. Three years later it would be declared functionally extinct.

In August, closer to home, news broke of the wildlife conservation crisis in Zimbabwe. The Parks and Conservation authority was unable to pay its staff; game scouts had to drastically curtail their patrols as vehicles had run out of fuel; and they were told to shoot game to make up for the shortfall in their rations. More than 3000 cheetah had been lost to illegal settlers hunting with packs of dogs. Rhino poaching was on the rise, and in four years almost 4000 poached elephant carcasses had been discovered in the Zambezi Valley alone.

In September, the 5th IUCN World Parks Congress held in Durban, at which Clive was a delegate, heard that there was simply not enough funding available for the management of the earth's protected areas – an annual shortfall of 20 billion dollars. The Durban Accord acknowledged that "environmental conservation today has to compete with urgent socio-economic priorities for funding and therefore needs to become self-sustaining in order to survive". The IUCN chairperson, Yolanda Kakabadse, made it sound slightly more noble: "Areas must be protected not against people, but for people."

What I would have preferred to hear, idealist that I am, is that wilderness in and of itself was worthy of our protection; environmental conservation ought to be a duty incumbent upon us for the privilege of sharing the planet with such a magnificence of other life forms. The realist in me knew that we had to be grateful that there was at least a perception in some quarters, though regrettably not all, that mankind benefitted from conserved and protected natural areas. The idealist had the last word: maybe such benefits would be seen not solely in terms of commercial exploitation.

Despite all the achievements reported by international delegates at the Congress it would have been a very naïve conservationist who couldn't read the writing on the wall: worldwide, and not least in a country like South Africa that had to prioritise the eradication of poverty, the fight on behalf of nature's other-than-human creatures could only become harder.

So for us at Doornleegte Munyane's news could not have been more welcome. Lapalala was a private reserve, every rhino counted. Naturally my delight outstripped everyone else's. Detective work by the rangers indicated that the father was Hatton, the large bull that Dale had named for Clive's grandfather. The Walker men agreed that Hatton had done the family name proud.

Munyane's next move was entirely natural, but intensely frustrating for me. She disappeared. There was no sign of her anywhere. Eventually I had to accept that either the birth had been disastrous for her and she died, or it had been successful and she was living as a fully re-wilded rhino somewhere in the reserve. Either way she'd left Doornleegte, and me, for good.

For a while I still kept hoping for reassuring news, that Clive or a field ranger had spotted her somewhere on their rounds. At least I would have known that she was alive. There was nothing. That was the worst: not knowing the fate of that animal which for me was not only the adult rhino, but also that terrified little calf with whom I had pleaded through a long summer night to accept my help.

November arrived and with it the shift to my hot-weather routine: household and administrative tasks allocated to afternoons when the stifling outdoors made it less of a penance to be indoors. So mid-afternoon on the first Sunday of the month found me at my work table, listening to rain sifting down, the end of the shower that had broken the mugginess of that day. Wonderfully cool air streamed in through open windows and doors. The rain stopped and I set aside the remainder of my work. The rain-washed air was just too inviting. I walked out onto the verandah.

Clive told me later that I'd given him the fright of his life. My urgent call had brought him rushing out onto the verandah where he found me with my hands over my face, weeping inconsolably. I couldn't tell him why, so he looked around for the cause of my distress. And then there were two of us in tears.

Approaching through the open driveway gate was a massive adult white rhino cow. She wasn't alone. Dwarfed by Munyane right up close to her, was the tiniest, most perfect little rhino calf.

They walked up to about halfway between the gate and the house and then stopped. Munyane's attention seemed to be divided equally between us and her calf.

"Go on," Clive whispered, "she's waiting for you. But carefully now."

I crept down the stairs and began calling her name as I'd done a million times over the years. At the foot of the stairs I waited a while, still calling. Munyane's full attention was on me now. I took a step and was brought up short by the change in her. There was no mistaking it. When a rhino means business you know it and that was as close as she was going to allow me to approach her calf.

I watched Munyane cross the lawn and walk up to the back of the kitchen. There she tucked into lucerne and pellets like someone who'd discovered a feast after a long famine. All the while her calf stayed tucked up close to her, a perfect miniature, still wet from the rain which in that light gave her as yet unmarked, baby-new hide the look of slate-grey smoke.

Suddenly that magical moment was over. As quietly as Munyane had arrived, she left again, taking her baby back to their world, out there somewhere beyond the umbrella thorns silhouetted in the failing light.

The rangers named the little one Mokibelo (Saturday). Her human grandmother, having been told to keep her distance, had to limit her need to spoil and indulge both mother and daughter to efforts at "improving" the veld around Doornleegte. Additional drinking water and a nutritional subsidy of lucerne and game pellets for mother; two newly created mud holes, one large, one small; a large heap of fresh, clean river sand for the little one.

I saw the circle completed: a rescued hand-reared rhino, re-wilded, teaching her offspring the ways of a wild rhino. From Munyane's precisely dictated safe distance I was able to observe

Mokibelo learning to use a rhino midden, a mud-bath and, among the choicest of Clive's specially planted indigenous trees in our extensive garden, acquiring her own adept manoeuvres for getting the most out of a rubbing post.

Mokibelo didn't always *want* to be taught – she had inherited some of her mother's stubbornness. With the aid of binoculars I watched as Munyane dealt with her headstrong daughter. Given her diminutive size at the time, Mokibelo was putting up a spirited resistance against overwhelming odds. Her ear-splitting squeals seemed to be, like the tantrum of any human toddler, a blend of indignation, complaint and frustration. Munyane had her head down, pushing her calf in front of her. Mokibelo kept protesting; Munyane kept pushing. I began to feel anxious: Munyane was getting rather forceful. Suddenly the squealing stopped. Mokibelo was jauntily trotting off through the grass ahead of her mother who, head still lowered, was following closely to ensure that the lesson was well learnt: small white rhino calves always run *ahead* of their mothers.

It was a happy picture which, alas, was becoming extremely rare in a significant conservation area far to the north of us. Garamba National Park in the Democratic Republic of the Congo, one of Africa's oldest national parks and a UNESCO World Heritage Site, was the very last refuge of the northern white rhino. In June 2004 we read the grim news: rebels from the Sudanese war zones had scaled up from wholesale poaching for bushmeat (devastating as that was for the wildlife of Garamba) to wholesale poaching for rhino horn and ivory. Michael Fay, Conservation Fellow at the National Geographic Society, warned that for the northern white rhino extinction was not far off. Little more than a year later he was proven right. None remained in the wild. Only three survived in captivity.

In my memory now that picture of Mokibelo, gambolling through the tall summer grass, seems all the more precious, a tiny hedge against extinction of the single remaining subspecies of white rhino.

Some time later there was another picture that was to engrave itself on my mind. It remains there to this day, ready to unleash an avalanche of memories against which I have very little defence.

It was high summer. A good year. The rains had arrived late, but then continued to hammer and inundate us as if the season was intent on a lavish, unsparing outpouring of its riches, as if there was a deadline to its generosity. When I got out of the Pajero to open the gate into the oldest section of the reserve, the gluey mud stuck to my boots. There were deep tracks and a few skid-marks: zebra and blue wildebeest which had crossed a short while earlier. All the way up the steep incline the road showed fresh scars from the previous afternoon's thunderstorm, but Clive had no trouble getting the vehicle to the top. In any case he could probably have driven that road blindfolded. More than 23 years earlier he'd taken me up there for the first time, for my first look at Lapalala. Then, with Malora lowering over us, we had had a celebratory picnic on the cliffs above the Palala, at the bend of it where Lepotedi would one day be constructed.

Twenty-three years, I thought, between that trip and this one, how could it have been so long? Almost a quarter of a century between that picnic and the one we were heading for now. We drove past the turn-off we took then, and past the other ill-defined almost secretive ones to the left and right to other hideaway bush camps. Without hurrying we followed the twisting route, a well-mannered little road that submitted to the land, and gave way to clumps of trees and rocky outcrops. Nowhere did it force its way in or through or across. With the consent of all the natural features of that landscape it took us deeper into the heart of the reserve. There were no vehicle tracks; if anyone had passed that way recently the rain would have erased the evidence anyway. There were no signposts, but like Clive I didn't need any.

It was midday – we hadn't managed to get going as early as we'd wanted – but even so there was plenty of game around. Most of them with youngsters. It was the season for it. We didn't stop anywhere. Neither of us felt like talking. Clive frequently had his head out of the window, reading the tracks as was his habit. Unusually, though, he didn't tell me what he'd seen or what his interpretation was of what he'd seen. When at last the road – no more than a jeep-track now, rutted and rather overgrown – dipped down towards the river there were impala everywhere. The beautiful heads turned to look at us. None of them ran away. All the way down that rock-strewn slope I spotted more of them in the sparse shade of wild syringa and cabbage trees. Then we wound in among bigger trees, the deeper shade of tambuti, knobthorn and river bushwillows.

Our arrival at the bottom disturbed a family of warthogs busily ploughing up the mulch of damp soil and leaf litter. The boar had his muddy snout and tusks up at us, the whole of his tough russet-maned body at full alert. And then they were off, tails to the sky, adults in front, five piglets following – seven erect aerials speeding through the undergrowth. I opened the door so that Button, barking madly, could indulge in her favourite chase. It was all bluster and no bite; she couldn't have caught up and wouldn't have done any harm anyway.

We walked up to the first of the buildings. There was no door. The screed floor was sandy and damp, strewn with leaves, bits of bark and sticks and dead insects. There were drifts of brittle, transparent wings without the insect bodies they once belonged to. In one corner there was the muddy granular foundation of a termite turret. Marks on the walls betrayed that there used to be cupboards there, beds, blinds. The next room used to have a basin, a shower, a toilet, a mirror. We wandered to and through another of the buildings which once housed a stove, fridge, freezer, tables, food storage cupboards, shelves, gas cylinders, basins and taps for the water which used to flow from the big green tank halfway up the slope. The tank was still there, surrounded by what seemed like a solid curtain of sound – the throbbing hum of what must have been thousands of bees.

In the shade of the wide sweep of a thatch roof, sagging and fraying at the edges, Clive put down our camping chairs and, on a few stones kicked together, our picnic basket. There used to be many more camping chairs there, and a large wooden table, shelves for lanterns and books, easy chairs and recliners and people relaxing in them, dozing or having meals or conversations or passing along binoculars to each other to admire something in the view stretched out in front of them. Children laughing and playing.

Tambuti, an eight-bedded bush camp at the confluence of the Blocklands and the Palala, had been a favourite with families. When the news of its closure broke, we were swamped with letters and emails of regret and protest, pleas to reconsider, and floods of personal recollections. Of course it wasn't just Tambuti. The entire bush camp operation was being discontinued, all the camps closed. The loss our bush camp aficionados were lamenting was not of only Tambuti, or Rock Lodge, or Mukwa or any of the others. It was the loss of access for the ordinary man, woman and family to the Lapalala wilderness.

I comforted myself with the knowledge that they had their photographs, their home movies and memories, and whatever changes the wilderness had wrought in them. Their Lapalala would always remain exactly the way they remembered it. They would not see the slowly disintegrating shells of rondavels and log cabins, the floors with cracks and puddles and piles of bat or bird droppings. They wouldn't see vines curling in through window and door openings, grass pushing up through cracks, thorny pioneer plants taking hold in the paths and around the fire pit. The bush reclaiming its own.

Outside of the campsites there wouldn't have been anything the bush needed to reclaim. The visitors had left footprints only; their presence as light and transient as the breeze I now felt through the sweaty back of my shirt.

I settled down with my binoculars. The view was still there. The same skyline, the same reed bed, and after a few moments the same highlight that had drawn me to that rendezvous year after year. A flash of snow and amethyst: a male plum-coloured starling. I couldn't spot any of the rather drab speckled females. I expected them to be at their nests, somewhere in the trees along the riverbanks. But it was the males' brilliant plumage I'd wanted to see, the striking contrast of white underparts and iridescent purple head, wings and back. In the course of the afternoon I saw several of them as they flitted in and out and across the reed bed.

The same breeze that cooled my back played among the reeds, played *with* them, I thought. I was beguiled by that movement of air – a thing alive which ruffled the fronds with their heavy, creamy seed-heads, made them sway and bend in one direction and then in another, or for minutes at a time left them undisturbed, immobile, an artist's etching of lines and angles and planes. And then I'd hear a whisper starting in the trees behind the camp, feel it passing over me and wait for it to reach the still patch framed in my binoculars. The reeds would come alive again, dip and wave and flow as the breeze willed.

In that picture is everything I felt that day. A connection with the place, the birds, and all those visitors who had seen them there. Gratitude that we could have facilitated such an experience for so many thousands of people. Acute regret too for so seldom allowing myself what we gave them: the chance to surrender wholeheartedly to simply *being* in the wilderness, so different from working as I did while based in a wilderness area. I felt the need to lose myself somewhere out there in the wild. To walk without route or plan or schedule except to follow the lie of the land where it led until exhaustion overtook me, or I arrived at some natural destination: a cliff-top, a lone tree, a bend in the river, a renewed serenity.

Like that airy current in the reeds, events had affected Clive and me in our almost four decades together. We'd been nudged in this direction, then another, then allowed a respite for a time, before being tumbled and set a-playing again by the next change blowing through our lives. Now another re-ordering had come. Or more accurately, several of them that had piled one on top of the other and coalesced to shake my world.

The decision to close down the bush camp operation was not easily taken, and was moreover not ours to take. It was but one of the cascade of unavoidable changes that had to follow in the wake of Dale Parker's death. It was a fluid time, for Lapalala and for us. Dale's son, Duncan, who had known Lapalala since he was a boy canoeing in the Palala, was ready to take on his father's legacy, but it couldn't happen overnight. Transitions, if they are to be wise, have a measured tempo to them.

The focus of our own responsibilities was also shifting, widening to include the Melkrivier Museum complex. The Lapalala Wilderness School was well-established now, widely known with an excellent reputation; Clive could hand over the reins while continuing as patron of the school. Inevitably we arrived at a moment when one of us had to say it: What if we were to relocate away from Doornleegte? Wouldn't it make more sense to be based at Melkrivier? Many discussions later, with our family and with the Lapalala directors, only one obstacle remained. But it was a big one: Bwana.

With his history he couldn't be released into the reserve. At Doornleegte he was integrated into a conservation education programme that everyone agreed had to continue. But who would take care of him? In the end there was only one conclusion: if we moved, Bwana had to move too. It wasn't a simple solution; for one thing we'd have to construct rhino enclosures at Melkrivier. But at least the last of a series of difficult decisions had finally been taken. It was a relief. At last there was a definite shape to the future. We could begin our planning for the move to be as ordered and effortless as possible. I began making lists.

Then one morning in August 2004 Lapalala received a phone call from Karen Trendler's Animal Rehabilitation Centre: a decision had to be taken about Moêng, Lapalala's black rhino calf rescued on Boxing Day 2002. After 20 months at ARC, although she was by no means fully recovered, the worst of her injuries seemed to have healed. Unfortunately she'd suddenly taken a turn for the worse. Her decline was so drastic and rapid ARC didn't feel they could do anything more for her. They recommended that she should be returned to Lapalala immediately. Given that she was in such a desperate state, an attempt at rehabilitating her in her natural environment might not succeed, but without trying it she would die anyway.

For the second time, Moêng's life hung in the balance, and again the decision lay with Lapalala's owners and directors. They couldn't themselves manage the round-the-clock personal care required by such a sick animal, so they gave ARC the choice: try to sell Moêng to anyone who would be prepared to take her, or try on their own behalf to pull her through once more and should she make it then decide what to do with her, or just put her down immediately without incurring any further trouble or expense.

ARC called us. They couldn't bear to simply give up on her; couldn't Conita take her? There was no easy answer, just more questions. How long would it take to nurse Moêng back to health? How long after that to re-introduce her to the wild? We wouldn't be at Doornleegte for very much longer, how could we possibly take on such a charge? I remembered the hot day of her rescue, and myself agonising over her survival. Then, the decision wasn't mine. This time it was.

If we were to take her on it would have to be at Melkrivier. It would mean more enclosures to be constructed in record time, and I'd be committing myself to another wild orphan. After raising Bwana, Mothlo and Munyane, I knew exactly what that meant.

There were many reasons to say No, all of them rational, reasonable and justifiable. There was only reason to say Yes: I couldn't say No.

Clive and I pooled our finances and bought Moêng for an amount more-or-less equivalent to the cost of her 20-month stay at ARC. They were so keen for us to give that poor animal a last chance that they negotiated a reasonable price for which we were grateful.

Months later, as I sat among the bedraggled remains of Tambuti, the worst of the relocation to Melkrivier was over. I was deeply thankful that Mother had been spared the upheaval at Doornleegte – she had moved into a frail care home in Bedfordview, Johannesburg, the previous year. Most of my household had already been moved, and there were two black rhinos in suitable enclosures close to where I would be living at the Melkrivier Museum. There Bwana would be waiting for me to pick up where we left off. Moêng was just waiting: for death or for someone to help her survive.

I tried to look on the bright side. It was an exciting time to be involved with black rhino conservation. In July 2004 the World

Conservation Union's Rhino Specialist Group was able to state that, even in the face of continued threats like habitat destruction and poaching, black rhino numbers were finally edging away from the brink of extinction. The species remains critically endangered but it seemed that conservation measures put in place by the Southern African Development Community, aided by agencies like WWF, the Frankfurt Zoological Society, and the U.S. Fish and Wildlife Service, had turned the tide. The dreadful rhino war that had begun in the 1980s was one which we couldn't afford to lose, and we didn't.

WWF was responsible for another bit of welcome news. The organisation partnered with Ezemvelo KZN Wildlife (the former Natal Parks Board), the Eastern Cape Parks and Tourism Board and the Mazda Wildlife Fund, and established the Black Rhino Range Expansion Project. It was aimed at creating partnerships between neighbouring landowners who had suitable black rhino habitat. In conservation, land is always an issue – always in short supply, or threatened in some way. And the bigger the animal, the bigger its range, the bigger the land issue. Cooperation across boundaries, ideally virtual boundaries rather than fenced ones, could only be good news.

I lifted my binoculars to scan the slopes beyond the reedbed. Not a single fence. No wall or obstruction to impede the movement of air or animals. A very very long time ago it was like that too, before man put his much vilified (and justly so) footprint in the Waterberg. Then the fates brought us here, and we became part of the effort to return the land to a pristine state – I saw firsthand that the human footprint didn't always have to be such a negative one. The long life of the Waterberg, including the human-dominated period with its herds and herders, guns and fences and the mindset with which they ruled the land, would be remembered in the Melkrivier Museum. But out here all those people, and us, would be forgotten. The land would always outlast us. I found that comforting. I was surrounded by something ancient and enduring. A deep, living silence held me and consoled me that day between the Blocklands and the Palala.

Button announced Clive's return. They were dripping wet. Both rivers were running strongly and between rocky barricades where the water cascaded into foaming pools there were beautiful stretches for swimming, hopefully crocodile-free. I wondered how many times Clive would have had to rescue Button – she was notorious for under-estimating the current, over-estimating her own paddling prowess and getting swept away downstream. Lapalala's rivers aren't major ones, not to compare with the Limpopo or Zambezi, but send enough water hurrying down their twisting, dramatic gorges and to underestimate them is to die. It has always struck me as one of life's paradoxes: we cannot live without water, but it has to be doled out to us in manageable rations. Too much and it becomes our executioner.

The whole of that week we'd been watching television reports of the almost incomprehensibly destructive power of water – the Boxing Day tsunami. In a part of the globe that was the quintessential image of paradise, an undersea earthquake had triggered a killer surge that left hundreds of thousands dead in 14 countries. Thirty-metre-high waves engulfed coastal communities of Indonesia, Sri Lanka, Thailand, Malaysia and India. Even 8500 kilometres away, on the other side of the Indian Ocean, it registered on our African coast. Kenya, Tanzania and South Africa reported drownings and structural damage to harbours where cars and boats were submerged under waters two to three metres higher than normal. I couldn't begin to imagine the power of the natural forces unleashed in such an event, 9.1 on the Richter scale. Scientists were saying that for almost 10 minutes the entire planet vibrated. It set off other earthquakes in other places, even as far away as Alaska. The earth convulsed and people, buildings, animals, trees, anything that couldn't escape, were destroyed.

And this was the same earth that cradled me and soothed away my agitation and trouble. Was it nothing more than a fancy of mine, this notion of Mother Earth being a benevolent nurturer of life, including human life? Surely all those people killed by the tsunami couldn't have been collectively guilty of some cosmic transgression and therefore deserving of punishment in the form of an immense calamity. Execution by water, like a latter-day Noah's flood. Were their deaths random then? Caught in a cataclysmic readjustment of the earth's own internal discomforts? The earth going about its own business, with no regard to the infinitesimal specks of life crawling its surface? Impersonal, uncaring earth, with no concern for one particular infinitesimal speck of life sitting for one brief unremarked moment at the confluence of two insignificant little watercourses and fancying herself known and noted and fed by the earth.

I sat with my binoculars and watched the starlings and understood nothing.

Clive and I finished our picnic, a modest one: sandwiches and tea. We took a few more photographs, shared a few more memories and then were startled by loud barks, unnervingly close-by. A baboon troop had begun their afternoon trek down the slopes to the water. Clive was thrilled and, in an effort to lighten our moods I suspect, insisted on seeing significance in the arrival of the baboons. It was 9 January, the birthdate of naturalist-poet Eugène Marais. Marais was famous for *Soul of the Ape*, his ground-breaking study of a Waterberg baboon troop. Our picnic had been intended to commemorate my survival, two years earlier, after the snakebite. But we couldn't do it on the right date, the 6th, a Thursday. It had to wait until the Sunday, and so we found ourselves among Tambuti's baboons on Marais's birthday. We watched the troop moving down to the river, juveniles scampering and squabbling among the dishevelled bush camp structures while the largest male postured and barked from the crown of a mighty ficus. Since the Melkrivier complex which would be our next home also housed the Eugène Marais Museum, I allowed myself to be convinced: it was a sign, surely, of good fortune.

We'd come to say goodbye, to Tambuti and to much else. I had braced myself for a painful experience, and it was. I will not pretend that there was no sadness. I was leaving a sanctuary. More: a way of life, a way of being.

And yet there was no wish to stay. In the midst of packing up our lives at Doornleegte I'd become aware of a growing excitement. A new life was calling to us. Clive, as always, was looking ahead. For him, even more than for me, Lapalala had been a mission, and being Clive it had been a mission of the heart. At the end of every day over sundowners our conversations were, as they'd often been before, of the future. The Doornleegte verandah was still our favourite spot for planning and for dreaming, but now our plans and dreams centred on Melkrivier.

Still, on that January day when the sun set – for me for the last time – over Tambuti, and I was overtaken by that particular brand of melancholy that belongs to quiet Sunday afternoons and farewells and guineafowl at dusk, it wasn't easy. The light faded and stole the starlings from me, and then the reed bed, and then all the green of the bush. Swifts were still slicing through the darkening sky when I noticed the first bats flitting in and out between us and the ragged thatch roof. Then the night took over. Frogs – numberless tinkling, glittering voices. And two small rivers rushing to go and find the ocean.

As we drove away through the dark I thanked the kindly fates that had arranged circumstances in such a way that there was important work waiting for me. It was work I loved, and it was waiting for me in a boma at Melkrivier. On the day of Moêng's finding I had surprised myself with the urgency with which I'd prayed for her rescue to succeed. How could I have known that there would come a day when she would be the one to rescue me?

FIFTEEN

Moêng

WITH A SICK RHINO on your hands you cannot be a delicate flower needing to be shielded from every ill wind. There will be many ill winds, literally. You'll try to dodge the worst expressions of the animal's discomforts, you'll dance, contort, cavort and anticipate, but more often than not you'll still find yourself at the wrong end of the beast at the wrong time. You *will* need a robust sense of humour.

On a daily basis your sensory faculties will come under assault, you'll see, touch, hear and especially smell things you'd much rather not. But wince and wrinkle your nose as you may, that animal will get under your skin. Your capacity to care for it will be stretched until there is no limit to what you'll attempt and endure for its welfare. After more than a decade of rearing wild animals I knew this, but nothing had prepared me for Moêng.

When she was off-loaded at Melkrivier I had the distinct impression of an animal that had held on only long enough to have reached the end of her journey. Now that she'd arrived, anything more was beyond her. There was not enough strength or spirit left in her to investigate her new surroundings. On that beautiful spring day she just stood there, fully taken up with the effort of breathing and remaining on her feet.

It was only when I got closer that I heard her groaning. A weak, unprotesting confession of her misery. Her hide felt dehydrated. Under my hands the ridges of her ribs and hipbones were sharp and felt fragile. She was small for her age, emaciated and incontinent. Constant diarrhoea had left her with a raw and bleeding backside. But her poor physical condition was not the only problem. She seemed unbearably sad. I didn't know if she had sufficient will to survive.

By rights I should have been able to do what I had done with Munyane: stay with her, sleep next to her, and if I could, *will* her back to life. But that wasn't possible. Clive and I were still living at Doornleegte, and so was Bwana. Until such time as my responsibilities had consolidated to Melkrivier, I had to leave Moêng in what I hoped would be capable and trustworthy hands. I will always be grateful for the fact that they were.

Anton and René had been running a project for gap students from the UK, and since their focus was on environmental conservation work, Moêng's basic care fitted right into their programme, and it must be said, their hearts. These young women had already assisted conservation officers in the construction of Bwana's new enclosure at Melkrivier, and now cheerfully pitched into the unglamorous tasks of cleaning and caring for Moêng.

I could guide and advise over the phone, but it was soon clear that they couldn't devote all their time to Moêng, and equally clear that she needed more intensive care than the situation allowed. I rushed through my packing at Doornleegte. Our new home, the former Melkrivier Primary School headmaster's house, was just about ready for us. Since I had already taken care of rodent-proofing the floors and skirting-boards, all it still needed was a crisp new coat of white paint to brighten the interior. A modicum of emotional blackmail, judiciously wielded, cornered Clive into volunteering for the job. The result was delightful: the little house sparkled as with a new lease of life. So did Clive, with his paintbespattered overalls, shoes, hair and glasses, as he threw open the doors for my inspection.

Our move, in typical bushveld fashion, involved an open truck, friends rallying around with farm bakkies and labourers and endless cups of tea. For a while my sense of order was severely challenged, but then came the moment when Clive handed me my sundowner, and I looked around and there were our homely worn-in easy-chairs, their seats and backs moulded to ours; there were our family pictures, Keith Calder's bronze rhinos, our collection of art works and antique maps and ceramics, Persian rugs on the floors.

We went outside to look west. A different skyline and around me a different garden. But there were Clive's favourite stones, accumulated through many wilderness years, and the gigantic leopard orchid he'd rescued from certain destruction under bulldozer tyres during the construction of a powerline. From the fever trees over to our left came a cascade of descending notes. A few seconds' silence, and then another one. *Du-du-du-du-du ... du-du-du ...* Wine poured into a glass, then into another. It was a Burchell's coucal. Our African rainbird.

It had been nine years since I first saw the derelict site of the old Melkrivier Primary School. Then too a coucal was calling. Like Clive with the Tambuti baboons, I took comfort where I found it. It was a good omen.

The journey Moêng and I were to take together began the next morning. She was standing at her feeding area. I cannot say she was *waiting* there, not the way my other animals waited for attention or food, with eager anticipation and bright eyes and vocalisations the moment they knew I was approaching. She was just standing, apparently staring at nothing. I began calling to her when I was still some distance away, knowing that her eyesight might well be too poor to spot me. Her ears moved, focusing the sound. So I knew she had at least that much instinct and interest left. And she was still on her feet.

She didn't move when I opened the gate and, still talking to her, entered her enclosure. Her eyes followed my movements until I was right next to her and stooped to be able to look into her face. I rubbed the wrinkly folds around the base of her ears. After a moment she leaned closer, then more and more, until she had her head pushed into my lap. When I tried to move, she leaned even more. She didn't move her feet, just leaned into me until she was about to topple over. I melted: a toddler, two years and nine months old, needing to be held. A very sick little toddler, occasionally uttering muted groans, very softly as if she was trying not to complain. Every idea I might have had about not crossing the line between wild-care and domesticating an animal was gone. I hugged her and told her she was my little girl and Mother would make it all right. I could have put it more dispassionately. I could have said she was my responsibility, bought and paid for, and I would employ rhino care of the highest standards to give her the best chance of healing. But I didn't. This was the first rhino calf I actually owned myself. Damaged and desperate and only mine perhaps because no one else wanted the bother of her, but she was mine and for her recovery I would fight as I'd never fought before. I *would* make it all right, and so I told her.

I sat down next to her, and from that vantage point, that of an undersized little rhino calf, looked around. Everything was in order, except that the railing of her enclosure appeared unnecessarily serious and solid for the pathetic little creature it had to confine. But it was, in a way, a last gift from Dale Parker.

In the early years of Lapalala's formation there was an enormous amount of rubbish to be removed, buried, burnt, or otherwise disposed of. There were other items too, not rubbish, but also not suitable for a wilderness reserve in the making. The iron railings of the bridges over the Blocklands and the Palala fitted into this category. Clive and Dale agreed that they spoilt the wilderness atmosphere; they had to go. The railings were dismantled, carted away and stored in a heap well out of sight, with the vague expectation that they might come in useful someday. When, in the midst of moving to Melkrivier, we needed to construct an enclosure for our newest rescue-rhino in record time, that day had arrived.

The vintage iron bridge railings went up quickly and securely, and in no time at all and with far less expense than might otherwise have been the case, the enclosure was ready. Since Moêng was, by birth, a Lapalala rhino, injured and rescued there, it seemed fitting that something so helpful should have come from her old home to contribute to what was in fact only the continuation of the process of rescuing her.

As unlikely as it might have seemed at that point I was determined that Moêng would, in a manner of speaking, grow into her railings. Like a proper black rhino she would get large and powerful enough to convince anyone of the need for such a formidable barrier. Looking back now I realise that the determined woman in Moêng's enclosure was not the same one who, more than a decade earlier, had waited with her stomach in an anxious knot to receive Bwana at Doornleegte. With Moêng much of the insecurity was gone. Experience being the best teacher, I had a far better idea of what I was doing. I was not above needing approval, but it was that of the animal that looked to me for her recovery and would show her disapproval by dying, and my own conscience. That was quite enough: my conscience had always been a sufficiently merciless slave-driver. So although I was not prey to the same fears anymore, it would be incorrect to assume that I was brimming with arrogant assurance. I was old enough to have had many reminders of my own fallibility, and had accepted long ago that humility was my lot. But I will confess now, as I was too embarrassed to do then, that as I sat there in the dust with my arm draped over the shoulders of my sorry charge, I just knew that Moêng and I were meant to find each other. In a way I will not even attempt to explain to myself, let alone to others, we were destined to travel that road.

I ran my fingers along her too-knobbly spine. Why was she still so underweight? Why was she still incontinent? Why had the diarrhoea not been arrested? When she arrived at Melkrivier I immediately changed her diet from the one she'd been fed at ARC. There they had to rely on what was available to them in their peri-urban environs, but in her Melkrivier enclosure she was in black rhino country, surrounded by the kind of vegetation on which her digestive system should thrive. I firmly believed that the secret to her healing, or a good part of it, lay there. So, no more lucerne, just natural black rhino browse, amplified with some game feed pellets. The gap students were instructed to cut fresh browse every day, and as far as I could gather, they did. What was the problem then?

On my way over from the museum grounds I crossed a gravel road. Along both sides the riotous vegetation was smothered in red-brown dust. A few months earlier it had looked worse: underneath the dust just the desiccated remains of the previous summer. The jeep track that led on to the rhino enclosures had been less dusty, but also surrounded by mostly brown. Not the rich mahogany, tawny or sienna of the Waterberg's autumn or the coppery tan of seed capsules waiting through the winter for the next rain to spur them into new life. It had been the barren, lifeless brown of drought. Just Moêng's kind of luck, I had thought at the time, to have returned to the Waterberg in such a tough season. The students would have had to scour the entire 90-hectare site to obtain enough healthy browse. They'd have had to venture into difficult terrain, gullies in the foothills some distance away. Perhaps that was the problem. Without someone dedicated specifically to the task, it wasn't possible for enough high-quality browse to be cut. And maybe there just wasn't enough of a supply on the site in the first place.

A neighbour, Jannie Nel, and his parents, Louis and Ansa (the same Nels who had sold the Melkrivier property to us) came to our rescue. They generously threw open the doors, as it were, of their adjoining 1000 hectares of prime bushveld. We could come and go as we pleased and take whatever we needed. So that was the supply taken care of and with the late rainy season well underway nutritional quality was no longer a problem. Labour, though, remained a stumbling block. The gap students, with my thanks and my blessing, had moved on to their next project. I urgently needed an extra pair of hands. Ideally it would be a replacement Titus Mamashela, someone with his ready understanding of the animals and their needs, his diligence and his meticulous attention to detail.

But he was now a field ranger in Lapalala, and very good at it, everything he'd learnt at Doornleegte put to excellent use. I was wishing for the moon: people like Titus were not readily available. They were fully occupied professionals, engaged by employers who valued their services, they were not sitting at home waiting for a job to arrive. Well then, I thought, I'll give up on all the other requirements, just grant me a willing pair of hands.

Early one morning while I was busy with Moêng, Button suddenly let out a volley of threatening barks and streaked off. I yelled her back and she reluctantly obeyed, still barking and bristling with protective zeal. A lanky figure, neatly dressed, came into sight. He walked fast, a man with a purpose. I kept Button clamped between my boots and waited for my visitor to approach. He lifted a hand in greeting, ducked his head and we exchanged the customary Sotho Good Mornings. The smile, which had been firmly fixed since he first caught sight of me, was still in place, but it was a nervous one. He seemed dreadfully anxious.

Lazarus Mamashela had been a gardener on a neighbouring property. He'd heard that there was a job going at the Melkrivier Museum and had come to apply for the position. In addition to his own language he could speak both English and Afrikaans. He had been to school and had learnt to read and write in English. He was a hard worker. He never touched alcohol – never have, never will. I asked if he had ever worked with animals. He nodded while ducking his head. I realised that Lazarus's head always said yes before his voice did. Oh yes, he'd worked with horses before, and before that he'd been a cattle herder. Would he like to learn to work with rhinos? Several nods and ducks of the head: Oh yes, he'd like very much to work with rhinos, if Magog will teach him. More nods and affirmative ducks of the head while his eyes remained apprehensively fixed on mine. I asked if he knew Titus – with the same surname, they might be related? He shook his head. No, no relation. Sorry Magog, sorry, sorry. He looked so dejected that I hastened to reassure him: a family-bond with Titus was not a job requirement. I held out my hand to him: "Come, I want you to meet Moêng."

My extra pair of hands had found me. Lazarus brought that same earnestness with which he'd come to apply for a job to every task he was given. And since some of those tasks were really not very pleasant, it goes to his credit that he never complained or took shortcuts. As it happened the least pleasant tasks were often the most important ones.

When I had taken over from the students I was relieved to find that the hygiene routines they'd kept were really quite high. But Moêng was still ill, so we had to aim higher. Every excretion had to be examined, buried and the area all around her ablutions cleaned and sanitised. Often this was her mudpool, but we still had to gather what she produced, gauge her state of health from it, bury it so that there could be no risk of re-infection, drain the pool, clean and refill it, and then scrape in enough fresh soil to stir it into the kind of muddy mess beloved by rhino. I'd had those challenges before: animals with acute diarrhoea and the resultant necessity of sanitising their environment. It was exhausting. But with Moêng it went on for much longer and her incontinence added yet another layer of trouble, for her and for us.

That little rhino's damaged, dirty, bleeding behind was my constant preoccupation. I knew she had to heal from the inside out and put my faith in an increased allocation of game feed pellets and her now excellent supply of the best browse, but in the meantime we had to prevent more damage to her rectal area, and guard against infection. That meant washing the sore, raw, eroded skin and coating it with a healing spray. Wash and spray, wash and spray, day after day. I shall refrain from describing in greater detail the consequences of spending so much time with your face in close proximity to the rear of a sick animal. Suffice to say that when Moêng finally produced a normal bowel movement it was a happy day for all three of us.

Lazarus took our good news home, and I hoped that his family received it with as much understanding and support as Clive did when he came to meet me en route home at the end of the afternoon. He waited for me near the other rhino enclosure, Bwana's. My first black rhino orphan presented about as big a contrast with my latest one as could be imagined. Bwana had grown into an impressive 12-year-old in superb condition. If ever one wanted an ambassador for this flagship species for wildlife conservation, it was him. New visitors had already come to meet and admire him since we resumed our sessions after moving to Melkrivier. I had not an instant's regret about bringing him from Lapalala. He couldn't have stayed there anyway, no one had a plan for him; and as the prized, living exhibit of our Rhino Museum he was in effect serving the cause of preserving his own species.

We'd taken trouble with his new home. It took six weeks for a builder and his team, plus the gap students and their education officer, to construct and equip the large, secure enclosure – sturdy wooden poles sunk and cemented in, wooden railings, a pool for bathing and his favourite muddy relaxation, a drinking trough and a covered feeding station, situated in such a way that it facilitated lecturing to visitors while also allowing them to get close enough, in safety, to be able to hand-feed Bwana. Lazarus was invaluable in keeping it all neat and tidy, and I quietly formed the intention to gradually groom him into a more prominent role. It was a little plot of my own, hatched one day when I was observing him with Moêng.

Lazarus was a blessing, but perhaps not an unmixed one. He performed best under supervision, and I'd made my peace with investing the necessary time and patience for him to master all his responsibilities. He took his work seriously and I had no doubt at all that he tried as hard as he could. But on that day I saw something more. Both he and Moêng had their backs towards me as I approached up the jeep track. It was too far for me to hear what he was saying, but he was clearly talking to her while he was busy cleaning out her pool. Every so often she'd get in his way and he would calmly work around her or gently and patiently encourage her to make room for him. It was so exactly how I'd always wanted my helpers to treat my animals. Then, finished with the pool, the stringy figure in his blue overalls bent down and hugged the small rhino. She followed him to her feeding area where again he was telling her something and then, before beginning to cut up her browse, he gave her another quick hug.

Animals sense a whole lot more about people than we sometimes give them credit for. Bwana accepted the introduction into his world of this new keeper with less trouble than I had anticipated. Moêng with even less. When the time was right, I thought, I would ask him how he felt about sharing what he already knew about rhino care, and his evident affection for them, with visitors. If he liked the idea, he could share the sessions with me and, in time, conduct his own.

As Bwana's attitude towards Lazarus pleased me, so his attitude towards Clive concerned me. The relationship they had had at Doornleegte did not transfer to Melkrivier. The comfort, I would even say friendship, they'd shared was simply gone. Clive's presence invariably caused a dramatic transformation in the relaxed, trusting, friendly animal Bwana still was with me. Even when Clive approached the enclosure hidden, as we thought, in the middle of a large group of people, Bwana's switch to hostility was instant and unmistakable.

The reason lay at Doornleegte on the day of his relocation.

We had decided that I should wait at Melkrivier to reassure and welcome Bwana. One never takes a rhino relocation lightly, so I was relieved to have my morning fully allocated to preparing the enclosure and interacting with the reception committee. The gap students together with the museum and restaurant staff had gathered round to share in the excitement and, unbeknownst to them, bolster my hopes for the operation. Everything was going to be just perfect, they told me. I smiled and agreed and quietly agonised about what might be happening at Doornleegte.

The projected time for the arrival of the truck came, and passed. The champagne and orange juice went back on ice. We rehearsed, again, our manoeuvres for the crucial moment when Bwana would emerge from the truck. We ran out of things to do. Conversations dried up as more and more of us engaged in the pointless exercise of watching the empty stretch of road that led up to the open farm gate. There were several false alarms. Distant rumbles and billows of dust above the trees delivered a couple of farm bakkies with workers and drums on the back, a truck with a mysterious load bulging under tarpaulin, and a game ranger's Land Cruiser speeding past on some urgent mission. I was wrestling with the temptation to start phoning when there was yet another promising rumble from the direction of Lapalala. With the road largely obscured we couldn't see what it was, but it sounded like the right kind of truck moving at the right kind of speed. We heard it taking the left turn to the museum, and then where it could have turned into the museum gates it didn't but kept coming in our direction. At last it came into view and turned in towards us. While the large truck backed up to the enclosure, the reception committee scattered to take up their positions, out of sight and under oath not to utter a peep until Bwana was secured behind a locked gate.

It couldn't have gone better. On cue, Bwana appeared and proceeded as if he, too, had been rehearsing for this moment. He calmly strolled into his enclosure and sniffed and snuffled at a few items that caught his interest. Then he took notice of his new drinking trough and signalled his approval by drinking from it. He walked over to the feeding area with its extravagant supply of the most appetising browse I'd been able to find. Approved – he chomped a few branches. He concluded his première performance at Melkrivier by marking his territory in true black rhino fashion, with a few strong squirts of urine.

I felt like applauding. He could not have known of course how critical his first appearance would be, but I did. He was a rhino with a reputation. Even though his near-tragic encounter with David Bradfield three years earlier had been kept under the radar as far as possible, some information had leaked out, just enough to fuel rumour and speculation. The observers of his arrival at Melkrivier were mostly people who lived nearby. They needed to be reassured that having a huge black rhino bull, especially this one, in their neighbourhood would not pose any danger to them. Bwana's behaviour fitted the bill perfectly.

The celebrations over, I stayed behind with Bwana for a little while and then went home. I found Clive in a subdued mood, and after digging for clues got it out of him. The morning had not gone so smoothly after all. It had started well enough with Bwana calm in his Doornleegte enclosure. He knew something was up – animals always do – but didn't seem to be unduly alarmed. The game transporter truck with its crate stood ready. The veterinarian prepared the tranquillising dart. Clive helped him to position for the best shot, and then watched as it went wrong. The dart missed the rump muscle and hit the hip bone. It must have been painful and with only about half the correct dose of the drug in him Bwana reacted with extreme agitation. A second shot had to be prepared, in haste and with some guesswork involved, since there was no way of knowing precisely how much more of the drug needed to be administered, and how much more of it would be too much. Bwana was stressed, angry and confused and presented a tricky target. Fortunately the second shot went home. The relocation, though an hour late, proceeded without further hitches. At Melkrivier Bwana emerged from his crate none the worse for the experience. So we thought.

Late that afternoon, having finished with Moêng, I allocated some more time to spend with him. It wasn't just for the pleasure of seeing him settle so easily into his new home, it was also to guard against a break in continuity. I wanted the only change to have been one of location, everything else had to continue as before. Bwana was lying in the shade of violet and horn-pod trees deeper into his enclosure. At least it might have been shady when he went to lie down there, but with the sun dipping towards the horizon the light was angling in underneath the foliage. He was dozing or perhaps simply too comfortable to move. It was such a tranquil scene I was almost sorry to have to disturb it. I called, he lumbered up and stretched. He had done some more investigating since the morning: the mudpool appeared to have also met with approval. He walked up to me, hinted for the usual head-rubs and handfuls of game feed pellets. Everything just as usual. But then, a couple of feet away from me, without any warning whatsoever he was suddenly in a mood I'd never seen him in before.

I was jolted into stepping back a few paces. But Bwana's attention wasn't on me. I looked around: it was Clive. He was still some 20 metres away, so I thought maybe Bwana didn't realise who it was. I spoke to him and stretched out to touch him, but it was an angry wild animal in front of me. He wouldn't be touched. He appeared to not hear my voice.

Clive had stopped: "Careful Conit." It was that quiet, dead-steady voice I'd got to know in dangerous situations on wilderness trails. The very first time I walked in the wild with him, he had told me as he told every new group of trailists: "Don't think you know better." Don't think you'd be able to predict a wild animal's behaviour, or read his intention to attack. Only the most experienced bush guides can read a warning, sometimes. There may be no warning at all from elephant, rhino, buffalo, or lion – and they're all faster than most humans. Even a hippo, that overlarge, heavy, lumbering animal, can be frighteningly swift in water and can attack without warning. In his career as ranger and trails leader Clive had at some point or another faced all of these potentially deadly animals, and so have I. We both knew trouble when we saw it. An elephant, its trunk curled and ears pressed flat back, coming at you at terrific speed; a lion, ears flat, tail lashing, a fierce, hostile look in the amber eyes, every muscle in its body taut, ready for the electrifying charge; a black rhino with the same high head, eyes and stance of Bwana's right now, that same loud, sharp snort...

Very quietly Clive retreated while I remained at the railing, my pulse hammering in my ears. It was only after Clive had completely disappeared from sight, and I suppose from the reach of Bwana's acute hearing too, that I again had the familiar calm rhino with me.

At first I hoped that it was just his reaction to the disturbance of relocation – it would wear off. It didn't. And it was personal. Clive had become associated for him with the stress he'd experienced during the botched darting. He represented danger, and a black rhino has only one way to react to danger, with aggression. So unfortunately Bwana's enclosure became off-limits to Clive. I knew this saddened him and hoped that their previous good relations would be restored, Bwana would forget. After all, general consensus held that black rhinos were not the smartest animals, unlike elephants with their proverbial long memories. Well, in this instance, general consensus was dead wrong. From that day on, whenever Clive came to fetch me, he had to wait well away from Bwana's enclosure, at the gate.

So it was at that gate that I gave him the happy news of Moêng's improved gastrointestinal health. Insignificant as it was as an item of news, at least it was good news. And its inconsequential nature was in itself a blessing. So little of our news was either good or inconsequential enough to simply ignore or forget. Just that week we'd heard of another farm attack in Limpopo Province, in the Polokwane district. The farmer was killed, his wife left wounded by intruders who'd broken into their farmhouse while they were in bed, sleeping. We didn't know them personally, nor the other farm attack victims that we'd heard of. But we had many farming friends and we ourselves lived in rural circumstances. Security had become a national obsession. Wherever people gathered, sooner or later, the conversations turned to crime and how to avoid becoming a victim of it. Lately I'd heard too many such conversations.

Not for nothing was our new home situated at an ancient crossroads, it was still the place where people met and exchanged news. Several rural grapevines converged at Walker's Wayside, and not rural ones only. City visitors brought city news, and like their rural counterparts they also brought rumours, gossip, speculation and their fears.

Increasingly the news from the world beyond the Waterberg bore out the rumblings we'd heard within the Waterberg. There was discontent at the rule of President Thabo Mbeki, who, while his country was struggling with its own overwhelming burdens, was often away attempting to sort out the problems of other countries. Admirable, perhaps, and appropriately statesmanlike, but puzzling to a large portion of his electorate. And then, while the entire civilised world committed to fighting the HIV/AIDS pandemic, like Nero he picked up the fiddle and started to play. Already in October 2002 he'd declared himself an AIDS denialist. HIV was a fabrication of the West, he propounded, it didn't cause AIDS, and the origin of the disease was to be found in poverty and, in South Africa, in oppression by the previous regime. His Minister of Health, Dr Manto Tshabalala-Msimang, advocated the use of beetroot, garlic and the African potato as a cure-all. Anti-retrovirals were believed to be toxic and would not be made available in the public health sector. While doctors, NGOs and scientists lobbied for greater sense in government, cartoonists had a field day with Dr Beetroot and her African cures, and the statistics of AIDS-related deaths climbed steadily. In rural districts like ours, clinics knew they were dealing with AIDS and that HIV infection rates in South Africa were among the highest in the world.

Something else was also spreading, virus-like, through South African society. In 2004 a report by the Southern African Migration Project confirmed rumours of escalating xenophobia in the Southern African Development Community (SADC) countries. It was most prevalent in South Africa. Foreign citizens were increasingly targets of not only hostility but also violence, the worst of it reserved for refugees from African countries further north. I found this sickening, but not altogether surprising. Floods of refugees from Zimbabwe were finding their way into Limpopo Province and into employment opportunities that local communities felt ought to have been reserved for them. It was the same all over the country, with Burundians, Somalis and others often at the receiving end of intolerance and stigmatisation. Small businesses were looted and destroyed, homes torched, some lives lost. I watched the television reports and listened to the angry voices of attackers and the terrified voices of others. There were children ... watching, learning. It was a nationalistic and ethnically based discrimination that found a particularly nasty outlet too in the murders of white farmers, a trend which was on the rise. My heart sank: anything that smacked of the kind of intolerance that marked someone of a different race or religion or nationality for elimination, scared me. How far to Srebrenica, to Dachau, to Rwanda?

The move to Melkrivier, undoubtedly much more of a social hub than Doornleegte had been, made it harder to avoid or escape news I would much rather not have known about. Alas, one doesn't escape news by refusing to hear of it. Like the Boxing Day tsunami it might have to traverse an entire ocean but it will eventually wash up on your shores. In 1939 Europe had not been far enough from Africa for its war not to up-end the life of a plump, moon-faced little toddler on a mission station in Sekhukhuneland.

As Clive and I walked back home from the bomas, we discussed the evening facing us. Clive, always more resilient than I, was looking forward to it. An opportunity to see many old friends, he said, and relive some of the best times we had shared. A couple of hours later it was dusk and we were driving through the Lapalala Reserve gates into what was no longer my world. Unwilling to delve into the mix of emotions that made that familiar drive now seem remote and unreal, I prattled on about the weather and whether the rain which was certainly on its way would hold off until everything was over, and whether I'd dressed warmly enough. The invitation had suggested smart-casual, and my smartest casual had put me in black. Too sombre, I thought, it didn't feel right.

Soon it was too dark to see anything but the hunched black shoulders of trees and the pale road threading between them. Occasionally I thought I saw a brief flicker of gleaming eyes, but then it was gone and Clive and I alone again in our noisy vehicle with its intrusive lights stabbing into the deep, uncommunicative night. In my mind I held roll-call of everything that I knew was out there: who was hunting, who was being hunted, Lapalala's most sensational performers appearing when and where we couldn't see them. If Bwana and Moêng had made it as free rhinos this would have been their time: black rhinos own the night, as do leopards and hyenas, jackals, owls, hippos and bats. Not us. We are not naturally equipped for the night, except in our capacity for awe. In a wilderness night we are cut down to size: we are blind and at the mercy of those who are not. We are dwarfed and silenced by the only things we *can* see: the moon, stars, galaxies of wonders we cannot comprehend. That is as it should be. We need our nights.

The road dipped and we slowed down for the left turn to Kolobe Lodge. The headlights swept through silver terminalia trees now in flower, but invisibly so. Like so many of our indigenous trees they are not showy flowerers. Only to the tree lover, to the birds and butterflies and bees who stop to peer into their hearts do they reveal their bounty. Or to moths, if they spread their fragrant lures at night. To flies perhaps, if they cast abroad the ripe smell of a well-matured balsamic vinegar or, like the terminalia, of rotting flesh. Did they do so at night? There was a time when I would have made Clive stop and we would have gone to investigate. There was a time when interrupting a journey to sniff flowers by moonlight didn't feel silly. Did that man, so silent by my side, also miss those days? I didn't ask.

The narrower Kolobe track wound, like a meandering stream, this way and that through a stand of wild syringa trees, and then straightened out and I saw the lights. Instantly I was back in 1986 and the lights were twinkling at the Lapalala Wilderness School. More than 50 guests were laughing and cheering and raising their glasses around a blazing bonfire, and then trooping in to a feast in the massive dining hall, lanterns and candles casting wavering shadows against thatch. Clive's mother was there, still strong and beaming with pride. His aunt Peggy. His brother Barry. Our sons, Renning and Anton. It was a gathering of the clan, which included the oldest staff member of Walker and Sons, Tom Locke, Clive's oldest friend, Leo van Vuuren, and friend and fellow elephant-lover, Dr Anthony Hall-Martin. At the end of a weekend of celebrations, of wilderness walking and game spotting and relaxing at bush camps, each guest left with a commemorative, specially commissioned ceramic candle-holder. Fifty candle-holders for Clive's 50th. A few months short of 20 years ago. It was winter then and the party mine to organise, the candles mine to light. Now it was summer, other people had gone to the trouble of organising and catering and brightening the night, and they had done so for Clive and me.

There were more than 100 people there and I knew every one of them, from the oldest (our old friends from EWE, and Charles Baber, elder-statesman of the Waterberg) to the youngest, the Nel's fearless little Twana and our own Tristyn who arrived on her father's arm, charmed everyone and made me want to weep at the joy she lit in her grandfather's face. Clive was born to be a grandfather:

endlessly patient, endlessly creative, with a youthful capacity for play and wonder that matched theirs. Ayden and Tristyn simply adored him.

Someone was calling to everyone to gather and as we thronged in to the lantern-lit boma I caught sight of two women a little apart from everyone else. One, a guest, was listening; the other one, beautiful, slim and elegant, was Elizabeth Parker. She was talking. It looked as if she was rehearsing something, running through a prepared order of items. A few minutes later she was standing alone, facing all of us, and I realised she'd been steeling herself for this moment. Her speech was all of gratitude and appreciation. It was a tribute to Clive and to her late husband, Dale. The charming woman laughing with all of us on the Doornleegte verandah was gone. The charm was still there, but that had been Libby; this was Elizabeth keeping her composure in a way I couldn't have.

There was applause and then Clive spoke, more applause, more speeches. Every story was a story I knew, they were stories I had lived, and so had many of the people around me. Clive and I were sitting together surrounded by our own history. The affection coming our way was tangible.

The dinner was splendid and drawn-out with the lodge dining room spilling chatter and laughter into the night. I knew, none better, just how much trouble it must have taken to give us such a generous farewell celebration. I was so appreciative of the effort that it embarrassed me to be feeling so tearful in the midst of such loving attention. But I hadn't wanted anyone to go to so much trouble, I hadn't wanted to be thanked and applauded and made a fuss of. I didn't need a farewell, I wasn't giving up any of our friends, I would see them all again. Clive, though, deserved it all. At least that much acknowledgement was due to him for his part in creating, with Dale, the Lapalala Wilderness Reserve. And to let him go without in some way ceremonialising the handover would have been wrong. It would in fact have been wrong for all of us. A party on the face of it, it was a rite of passage. Clive and I, the Parkers and Lapalala were freed now to move on from our joint and joined history.

Then it was our turn to thank everyone. I felt guilty to be going home while others were left with the burden of cleaning up after a big late-night party. But I was tired and at dinner I had thought Clive looked drawn, as if the emotional roller-coaster of farewell had taken a toll on him too. We drove away through the light rain that had held off long enough to dampen but not drench our departure. Just short of the turn from the Kolobe track onto the bigger road that would take us out of the reserve, there was a movement among the syringas to the right. Clive stopped and switched off the headlights. My eyes adjusted and there he was: a large kudu bull, shadowy and indistinct, a phantom in the low light and drizzle. After a watchful pause he took a few steps, arching back his neck, the beautiful horns angling horizontally along his withers to avoid tangling them in the low branches. He straightened up and walked out on to the road. He stood there, facing us, a thousand conservation and tourism emblems come to life. Behind him, his family emerged from the trees and quickly, furtively crossed the road. Then, with a toss of the proud head, he moved off to the left and was gone. We drove on, knowing that all signs of our midnight meeting would be gone too, rained away, by morning.

SIXTEEN

Lonetree

Was it some ancient memory embedded in my genes that drew me up to Lonetree? A bipedal ancestor hauling herself into a tree or onto a pile of rocks to look out over the savannah? Where's the danger, where's the food, where are the members of my family?

As long as I can remember I've sought out the high places, the lookouts, the perches above the rest of the world. On the Lobethal mission station it was the lemon tree behind the house, wickedly thorned as such old wild-grown trees are but eminently climbable even for someone whose ambitions stretched further than her short limbs. Grown-up, I took to flying and saw the African savannah passing far below me. Then the checkerboard patchwork of Europe. The hungry cities sucking in, it seemed to me, countryside, converging roads and rail links, and us, as we descended, landed and got swallowed up. With the next flight we'd escape back up to the clouds and the views. I liked it better there.

Then followed my wilderness trekking years with Clive and always somewhere along the trail there was a magnet pulling us up higher, to see wider and further and feel safer and freer because of it. After that we found ourselves in Lapalala, an inexhaustible supply of cliff-top view-sites stitched together by gorges and winding valleys. And behind my home there was Bwana's hill where I could go to see further than Doornleegte and follow the Palala to the horizon.

We moved to Melkrivier and I found Lonetree. There really was a tree, a mountain syringa – my favourite Tree of Heaven – and it stood alone, shading a rocky outcrop that became my eyrie. Eagles soared alongside me. A sea of Waterberg green flowed all the way to Lapalala and through it to the sky. If I had had the time I could have sat there for hours staring at that shimmering horizon, especially on searing summer days when it drew mysterious undulating escarpments of dull green up into the sky, or lakes of blue onto the land until the angle of the sun or the temperature changed and everything solidified, reduced again to what was real and familiar.

2 February 2005 was such a day. From Lonetree I looked down onto the narrower confines of my new world. There, on the right was the two-hectare Melkrivier Museum complex, its garden, restaurant, chapel and the parking area with the cars and minibuses of early visitors. Obscured from my view was the small house that was now my home and where Clive was working his way through a mountain of conservation reports. To the left, on the other side of the road that ran past Lonetree, past the museum and on to the junction with the Lapalala-Vaalwater road, was a 10-hectare piece of land and, hidden in indigenous bush, a house (Magog's, named in my honour) with – set apart and completely hidden from every view – a smaller cottage. These had been built several years earlier to Clive's design and under his supervision. It had been our guest accommodation for friends and family who'd come to visit us in the Waterberg. At Doornleegte there hadn't been enough space for everyone, and especially when Dale had been staying with us he needed all the privacy we could provide. Now post-Lapalala, in our revamped headmaster's house at the museum, we still found ourselves with more friends and visitors than bedrooms, so Magog's remained handy.

From Magog's up to where I was sitting and all around me were the 90 hectares of Lonetree. It belonged to Anton and was undisturbed bush except for the house where the gap students' programme had been based, and right at the bottom, virtually across the road from the museum, where we had our rhino enclosures. We had cleared as little of the bush as possible, lots of small game dwelt there. Bwana and Moêng were living in an all but natural environment, and from my perch I couldn't see them or their enclosures. They were also invisible from the roads, the one running past the museum and the smaller one running in between Magog's and Lonetree, from the museum road on to farms further to my left. There was passing traffic, some of it on foot, mostly people going to and from work on the surrounding farms. All remote and incidental to my reality up there on the rocks.

I had a reason for coming up to Lonetree. The view could have been enough and often was, but February was remembrance month for me. No one gets to my age without every month gathering its own crop of anniversaries. In my case a whole of lot of them pooled in February. My father's birthday, my elder brother's, and mine. My granddaughter's birthday. My youngest brother's wedding anniversary. My mother's death. It was the month in 1945 when almost 25 000 people died in the ruinous bombing of Dresden with its resultant firestorm which, for the German people, must have been a vision of hell. Two hundred kilometres away from that deadly conflagration, I was in an underground bunker, hiding with my family from the bombs that punished Berlin.

But it was also the month that brought hope to my other homeland, South Africa: on 2 February 1990 President F.W. de Klerk announced the end of apartheid; on 11 February Nelson Mandela walked out of prison, a free man in a suddenly freer country.

Such days send me searching out the heights, so in 2005 it found me on a rock on a hill at the beginning of a whole new chapter of my life. I felt lucky and excited. And down there, at the foot of Lonetree, I had two thriving black rhinos. Bwana was my treasure, but he was having to make room in my heart for little Moêng. She had turned several corners and was now as engaging and playful as I could wish. Her appetite was boundless; she gulped her game pellets and always turned the heavy rubber bowl upside down to search for more. To her delight, and our despair, she'd detected the single weak point in our design for her enclosure. It had been such a scramble to get everything ready in time for her arrival that there had been no time to throw a concrete base for her feeding area, so we got creative and used heavy tractor tyres, halved, for feeding troughs. They might as well have been put there especially for her amusement. She pushed them around, up-ended everything, trampled her browse and made another delightful discovery: the mess she'd created was good to recline on, and since she was now heavier and stronger, she could simply by lying and refusing to budge, hamper our efforts to clean and tidy it all up again. She much preferred the mess.

She amazed us all with her recovery, but I knew we had only begun. After her traumatic start in life she had a lot of catching up to do. She was growing well, but was unlikely to ever reach what would have been her normal size. There was a lot she still had to learn or relearn about black rhino behaviour. Her internal injuries had been so severe that her chances of reproductive health, I was told, were zero. We'll see, I thought, plenty of time before we need to worry about that. Now it was still time to play and learn and get stronger.

I needed to teach her about rhino middens and how to use one. She failed to see what fascinated me so much about a scattering of her old dung in a particular corner of her abode. She was far more interested in returning to her favourite occupation: sharpening the fascinating appendage that had sprouted on her face. With studious concentration she'd rub her small horn up and down, back and forth across the iron bridge railings, uttering sounds that could only be described as satisfied cooing. As I walked down from Lonetree I had no doubt at all that that was how I'd find her, head swinging at her chosen section of railing.

I was wrong. She was resting on the trampled remainder of her browse, surrounded by the evidence of a vigorous workout session among the tyres. She got up and approached for the usual tickle around the ears. That's when I noticed the flies. Dozens of flies clustered around the bloody pus oozing from a hairline crack at the base of her horn. As if Moêng hadn't had enough trouble with her rear-end she'd now gone and caused trouble at the front-end too.

There wasn't much I could do except prevent infection. So I cleaned the area and applied a disinfectant and healing spray. We were back to wash and spray, wash and spray, day after day. I expected that, with its base cracked, the horn would eventually come off. It took several months of discomfort, and I suspected considerable pain, for Moêng. In the end the horn was literally dangling by a strip of strong hide from her purple-sprayed nose, a truly pathetic sight until we could pull the dried-out piece of hide away and the small horn with it. She stayed purple for a while longer but her main horn had begun to grow out again, matching the growth rate I'd measured on Bwana, about half a centimetre per month.

In the meantime, like the grown-up he was, Bwana did his part in our educational programme without fuss or bother. Every day except Mondays we had groups of visitors from game reserves and lodges in the area, from the Limpopo Department of Environmental Affairs and Tourism, people passing through on holiday, neighbours who had stopped to visit the museum or relax at the restaurant, busloads of school children. Because of the more accessible location at Melkrivier we drew many more visitors than we had had at Doornleegte. So from 3 to 4 in the afternoons I was a teacher again and loving it.

My previous experience of introducing visitors, especially children, to something as exciting as Bwana had taught me to not rank my attractions above his. As soon as they caught sight of him my carefully prepared lecture went for nothing. So I always began a short distance away in some attractive spot, within earshot of the rhino resting perfectly camouflaged in the deep bush of his enclosure without the visitors being any the wiser. Once the conservation message I'd wanted to get across had been heard,

I'd lead on for the climax. His emergence from the bush never failed to elicit gasps of surprise and excitement and I daresay sometimes fear. His sheer size (almost two metres at the shoulder, and just under four metres from hook-lip to tail) always caused a few of the visitors to back away from the railing, and rather touchingly attempt to hide behind me. From that point on it was a practical showing off of Bwana's charms: how he ate, what he ate, information about his biology, his behaviour, his impressive condition and good nature. He obligingly took his pellets from a variety of confident or nervous or clumsy hands, large ones or tiny ones barely able to hold a couple of pellets, and deftly, gently dealt with them all. I couldn't have been more proud of him.

One afternoon I finished a session and found that Clive, waiting for me at the gate, had news. Stirring events had been taking place in Lapalala and Anton had been right in the middle of it. In fact, exactly like Boxing Day three years earlier, he had been in charge of it. Another black rhino rescue.

In 2002, when they'd found Moêng, I was still anxious on his behalf: would he know what to do, did he have enough experience to be able to make the snap decisions required during difficult rescue operations? Did he have the right team to support him? By 2005 I'd stopped worrying, except about his safety.

As Lapalala's wildlife manager he'd put together an impressive team of field rangers. They were specialist rhino monitors who could identify Lapalala's rhinos by their tracks. Each rhino was an individual personality, known by the name which they, all locally trained Pedi with their innate gift for appropriate naming, had chosen. They watched over their rhinos with a commitment which was far more than professional, it was personal.

That morning they radioed Anton in some concern. A young black rhino calf, an 18-month-old male, who'd been driven off by his unusually aggressive mother, seemed to have fallen foul of other rhino bulls. He was lying next to a waterhole and looked hurt. Anton told them to keep watching, he was coming in on foot. When he got to the waterhole, the calf hadn't moved. Its injuries seemed serious. But, along with a love of the bush and of flying, Anton had inherited his father's inability to give up, and a stubborn dose of optimism. Besides, having seen Moêng's even worse injuries and her recovery, he knew what might be possible. So the debate next to the waterhole was a brief one: a helicopter and vet were summoned. Anton flew with them to the site. From the air they could plan the operation: the terrain, the estimated weight of the calf, who'd be doing what on whose signal. Then Anton was dropped off to lead the ground crew in a text-book operation. In under 30 minutes Dr Pierre Bester had darted the calf, completed emergency treatment and seen it safely loaded up. The helicopter lifted off, the field rangers cheered and then piled in with Anton and their dozy, patched-up young rhino for the drive to Lapalala's holding pens to begin their programme of bringing Meetsi ("Water") back to health.

Not long after that more news came from Lapalala.

Our first autumn at Melkrivier had been busier than I could have imagined, and we were delighted to have been able to lure our old friend and colleague from Lapalala days, Glynis Brown, to join us. Button discovered that Glynis's feet stayed in one place longer than did either Clive's or mine, so we'd frequently find her there under the desk, dozing and gently snoring while Glynis dealt with the day's administration. With the arrival of winter, traffic to and through the museum gained even more momentum. Schools closed for their winter break and families streamed out of the cities to holiday destinations. In South Africa the coasts, by and large, got the summer shift; in winter it was the bushveld. Since becoming a biosphere the Waterberg had been attracting more attention, and as I told Clive, his efforts at promoting it as a tourism destination had resulted in more work for his wife while he escaped into the bush to paint. I might have exaggerated a bit. As a board member of several governmental as well as non-governmental conservation organisations he was fully involved in the design and implementation of provincial and national conservation policies. It wasn't easy work, it was often discouraging, and always time-consuming. Even so, he made a point of still being available to the Lapalala Wilderness School. It had been his baby and his continued involvement as patron was important. Even more than the official business of board meetings, his occasional presentations to children there gave him, as ever, enormous pleasure.

Shortly after his birthday, mid-June, he returned from Lapalala one afternoon and came to collect me at Moêng's enclosure. "Fancy a walk?" he said. It was our usual leisurely stroll up the footpath to Lonetree, and ahead of us Button nosing her way through the intoxicating bouquet of wildlife smells. It was only once we had got to the top and Clive remained standing, staring out north, that I realised that on our way up he hadn't said a word. I'd been chattering on about my rhinos and doings of the day, but from him, not a word.

We sat down and with his walking stick he hooked Button closer. After a playful tussle she scrambled up onto the rocks and settled next to him expecting, and receiving, her ration of affection. With his hand still on her head Clive finally spoke. He'd been trying to work out, he said, just how many hundreds of kilometres of wire fencing had had to be removed to create the Lapalala Wilderness Reserve. How many kilometres of snagged and rusted wire he had personally hauled out of the bush, how many thousands of wire snares that had been set to maim and kill in the random, cruel way that resulted from such things. Twenty-three years for 18 farms to be cleaned up and consolidated and restored to ecological health, for that corner of the Waterberg to be brought back to wilderness.

"What did we do it for?"

I didn't know how to answer. He continued. "What was in it for Dale? Of all the things he could have done with his money," the walking stick stabbed to the northern horizon, "why that?"

There was a long silence, the only sound that of the breeze moving through the syringa's bare branches. In the distance a raptor was being harried by two small dark specks that dived and circled back and dived again. Tawny eagle and kestrels? It didn't seem to be the time to ask Clive for an identification. He was also watching the birds, but then he turned to me. "Remember Dale's snake?"

Dinner at Doornleegte, a cobra as startled at Dale's presence as Dale was at the cobra's – noise and profanity followed by much hilarity and Dale's admission that he was, after all, a city boy. He had loved the bushveld, but was not by nature a rugged outdoorsman. Lapalala was not his playground, it was his passion. It did not have to amuse or entertain him; he didn't expect it to turn a profit. All he expected of it was to become healthy, intact wilderness again. Wilderness for the sake of wilderness.

"Now he's gone," Clive said, "and I'm sitting out here. Lapalala has to go on without us."

I didn't understand. "I thought that was the whole point, that it *would* go on after you."

"But will it?"

"What do you mean?"

"There's a land claim, Conit. Lapalala is under claim."

We stayed up at Lonetree longer than was wise. We had to find our way down in uncertain light although the moon, one night before the full, did see us home without twisted ankles. It had got cold, it was our winter solstice after all. But in front of the fire-place, as around many millions of African hearth-fires that night, the day's news became less alarming once there was a small, contained world of leaping flames to stare into.

So a land claim had been gazetted on more than a third of Lapalala's 36 000 hectares. There was no need to assume that the outcome would be disastrous. The claim might be legitimate and all parties willing to negotiate in good faith. It might be possible to avoid the worst-case scenario: 12 000 hectares of wilderness carved up into dozens, even hundreds of fenced, overgrazed parcels with its unparalleled biodiversity reduced to four species: humans, cattle, goats and half-starved dogs.

"That won't happen," Clive said. "Not in this instance."

The Motse Community claim was made up of many individual claims, some people resident in the area, some not, some more affluent than others, but all of them looking to land restitution to better their lives. Clive had always maintained that a conservationist, and especially a conservationist-landowner, occupied treacherous moral ground when he had neighbours who did not have access to clean drinking water, adequate healthcare and decent schooling for their children. It is inevitable that for such neighbours conservation messages would ring hollow if they were delivered in the absence of concrete, shared benefit. A game reserve boundary could easily become a hated symbol of division: poverty versus privilege, and in South Africa unfortunately all too often still black versus white. An unsustainable situation in which everyone ultimately loses.

If Lapalala's future could be one in which a wide variety of legitimate stakeholders shared equally in both benefit and responsibility, with its core business still wildlife conservation, it could stand a much better chance of being sustainable.

"Let them just start talking to each other," Clive said. "This could be a win, for everyone."

We didn't know how the land claim might affect Anton: he was the wildlife manager there, and the house that he and René occupied was in the claimed section of the reserve. But apart from that, Lapalala was no longer our concern. It was time for the next generation. And beyond them another one, I hoped, who would watch over the claimed section's rock ledges and forested gorges, the white-water bend of the Palala below Dales's Rocks, the martial eagles that nested there, the blue-leaved cycads, the slender three-hook thorns – every spring the first to flower on the winter-brown slopes; the buffalo, rhino, giraffe that roamed that area; the herd of zebra which, early one chilly morning, thundered past me across a field of rose quartz pebbles; the group of eland that leapt, one after the other, across the road in front of me – muscular bodies in flight against a red-copper sunset. I hoped my grandchildren, and especially the grandchildren of the claimants who had yet to discover something so wonderful about their world, would get to see it all.

Our first spring at Melkrivier found me settled and contented. Living as we were right in the middle of our own investment it was satisfying to see the numbers of visitors streaming through the museum and Walker's Wayside. Although I'd never wanted to be in charge of a restaurant (a point which I'd made very strongly to

Clive) it had proved to be an excellent marketing strategy. People who might not take a detour to visit a museum might do so for coffee or a glass of wine and a meal, with the museum as an added attraction. The result was that we weren't only getting members of the public already converted to the cause of conservation, people who were coming anyway. We were also getting parents who merely wanted a break from travelling with their bored and hungry children and, having fed them, thought they might as well hang around into the afternoon so the kids could have a chance to see and feed a real live rhino. Bwana's sessions became an enormous drawcard, and as we moved towards summer I could look back on a good year, at Melkrivier and beyond.

Conservation had landed on the world agenda. Not only did the Kyoto Protocol finally come into force in late February, there was a general push from developed nations to focus more attention on assisting African countries with biodiversity conservation. The UN Secretary General, Kofi Annan, urged greater cooperation between Africa and the UN in order for Africa to achieve its Millennium Development Goals in 10 years, by 2015. The 7th of the Millennium Goals (Environmental Sustainability) aimed, with even more urgency, to achieve a "significant reduction in the rate of loss" of biodiversity in five years. By 2010 there should be more protected areas, it stated, and fewer species threatened with extinction.

Laudable goals – we could only keep our fingers crossed for sustained political will. I find it difficult sometimes to not become cynical about high-level summits and their crop of resolutions that barely last as long as the vapour trails of the planes taking the departing signatories to those resolutions back to other agendas and other priorities.

But we had reason just then to be optimistic about political will: the South African government had bowed to international persuasion and to the pleas of its own people and revised its policy on HIV/AIDS. A nationwide roll-out of anti-retrovirals was underway. Perhaps Nelson Mandela's public statement at the beginning of the year that he had lost a son to AIDS might have tipped the scales. Be that as it may, President Mbeki's turn-around had extended the lives and hopes of millions of South Africans, and in April his legitimate concern about the impact of poverty on health status was the focus of a World Health Organization meeting, held in Durban. The majority of people living with HIV in Africa could not access or afford even a basic healthy diet. Then came two statements from the UN Food and Agricultural Organization which, when taken together, painted an even more dismal scenario: climate change was set to impact food security, further reducing nutritional options for the most vulnerable people in developing countries. Most vulnerable of those: sub-Saharan Africa. And most vulnerable in sub-Saharan Africa: 11 million AIDS orphans.

As I read those reports I had to wonder, as I've had to do so often in my life as a conservationist: how could my concerns for wildlife *not* be swept off the agenda by such dire and pressing human needs? Of course I had my answer to that: conservation strategies that result in sustainable human-versus-environment relationships. But it was a long-term answer, one that required far-sighted implementation of unpalatable options. Politicians don't like those. Neither do the news media that need dramatic headlines about dramatic interventions that deliver dramatic, preferably immediate outcomes. That's how you sell newspapers and win votes most easily. The slow, undramatic, considered option that will only pay off in a generation or two struggles to get political support, and long before the argument is adequately made and disseminated to the public the media will be racing off to the next news hotspot that allows for screaming headlines. The world will always offer a sufficiency of those. 2005 was no different. In July terrorist bombs exploded during London's morning rush hour: 52 people died, more than 700 were injured. It dominated international news media, quite rightly. But then in August Hurricane Katrina came along and stole headlines as she slammed into the US Gulf Coast: New Orleans was devastated, 1836 people died. It was a huge disaster, appropriately deserving of its headlines. But in due course it too had to yield those to the next dramatic happening, someone else's big disastrous news.

Good news gets fewer columns, smaller headlines and seldom lands on the front page. One of those came on 30 October. In Dresden the Frauenkirche, rebuilt after being destroyed during the WWII firebombing of that city, was consecrated. I read the story a few days later.

In March 1945 when my family fled on that refugee train out of Berlin I didn't know the extent of the destruction we were leaving behind. Of what had been happening in the other cities of Germany I knew nothing at all. It was only well after the war, once we were back in South Africa and I was old enough to be able to understand such things, that I could look at post-war photographs in newspapers and books that came my way and begin to wonder at the wilful destruction of beautiful things. Architecture of the most exquisite design and execution, buildings that had graced skylines and served people for hundreds of years reduced to rubble. I knew the arguments of the war, I knew what had been at stake, but how could one not feel outrage at the loss of such beauty and heritage? I never knew the Old Germany of my antecedents, but I wept for it.

The Frauenkirche, built in the early 18th century on foundations from the 11th century, had been a Lutheran church, the denomination of my parents. It had a magnificent organ on which my father's great musical hero, Johann Sebastian Bach, had performed. The crowning glory of the church was a 96-metre-high, 12 000-tonne sandstone cupola, said to have rivalled Michelangelo's dome for St Peter's Basilica in Rome. It had been one of Germany's most treasured landmarks.

Two days of bombing in February 1945 and it was destroyed. For the next 45 years, while East Germany was under Communist control, the blackened mound of rubble that had been the Frauenkirche lay undisturbed. In 1966 it was declared a "Memorial against war". Sixteen years after that it became the gathering site for peaceful protests that were to grow and spread until eventually the Berlin Wall fell and Germany could become a re-unified nation. The remains of the Frauenkirche continued to be a rallying point, as much for the rebuilding of the German people as of the city of Dresden and of the church itself.

Teams of architects, engineers and historians gathered at the site to begin the painstaking process of sorting and labelling each individual piece that could be reused. But they were not the first to do so. More than 60 years earlier, in 1945, Dresden residents who had miraculously survived the devastating firestorm emerged from the ruins to try to salvage something of the Frauenkirche. One by one they chose distinctive stone fragments, numbered them according to the position in which they'd been found, and took them away, not as keepsakes but for safekeeping, should the day ever come when, *Gottes Wille*, the church could be rebuilt. An act of faith in more ways than one.

A lifetime later and thousands of kilometres to the south I sat in the lounge of my Melkrivier home, bathed in the warmth of a late spring afternoon, and tried to imagine myself into a wartime winter in a ruined city. I tried to see the handful of people, cold and starved and wretched beyond my imagining, as they scavenged the wrecked remains of their lives for something that could speak of hope and of a future. I was greatly moved by those survivors with their bits of consecrated stone. They'd seen something irreplaceable destroyed, but refused to accept that that had to be the end of the story. They were not powerful people, rulers who could write and rewrite the course of history. Yet they stumbled, crawled and limped up to the rubble and started doing just that.

It took many years and many of them did not live to see it, but after an international fundraising effort and inspiring participation from the descendants of Germany's former enemies, the Frauenkirche did rise again and at the end of October 2005 it was filled to capacity for its re-dedication as a place of refuge, of faith and of healing.

I put down the newspaper and got up to look out through the window at my safe, pretty world. What if everything around me lay in ruins? Was there enough in me of my German roots? Could I, like the courageous people of Dresden, face destruction and yet be the one to begin picking up the blackened and broken stones?

Not needing to find an answer, I didn't. With a few flowers from the garden I walked past Walker's Wayside, away from the visitors and the relaxed murmur of their conversations, and took the footpath down to the chapel. A while later Clive came home and followed Button's barking to me. We sat there, quietly watching the light move across the floor, until the sun dipped and then we went home. Everyone else had gone, leaving us the birds and the sunset and the contentments of that day.

Then November came.

Armistice Day, of course, and a few birthdays: my sister-in-law, my eldest son, my grandson. But this time it wasn't the anniversaries that sent me up to Lonetree.

When I strode up the footpath at first light it was because I couldn't bear any longer to be among other people. Too many voices down there, and unbearable silence when they ceased. So I fled. I didn't head for Lonetree particularly. I headed for nowhere except away. Finally I managed to pull out of the suffocating whirlpool of my thoughts to find myself cast ashore on a dew-wet sandstone ledge far above the shadowy places that I didn't want to see. My gaze stayed close, on my hands, on wilted syringa flowers gathered in, piled up and coaxed into little domes, 12 of them. A dozen little cupolas that broke when Button came racing back from some olfactory adventure. She scrabbled up onto the rock and along my ledge, scattering syringa flowers, to bring me her panting breath and muddy paws and unquestioning devotion. She licked my face and didn't get chastised for it. I pulled her onto my lap – something warm and solid to hold onto. Something alive.

More flowers dropped around us. A biting little breeze had stolen through the syringa branches and into the day just ahead of the sun. I looked at my watch: 5:14. Button and I sat, marooned and unmoving, as the light flowed over us and on down Lonetree's slope, canopy after canopy, spiny thicket, flaming creeper, the beseeching arms of a great tree euphorbia, on and on until the whole lowland of the Melk River was filled, a basin spilling light to the horizon.

And right in the centre – not its centre but mine – there was on this clear young morning with its birdsong chorales and fallen shrines of Tree of Heaven flowers, a smashed-up Toyota to prove the nightmare of the night.

It began with loud shouts and a banging on the kitchen door. Bwana had broken out. Late on a Sunday night with people, singly or in inebriated groups, finding their way home along a public road, a mature black rhino bull had broken out.

What was I expecting? A replay, I suppose, of our early morning coordinated manoeuvres a couple of years earlier at Doornleegte when Bwana returned from his nights out to give us an adrenaline-charged wake-up sprint into his enclosure. We managed then, we'd manage again.

From some distance away already the sounds told me what we were to discover in the light of our torches: Bwana was demolishing the gate between Lonetree and the road. It was a determined single-minded assault. Explosive bursts of raw power from an animal that only a few hours earlier had eaten from my hand. He didn't see me, he didn't hear me. Clive told me to go home and phone the vet – Bwana might need to be darted.

Six, seven sleepless hours later, alone on Lonetree to do battle with my questions, I wondered if that had been the decisive moment. I could have disobeyed Clive, stayed there longer; Bwana could have calmed down and eventually allowed me to lead him back to his enclosure. But what if the gate had given way before his mood did? There were people shouting, some of them stupidly drunk – that didn't help. Clive ran to fetch his Toyota bakkie: he would block the gate while we waited for the vet to arrive.

From the pool of kitchen light I watched as he drove off, then listened in disbelief as the vet told me No, he wasn't coming. Dark night, a black rhino already enraged – no, he was sorry, but he couldn't help, the risks were too great. I didn't take it kindly: What about *our* risks? Just stay out of his way for the rest of the night, he said. In the morning, if we still thought it necessary, he'd come and dart our rhino.

I put down the phone and hurried out again. There was suddenly more noise. Shouts and the dull percussive crashes of rhino on metal. I ran. My torchlight caught Clive sprinting across the road towards me, managing to leap at the museum's high game fence and clamber up and over, a heartbeat in front of the charging rhino. He dropped down at my side. Bwana wheeled and raced down the road, then up again past us, deaf to my calls.

Should we have left Bwana out there, to run off his over-excitement until, adrenaline spent, he got tired and felt ready to seek out the food and familiarity of his enclosure? But what about those people, shrieking from the bushes next to the road, escalating his excitement and their own danger? Three years earlier David Bradfield, an experienced rhino-tracker, had faced Bwana with all his wits about him, and nearly lost his life. Those Sunday-night revellers wouldn't have stood a chance. Should we have tried to get them out of the area before one of them became his focus? But Bwana didn't leave us that option. He attacked the gate to the museum grounds and broke through, to the consternation of the onlookers who'd been drawn there by the noise. Clive ordered them indoors and told me, in no uncertain terms, that I had to do the same. I refused. I'd noticed a change: Bwana was now also curious, no longer just blindly aggressive. I approached just far enough to be sure he could see as well as smell and hear me. His attention narrowed: the human he knew best, the voice he knew best – his movements slowed. A few more snorts, his head jerking in the direction of the men, and then he stood absolutely still. I continued to call and retreated into the garden, further away from the road and from people, further away from Clive. Bwana followed.

I was relieved when, after several tense minutes, Clive and Lazarus left to inspect the breakout site and effect whatever makeshift repairs might be possible, or to determine if an alternative plan should be put into operation, to have Bwana, once he'd been darted, moved back to Lapalala until his enclosure could be secured.

We were alone. My rhino and I again exploring a garden, as we had done so long ago when he'd arrived, a baby, at Doornleegte and he followed on my heels, tree to tree, leaning against my legs when he felt tired or in need of mothering. The beginning then of an almost 13-year-long conversation: murmured endearments and sniffing, snorting, moo-ing responses. I switched off my torch and accompanied him as he moved between hedges and around trees and tall aloes, a greater shadow among lesser ones – moved so easily, so confidently, so untroubled by the night. A magnificent creature, the mysteries of instinct and genetic memory so perfectly integrated in him, so superbly served and protected by an evolutionary design millions of years in the making, and by his fierce spirit and staggering power. His was an animal intelligence I could glimpse but not share or fully understand. What was he making of this night, this place? What subtle signals spoke to him, but not to me?

All at once I realised that all our walks together had been daytime ones. Safer of course, but still: more than a decade's worth of nights and I had not experienced even a single one like this. What might I have learnt? Would he have allowed it? More pertinent probably, would Clive have allowed it? Perhaps, but only under his protection. It wouldn't have been the same. It was a bonus then, this star-lit encounter of a woman – unarmed, unprotected, unsupervised, un-afraid – with the most dangerous of rhinos in dangerously exposed circumstances.

Was that my moment? A companionable ramble back to his enclosure, and to a different outcome? But I heard the men returning. Lazarus had brought a bucket of game feed pellets. I stretched out to take it from him, but Clive said, "No, let him. I'll go along." I couldn't make out Lazarus's face, and didn't need to. All of his earnest affection was in the voice with which he called to Bwana. The rattle of the pellet bucket had always been a reliable enticement – Bwana turned towards Lazarus.

As the little procession disappeared in the dark, I became aware of hushed voices and nervous laughter, faces appearing around corners and in doorways. We can all go to bed now, I told them, it's over. I walked back home. At the kitchen door I stopped, turned and listened. Nothing. Just the winding down of the evening, someone saying good night, then footsteps disappearing. From inside the house came the muted complaints of a small dog scratching at the door of the bedroom to which she'd been banished. It was too soon to let Button out; she'd be bound to go in search of Clive and might upset what could be a tricky situation. I called to her from the kitchen and she subsided.

It was 11 o'clock. A cup of tea when Clive returns, I thought, and come daylight we'd investigate the breakout: somewhere there had been a weak point in Bwana's enclosure. Probably a workman taking an unsupervised shortcut while sinking poles into concrete. A powerful, heavy, fully grown rhino leaning against a pole that gave a little, then more and more as he heaved a playful shoulder against it – that's all it took. But we'd take care of it in the morning.

I switched on the kettle, then switched it off. There was shouting, then screaming, then rapidly approaching pounding as Bwana stormed back into the museum grounds. Mere minutes between the calm animal sniffing through the museum garden, and this one wheeling and charging towards the voices of terrified people once more scrambling up onto vehicles and garden walls.

Clive yelled at everyone to be quiet and stay out of sight. He pushed me back indoors, "Call Anton. And get that vet!"

How many of those futile phone calls? Anton unreachable, and no one else able or willing to help. How many agonising arguments with Clive? He wouldn't allow me to approach Bwana again. I tried to edge away; I needed to gauge Bwana's mood. Aggression and fury, of course, but what was fuelling it? The smallest shift in temper, a hesitation in his rage, and I might be able to connect directly with the fear that drove this ferocious attempt to protect himself. He was aiming everywhere, turning in all directions. A darkly spinning shape, huge and prehistorically fearsome, half-hidden, half-revealed by dark and dust.

"Conit! Please!" Clive was pleading with me.

Did I retreat? Up on Lonetree I couldn't remember. But I must have, because at some point I became aware that Clive had left; he wouldn't have gone to phone again if he hadn't considered me safe enough for the moment. A loud snort, and someone screamed as Bwana charged towards a Land Cruiser on top of which staff members were whimpering and clutching each other. I called Bwana, again and again. He didn't seem to hear; there was too much noise and I was too far away. I moved in closer, imploring him to listen to me, to believe me that he was safe. I no longer cared about the danger, I had to reassure him – my beautiful brave rhino in such torment. I realised I was crying. He circled back, in that strangely swift-footed gait of heavy rhinos, and lowered his head as if to ready for the next charge. But then Clive was back, positioned between me and Bwana, and I knew he hadn't gone to phone. He lifted the rifle, and it was over.

There was another anniversary now for Lonetree. 13 November ended with Bwana's collapse after a faultless, painless heart-shot. No struggle, no sound. The only sound I heard, and that was enough to haunt me, was that of the man lying with his head and hands pressed to the dead rhino's massive, still-warm shoulder, weeping. The choice of the night, and the consequence of it.

What of me? Weeping too, I suppose. But more clearly I recall Bwana's hide under my hands, the great curve of his chest, so quiet; no last breath or heart-beat. I stroked his head, all the features and angles I knew so well. In the torchlight his eyes had dulled.

Then it was midnight, I was in the kitchen, someone was forcing me to drink something. I didn't want to drink or eat, I didn't want to speak or be spoken to, I didn't want to be helped to go to bed. I did not want to know what I had witnessed.

SEVENTEEN

Lonetree II

HALFWAY DOWN THE SLOPE a pair of francolin exploded into flight. They didn't go far – rapid wingbeats on the rise, gliding descent to disappear in vegetation a dozen metres further. Their indignant calls continued to protest the presence of what I guessed were Lonetree's kudus. I'd seen their spoor down at the enclosures, drawn there perhaps by the easy pickings of ready-cut rhino browse.

Had they been the trigger for Bwana's breakout? Had he been startled or annoyed by their presence? Unlikely. A couple of head-shakes, a bit of huffing, perhaps a mock charge, nothing more. If there had indeed been shoddy work on the construction of his enclosure, Bwana might have broken out, but not in such a blind rage, and not to get to kudu. There were no free-roaming rhino in the area. What else could have been there? Or who else?

From my rocky lookout I could see movement on the roads below. People walking and cycling to work. The previous night there had also been passers-by. Might some of them have climbed fences to get to the rhinos? A deliberate, perhaps drunken piece of mischief, to tease Bwana into breaking out? A poaching attempt? It was certainly no secret that we had a fully grown rhino, complete with impressive horns, on the premises. Small comfort to me that, if there had been such people, they didn't get away with their trophy. Bwana was still dead, his horns removed to be registered with the authorities and lodged in safe deposit. Clive was taking care of it. Clive was always taking care of things, putting himself between the threat and those endangered by it. That's what a conservationist does: he stands between elephant and poacher, between wilderness and exploiter. If he is, like Clive, a board member of both the national and provincial environmental conservation agencies he also has to stand between members of the public and his own rhino. And if that same rhino had already nearly killed a man and now appears to be threatening the lives of others and most immediately that of his wife, he is the one who has to pull the trigger and live with it.

Over the years he'd let slip something of his feelings when he'd had to shoot to kill. On more than one occasion he'd had to stand in front of an animal that had been terribly wounded by a poacher or an incompetent hunter, and relieve it of its pain. An elephant that couldn't walk anymore would just look him in the eye, and wait. He was the one with the gun, he said, but he felt as helpless as that animal waiting for death – he couldn't undo the grievous suffering inflicted on such innocent lives by humans. Sometimes it was nature's own cruelties that were hard to witness. A white rhino, weak and starving with a broken jaw after a plunge down a cliff, watched as Clive walked up to him, gun at the ready. He didn't move. Head raised, he held Clive's gaze. There was recognition and acceptance, a communion before death.

However merciful such a killing, there was no joy in ending something as magical and irreplaceable as a life. What then if the life you had to destroy was one you'd known intimately, had personally watched over from baby to adult?

In the dawn light, en route to Lonetree, I'd seen the Toyota, lying on its side, smashed beyond repair. Somehow, in between Bwana's raging charges, Clive had managed to crawl out of the rocking, up-ended vehicle and run for his life. Just in time. And yet, in order to protect me, he then took another risk and accompanied Lazarus to walk Bwana back to his enclosure. He was there when that attempt failed. Bwana had followed the pellet bucket all the way to the far end of the enclosure, but then raced after Lazarus who, in running back to the gate, had neglected to leave the food with Bwana on the far side of the enclosure. A mad fumble with gate poles, but Bwana was out again, running wild and heading for the museum. If I'd been the one to go with Lazarus, it might have turned out differently, either successfully or even more disastrously, with someone's death. Perhaps mine. The night had ended well then, you might say. No one was hurt or killed, except an animal. What's the big deal?

What *was* the big deal? Why did it leave me feeling so lost?

A conservationist's existential crisis? I'd dedicated so much of my life to saving that rhino. I followed all the rules, and devised ones for situations where there weren't any at the time. Through all his health crises, his breakouts, his attack on David Bradfield, I would not give up on Bwana. If he'd committed any transgression it was simply that of being a strong young black rhino bull in a world changed, mutilated by and for humans. We make concessions to accommodate wild creatures, but on our terms; our priorities always trump theirs. Even those of us, the conservationists who go against this deadly current, make mistakes, and almost invariably the animal is the loser. Perhaps Bwana's fate was sealed that day when I drove away to Johannesburg and left the coast clear for the Lapalala decision makers to release him into the wild. I wasn't there to caution, to protest or oppose, but might I not have agreed with them? Some risks have to be taken, and risks don't come with guarantees. 20/20 hindsight from the top of Lonetree was of no use whatsoever, except insofar as accepting that there had been lessons to learn and we'd learnt them the hard way.

But my grief was also personal.

Why couldn't I have been like those extraordinary black women I'd known over the years? Rosina at Doornleegte; before her, Constance Desimela who'd become our anchor and indeed family member during our Johannesburg years; my parents' friends among Modjadji's subjects at Duiwelskloof; and further back still, my first introduction to the open heart of the African woman: my childhood friend, Regina, and the tribal women of Sekhukhuneland. They could gather in their dozens, hundreds sometimes, and give way to their grief. Wail and writhe in a full-bodied lament for their loss. I envied them: they could shatter in community, the splinters and shards of their lives held by many hands. That wasn't my way. African to the bone as I regarded myself I still had to flee – to be alone, to bleed in private. Perhaps I felt unjustified in my mourning. Bwana had been my job, no more; life goes on. Yet, who decides the conventions of grieving anyway? Who's to say which death is worth mourning and which one isn't? Who's in charge of weighing the allocation of sorrow appropriate to each kind of loss? And how does one prevent one grief from unlocking others?

Up on Lonetree there was no need to be brave and quiet, and I wasn't. I wept for everyone I'd lost, and for the ones I feared to lose. For every graveside and sickbed and heartbreak where I'd had to be strong, I now howled from some deep, ruptured place that I hadn't acknowledged before.

Halfway through the morning I left Lonetree, not really sure anymore about who it was who was walking down to her most important tasks of the day: to reassure Lazarus and to comfort Clive – the blame was not theirs.

Moêng was my lifeline. Responsibility, work, distraction. Our environmental education sessions continued with her as the star attraction. And on my walks to her, past the museum garden where Bwana was buried on the exact spot where he'd fallen, through the repaired gates and up the winding track past the now mended, empty enclosure on my left, I could face my demons in private. Every day another batch of questions, another insecurity or disappointment or difficulty. Long-buried vulnerabilities resurfaced and had to be wrestled into acceptance. Until one day, all at once, it was done.

I was crouching, eye-to-eye with Moêng. She teased me with

a mock head-butt and pranced away, then spun around and stood waiting, swinging her head at me in expectation of a game. Several rounds of pretend-chase and counter-chase later she was positioned exactly where I wanted her. I lifted the catch, the gate swung open and I walked through.

She didn't know this part of the game. After a few hesitant steps towards the open gate she stopped, gave a small snort and then shuffled back a little way. I kept walking, slowly, and calling to her to follow. She had her head up, ears searching for clues, with as puzzled a look on her little face as I'd ever seen on any wild animal. I walked a little faster and took the turn onto the track. She bleated after me and then, in a nervous little rush, dashed through the gate and headed straight for my knees. After a reassuring hug and scratch around the ears, we were off.

Just as well I didn't expect her to do the predictable thing and stay with me, because she didn't. As a little rhino whose only experience of freedom in the bush had been as an infant, it wouldn't have surprised me if she'd felt too insecure to venture far on her own. But she raced off towards a large hornpod tree – I assumed for a snack of her favourite food. But not even a pause. She disappeared behind a tangle of old raisinwoods. I kept on down the track, calling to her all the time. The brittle crackling of twigs and clatter of dislodged stones signalled her progress as she charged through the undergrowth until, to the right and ahead of me, there was the screeching protest of francolin and suddenly there she was on the track, panting, looking around excitedly. She spotted me and charged back up the slight incline, overshot, and all but knocked me over. Reassured as to my approval she shot off to the left and was soon gone from my sight again. A hundred metres further on she emerged from the bush, and proceeded to jump up and down as if spring-loaded, before darting off and flushing the harried francolin once more.

Seldom had there been a happier walk at Melkrivier. My little rhino was revelling in her taste of freedom, and she was proving me right. Black rhinos have a reputation for unpredictability and aggression, but I knew my rhino and felt confident about letting her out without any safeguard other than the trusting bond between us. I hadn't wanted any other people around, certainly no one with a rifle. I was not in the mood to be cautioned and second-guessed into doubting my own instincts about a rhino.

I would not pretend to be an expert, certainly not a scientific one, but more than a decade of rhino care, with all the learning that had gone along with that, had been useful. Just that morning the phone had rung with another cry for help. The caller was terribly apologetic: he'd called before, more than once, with the same problem. I was happy to reassure him, again, that this particular problem was more likely his rather than that of the baby white rhino, the first on his property, over which he was watching with such anxious care. The problem was simply lack of prior experience. I told him he could trust the mother. It sounded as if she knew exactly what she was doing, just as Munyane without being taught had known how to raise Mokibelo.

Over the years there had been calls from owners or carers of rhinos that had been wounded, or were otherwise ailing, or behaving in an unusual way. I've answered the phone and heard a worried voice saying, "What does it mean when it does this ..." followed by a sometimes rather amusing attempt at rhino vocalisations – coughing, barking, snorting, grunting, bleating, moo-ing. I was very sympathetic because I well remembered the days when rhino behaviour seemed to me too to be just one puzzle after another. And how well I understood the anxiety of dealing with serious illnesses or wounds. One desperately wants someone to tell you exactly what to do, and precisely how to do it. But I could only share my experiences, tell them what I'd done in similar situations and refer them to the same excellent veterinarians, like Dr Richard Burroughs, who had helped me with advice.

No one in my extended family of fellow rhino carers had yet called to tell me that their rhino had been killed. After Bwana I hoped and prayed that no one ever would.

I took my time down the track, all the while calling to Moêng, and as was my habit stopped here and there to pick up bits of broken glass or rusty wire or tins; even after years of veld restoration one could still find evidence of the reckless and wasteful presence of man. The track straightened out and I saw Moêng up ahead. She was standing completely still, her sides heaving after all the exercise, and staring intently at something in front of her feet. Water. Good rains had set seasonal streamlets flowing down off Lonetree to the Melk River, and one of them crossed our path. Moêng didn't know what to make of it, and it was only after I had walked through – it was no more than ankle-deep – that she dared to put one reluctant foot after another into the water. She crossed at the pace of an elderly chameleon and at the other side turned back to stand and stare at the water some more.

We strolled on, her energy somewhat abated, and came to the wooden railings and open gate of Bwana's boma. She went straight past, sniffing at everything. I walked into the boma and called. Oh, the temptation: she heard me clearly of course, wanted to obey, but couldn't. Indecisive pauses to glance back at me and then, with a toss of the head, she bounced away in pursuit of the next fascinating smell. Eventually she circled back and joined me. That was when I realised that however unpredictable black rhinos might be they'll never match Lazarus. He was supposed to have lain in wait for the right moment and, as soon as Moêng was inside the boma, quickly close the gate without spooking her. Early that morning, after we'd scrubbed and refilled the water-trough and dug out and replenished Bwana's mudhole, we'd rehearsed Lazarus's manoeuvre, and he'd repeated his instructions back to me, but here we were, Moêng and I in the boma, and Lazarus – predictable in his unpredictability – nowhere to be seen.

I enticed Moêng over to the feeding area, piled high with the most delectable selection of freshly cut summer browse. A handful of feed pellets, scattered among the branches to keep her interest, allowed me to dart back and take care of the gate.

Eventually Lazarus did appear, but by then I was too happy with Moêng's presence in Bwana's boma to even bother with reproaches. All that way from her old home to her new one she'd walked and run and explored and played freely. No crate, ropes or blindfold. No dart-gun, no shouting, no trauma.

I went home and updated my rhino-care records: "Moêng moved to Bwana's boma." Five words with no hint of what that walk signified. A far greater distance had been covered than the length of the track between the two bomas, and over much more treacherous terrain. But that is the way of all such record keeping and other factual writings – a mere distillation of the experience makes it to the page.

Every time I held the newly printed copy of one of Clive's books I'd been aware of just how much more had been lived through than had been passed on to the reader. An example was *Okavango from the Air*, the result of a collaboration between Clive, aerial photographer Herman Potgieter and pilot André Pelser. The pictures are stunning and the writing eloquent, but it gives barely a hint of Clive's love affair with the wild areas of Botswana, or how deeply meaningful those flying hours had been for him. Every day, from their headquarters at the camp of our friend, Lloyd Wilmot, they took to the sky to see the Okavango as its eagles saw it, and with him in the plane was Anton, spotting game to photograph and vultures to avoid. Anton flew with him too, as chief navigator, when the Rhino and Elephant Foundation conducted a major survey of white rhino in the Chobe National Park. Ten days of exhilaration shared with another close friend, Peter Hitchins, as project leader. Again the project report dealt only with the facts; it couldn't fully convey their elation when the two-plane team located Botswana's last five white rhino, nor their heartbreak at the realisation that all but those five had been poached.

If one really wants to see the scale of a problem, you cannot do better than take to the air. The extent of a fire or a flood, and the animals caught in it; a poaching band's field of slaughter in a valley strewn with carcasses; the spread of pollution down a river or into a lake. But it's from the sky too that I've had my favourite views of my favourite landscapes.

"You haven't seen a tree until you've seen its shadow from the sky," Amelia Earhart said, and how true that is of our African savannah.

When Renning and Anton were still schoolboys we used to fly

up to Lloyd's camp on the Savute Channel in Botswana. He was then just starting his operation there and it was an enormously exciting time for all of us. It's a different Africa now, but in some places it's paradise still. I've flown up to Xaxaba in the Okavango, to Chobe, to Xugana Lagoon, to Shakawe for the tiger fishing, and although you might now have to filter out some unwelcome signs of human encroachment, on the whole you look down on the same magnificent wilderness. Perhaps Botswana has done better than most in its custodianship of its natural environment.

Delighted as we'd been to discover Anton's natural aptitude for flying, the day he phoned with the news that Ayden, at age six, had also joined the Flying Walkers, we were over the moon. Since that first flight with his father, Ayden has become completely at home in anything from ultra-lights and the micro-lights used for low-level reconnaissance and anti-poaching work, to the giant Russian helicopters used in rhino capture and relocation programmes. Whenever possible father, son and grandson fly together. And whenever duty relents, I'd be up there too.

August 2006 gave us another anniversary to take up to Lonetree: Mother's passing. Born just two months before the start of that great war that had made allies of the bitterest of Anglo-Boer War enemies, she survived the terror of the 1918 influenza epidemic, as did another South African baby, born just a few months before the end of the war, Nelson Rolihlahla Mandela. She saw apartheid come and go; she saw Mandela's ascendancy to power and fame, and then, with considerable sadness, she saw what remained of the Mandela dream once he'd handed over to others less able.

It had been a long life, 92 years, and when Clive returned home after visiting her a couple of days before her death, he told me he'd known it would be for the last time; she was ready to go. On a lovely early spring morning in St Margaret's Anglican Church in Bedfordview I watched as her casket was carried in, by her two sons and four grandsons, to a gathering of family and friends. It had been a life well-lived, with courage and honour. I was blessed to have known her.

There was another landmark that year, though its significance registered only well after the fact. It was a small thing at first. A rounded stone in the path that, annoyingly, shifts under your boot and breaks your stride. You kick it to the side and walk on. But tomorrow there's another one, and the next day yet another, day after day, until you realise you'd better get a spade and start digging. So you spend some backbreaking hours excavating that section of your path, and rebuilding it with a more solid substructure, firm enough to withstand the impact of your and many other boots. For a while you walk easily. Then the first rains come. One day you set out for your walk, but your path is gone. Those stones you'd so carefully cemented in are lying tumbled and broken at the bottom of a muddy pit.

We were informed that a land claim had been lodged on our Melkrivier property. This wasn't welcome, but hardly the biggest surprise. Land claims had become the background rumble to our national discourse. Whenever an election manifesto needed some punch, land redistribution shifted up the agenda – easy to promise, less easy to deliver. As it had been since 1994, it was again handy for sloganeering during the 2004 national elections and the government was able to assure the nation that by the end of that year more than 57 000 claims had been settled. That left around 22 000 outstanding claims and for that they allocated an additional 6 billion rand over three years. The numbers dazzled those people who'd been holding their breath until they could receive land, or have it taken away. Thousands of families had been living with their lives suspended – they would get moving, start working, start over, get their lives back on track, just as soon as the land claim was settled.

Sadly, for all its good intentions, the system was increasingly open to exploitation, mismanagement and soul-sapping delays. As deadline after deadline for settlement passed with many cases remaining unresolved, the deadline for new submissions of land claims was being extended. Inevitably the number of outstanding claims kept rising, and equally inevitably I suppose, so did the percentage of ones that would turn out to not have been legitimate.

Clive read the paperwork, pushed it across the table to me, and said: "Don't stress. Let's just make sure of our facts."

It wasn't hard. Before purchasing the land almost a decade earlier we'd done our research, and in 2006 another round of enquiry delivered the same conclusion: the claim was not legitimate. The stone in the path could be kicked to the side. The Melkrivier Museum would continue to operate as a cultural, environmental and educational service to the Waterberg.

A few months later that stone was back. It dawned on us that reason and rational argument had very little to say in the transaction. An annoyance and a waste of our time, but it could not be ignored. We would have to take the legal route and contest the claim.

I had little stomach for a legal battle. More than likely it would turn out to be a battle with intermediaries benefitting from the protracted process while making grandiose promises to their perhaps less legally astute clients.

It was on Lonetree that I discovered that Clive had even less appetite for such a fight. It was Sunday at the sundowner hour. Below us the valley of the Melk River was too pretty to be painted without the artist being accused of kitsch. Far below was our museum complex: a toy habitation in an ocean of Waterberg green. Impossible to look out over such a landscape and think of anything but peace. In the same way, at various times, we had sat on top of the sandstone cliffs of Mmammagwa in Botswana, and on Dale's Rocks in Lapalala, on the Brandberg in Namibia, on the edge of the great Fish River Canyon there; many other places too where one is silenced in front of a vista beyond your full understanding. I had flown over the cloudscapes above Africa with that same sense of being given a glimpse of a truth beyond our human agenda.

"Who owns this view?" Clive shook his head. "No one owns the sky."

We decided not to contest that claim on our property, invalid though it was. The whole point of the museum complex had been to serve the Waterberg; there was the potential that it could continue to do so even if we were to give it up. Since that unwelcome little stone in our path would not be kicked aside, we would go one better: get out the spade and begin to construct an alternate path, one to suit other walkers. We began by presenting a proposal directly to the claimants themselves. They would have ownership and if they did not see their way clear to keep the whole operation going by themselves, we offered to take on a 15-year lease; they would have title and income and not have to do any of the work. The offer was declined.

I was taken aback and quite frankly indignant. All our resources had gone into the development of the Melkrivier Museum complex – the investment was far more than financial. Yet we were prepared to give it away to people who had no proven or indeed provable right to it; we would maintain and promote what would be their asset, its real estate value accruing all the while, without them having to lift a finger, except to cash the generous monthly cheques for 15 years.

Did we misunderstand their needs or intentions? They didn't have a plan for the site, they didn't wish to run the museum complex themselves, they didn't want anyone else to run it for them. Was there anything else they wished to do with the land? Apparently not.

I was disappointed enough to consider the prospect of a challenge in court with less reluctance. But it couldn't last – belligerence had never been my strong suit. There followed some rather sombre walks up to Lonetree, to watch the day begin or end. Invariably we found more serenity up there as we watched the play of light all the way to the north where Lapalala too was dealing with a land claim. How many other people, all over the country, found themselves in a similar situation to ours? For most, if not all, it was probably an equally exhausting process. Even when all parties were willing to work together, progress was slow. It didn't help that rumours had begun to surface: the Land Bank (the government institution responsible for financing land claim transitions) was running low on funds.

If we were to contest the Melkrivier claim the whole business could drag on for years, courting the risk that the Land Bank might indeed run dry, and we'd be left without even the nominal financial compensation due to us. So once more we got out the spade and tried to dig deeper.

Our next offer was for a five-year lease, with the Waterberg Biosphere undertaking to establish an office and auditorium at the museum, for which a considerable rental would be guaranteed to the new owners; we would also continue to carry all responsibility for maintenance and insurance. The answer came back and sent me up to Lonetree with the sure knowledge that no offer, however favourable to the claimants, would ever be accepted.

I cannot remember now what day of the week it was, or how it happened that I was able to take the time to go up there in the middle of the day. But I remember that down below, beyond my hearing and hidden from my sight, a vehicle was slowly pulling its trail of dust across my view. All I could see of the over-familiar Melkrivier road running from Vaalwater to Lapalala was that silent slashing of the land. For a long time I watched the brick-red gash, until it had thinned, bled out over the trees.

This then became the next marker on my calendar: the end of our path with Melkriver. It wasn't a swift, clean severing of that life. It died in stages. At first, since we were on the premises and I had a grandstand view of the day-to-day affairs there, I felt compelled to help the claimants, but came the day I had to accept that my attempts at stemming the tide of neglect had achieved little beyond my own frustration and exhaustion.

Then it was time to pack again. We had to vacate our home and our place of work. No sale, no finalised transaction, no closure, but the museum, the old headmaster's house, the little chapel, the restaurant, Walker's Wayside, the garden where Bwana had been buried, everything we'd created there wasn't ours anymore. With luck the giant Schotia would remain; the paradise flycatchers would continue to raise little ones there, but I wouldn't be there to see it.

Fortunately, or unfortunately, we were able to move across the road to Magog's, our erstwhile guest accommodation. Fortunately, because it was conveniently close-by and didn't affect Moêng in her boma. Unfortunately, because it *was* so close-by – the signs boded ill for the continuation of the sole environmental and cultural museum centre in the greater Waterberg. I tried to look away, to not care.

Clive's way, as ever, was to draw a line and move on. "Water under the bridge, Conit," he'd say to me and turn the conversation to our future, to a next chapter to be lived beyond Melkrivier. Just like he did decades before when scouting for a location for our wilderness school, he again took the scenic roads to and from work assignments in order to investigate relocation options along the back roads of the Waterberg. He had my wholehearted support. His trip de-briefings over sundowners or supper were my therapy. We pored over his photographs and impromptu sketches of landscapes and landmarks. Another life began to seem possible, another home, something that still lay ahead of us. Something good. And heaven knows, I needed it. I'd told my children I was fine, and my grandchildren that it was all a grand adventure, exactly what we had wanted, but it was an unsettling time.

For some reason, or for many reasons, the Land Claims Commission just did not get around to finalising the settlement of the claim, leaving us in limbo. We still felt some responsibility to keep the museum complex afloat and functioning, since the collapse of the enterprise would affect the valuation of the property and hence the compensation due to us. Low as the promised compensation was, we could not make a new beginning elsewhere without it. But I'd had to put limits on my emotional investment there.

So, for two more flowering seasons of the massive stand of mountain aloes behind Magog's, I resolutely kept my focus closer to home, on Moêng and on my family. And like all grandparents the world over we found in Ayden and Tristyn our greatest delight. Together we watched kudu, bushbuck and grey duiker coming down to drink at the stretch of the Melk River that ran below the house. There were birthday treats on trips to Polokwane, and on sleep-over nights at Magog's we'd all snuggle up in front of the TV set for cartoons or a movie. They accompanied me to Moêng's boma, helped to feed her, and often amazed me with their knowledge not only of rhino but of all wildlife-related matters. Of course they were growing up in a conservation family, and occasionally they were playing around the boma while I was teaching Lazarus. He was an eager student but fared best with plenty of repetition, so I suppose as Lazarus learnt, the little ones did too.

Moêng remained a drawcard for tourists and offered an opportunity for Lazarus to shine. When he handled a session I watched from the back of the visiting group and felt inordinately proud of that little partnership. A rhino who'd entered her life with so many odds against her, and a man who had had to face different, but equally limiting odds. My path with Melkrivier had not been for nothing.

There were many such moments around the boma. Small for her age and the possessor of the sweetest nature I'd yet seen in a black rhino, Moêng became the closest and least alarming contact with such an animal that some elderly or disabled people could have had. I always allowed them to take their time, to stay as long as they needed. Sometimes when I watched a child in a wheelchair reach through the boma railings to touch what every book would have told him is a fearsome beast, I did so through my tears.

What was Moêng's experience? She obviously liked being stroked and fed and petted, but perhaps there was more. Animals always know and understand more than we give them credit for, and they *feel* a whole lot more than is sometimes comfortable for us to admit. From her behaviour I knew that Moêng felt safe; she trusted the people around her and the strangers' hands that stretched out towards her. I swore that it would always remain that way. And it didn't even need to be mentioned between Clive and me: wherever our next home were to be, there would be a place for Moêng.

Shortly after the 2007 summer rains had begun, Clive's scouting forays took him to the area to the north-west of Lapalala, the district of Lephalale (Ellisras). He looked at several properties there, found them wanting, and then one evening told me he was on the trail of another one which sounded promising. We were on the verandah, keeping that same appointment with the end of the day that we'd kept for more than 25 years on the Doornleegte verandah. A little bit of conversation, a lot of listening as dusk turned to night – the time for jackals and bush babies, nightjars, bats, crickets and frogs, when the eagle owl comes to perch on the roof of your house, according to Shangaan folklore a messenger of doom. Death is sure to follow unless you were to capture the owl and decapitate it, thereby ensuring that the evil spell, like some bewitched boomerang, speeds back to kill the sorcerer rather than you. I had no such apprehensions about our nocturnal hunters. At Doornleegte we had spotted eagle-owls, a couple, mated for life, whose softly hooted cadences and duets we heard after sundown. At Melkrivier we had barn owls, again a devoted pair, who nested above the door to Clive's office. From Magog's we could still hear their unearthly screechy calls as they set out to hunt at nightfall.

"Hope they're allowed to remain," I said. Many a morning I'd complained about having to clean up below their nest, but now I was feeling protective. Barn owls are known to use a single nest for many years, so if left undisturbed they would in all likelihood stay there and continue to keep the Melkrivier rodent population under control, a benefit to the new owners as it had been to us.

"Never mind, there'll be owls up there too," Clive said. "Up there" was the Lephalale property. He'd been singing its praises. Even though he'd not yet seen it himself, hearsay and photographs had done enough – he was itching to go and investigate.

I tried to join in his enthusiasm but for all its attractions the place had one major drawback: we'd be several hours away from our grandchildren. No more spur-of-the-moment popping in by Anton and René with the little ones; I didn't relish the thought. Clive didn't either, but he'd already criss-crossed the greater Vaalwater area and had found nothing even remotely suitable. All our friends knew we were looking, and so did the estate agents - if there had been anything closer that could have worked for us, we'd have heard about it. And how much longer did we want to wait around with our lives suspended? No doubt the Land Claims Commission was overburdened, perhaps understaffed, we didn't know. Rumours of its financial woes were growing. The whole process had become very trying: meeting after meeting, reams of correspondence, all kinds of assurances that had led nowhere. Time was passing and we weren't getting any younger.

"We have to be realistic. Maybe it's not ideal, but I can tell you it'll be better than this. Over there," Clive nodded in the direction of the museum grounds, "the only thing that moves is time slipping by."

That was unarguable. I was weary of trying to rationalise away what I was witnessing. In conversations with people who were critical of what the claimants were doing, or not doing, across the road, I got defensive on their behalf and placed the blame elsewhere: the legacy of apartheid, of course, prior lack of opportunity, education, different cultures and value systems that perhaps we didn't understand. But by late 2007 the excuses were wearing thin, and I had to concede that they weren't always applicable.

By the time we left the verandah to the mosquitoes and the dark, and went in to dinner, I'd agreed. "Let's go look at this place. Let's go tomorrow."

I went to bed with a mixture of excitement and apprehension. Like Clive I was ready for something new, but did it have to be Lephalale? What did I know of the place, other than that after my 2003 snakebite it was in one of the hospitals there that I nearly died, and in another that my life was saved? I did know that at the D'nyala Nature Reserve, 15 kilometres out of town, history was made. In 1989, South Africa's President F.W. de Klerk summoned his entire cabinet plus attendant advisers to an *indaba* (bush summit) there. I like to think that De Klerk must have spent some time out there under the stars, feeling himself humbled by a universe so much greater than our human concerns, because two months later he was able to step into the role that destiny had designed for him. He stood up in Parliament and stated that his government undertook to end apartheid and negotiate a new future for South Africa. He announced the unbanning of black liberation organisations and the release of many hundreds of political prisoners, including Nelson Mandela. De Klerk returned to D'nyala again and again, negotiating with the ANC, resolving disputes and crises, and beginning to design a new constitution for post-apartheid South Africa. Those of us who lived through those years remember how tense and dangerous it felt, the likelihood of civil war never far away. But somehow, with every return from their session in the Waterberg bush, De Klerk and his co-negotiators were able to push ahead with their agenda for a peaceful transition. In April 1994 when I drove away from Doornleegte to go and cast my vote in our first democratic election it was because of a deal that had been wrought right there, in a stunningly beautiful patch of Waterberg bushveld outside Lephalale.

I switched off the light. I would raise no more objections. *Es kommt wie es kommt.* (What will be, will be.)

Early the next morning we drove past the museum gates, still closed, nothing stirring at any of the buildings. We turned to take the road than runs away from Lapalala, away from Melkrivier, away from Lonetree. Two people, no longer young, searching for a home.

CHAPTER 18

Walker's Islands

IF THE GRANDCHILDREN HAD been with us we'd have been counting raptors on telephone poles. Etched against the pale early-morning sky, immobile like chess pieces or those iconic soapstone carvings from Zimbabwe – eagles, hawks, buzzards and kites, a representative collection of the Waterberg's forty-plus raptor species. We were keeping an eye out for kestrels, and just before we took the turn onto the tarred road there was one, lifting off from the grass next to the road, with what I guessed was a lizard dangling from its beak. It was a lesser kestrel, one of three migratory falcons of great interest to us.

In 1995 Clive's Endangered Wildlife Trust had noted a decline in lesser kestrel numbers. Further investigation yielded an alarming statistic: the number of the little falcons over-wintering here in South Africa was down by 25%; in their breeding grounds in Europe, Siberia and Kazakhstan it was down by almost 50%. In response, EWT launched their Migratory Kestrel Project (MKP), involving scores of volunteers in the drive to count kestrels all over the country. In 2002 the MKP was expanded to include two other falcons: the red-footed and the Amur. I have a particular fondness for the latter, the greatest migrator of the three with its annual roundtrip of 26 000 kilometres between East Asia and South Africa.

Every year thousands of tourists flock to Tanzania's Serengeti to marvel at the annual wildebeest migration, and a wonder of the world it is – one of nature's last remaining grand spectacles. But give me the great bird migrations. Around 4000 species of birds migrate. Most of the migrations have been mapped, but there's much still to investigate and understand. The fact that we cannot watch, in real time, full migratory flights around the globe just adds to the mystery and wonder.

One autumn morning a Falklands Islander looks out to sea and discovers that the sooty shearwaters are back: they've completed an immense journey between feeding and breeding grounds, between the Arctic and the Falklands. Some of them travel on to New Zealand, racking up a total of 74 000 kilometres annually. In Australia someone spots another of the shearwaters, the short-tailed, which flew in from Kamchatka or the Aleutian Islands in the far northern Pacific. And in the Waterberg I wait for our summer migrants: the swallows, the red-chested cuckoos, the plum-coloured starlings, little Amur falcons that had crossed oceans to get here.

One late spring morning I'll suddenly hear a distinctive call: a sharp grace-note followed by a descending trill, and I'll know the woodland kingfishers had survived all of the hazards of weather, terrain, trappers and predators in their flight down the length of Africa to come and breed here again. I'll pull on my boots, take my binoculars and go in search of that radiant flash of aquamarine as they open their wings in display on every call. Where, in which trees, would I find their nesting holes? While we're still at Magog's perhaps a big bushwillow at the foot of Lonetree and others along the Melk River. And next year, somewhere in the Lephalale district, I might see and hear them there too. It would still be Waterberg, though not included in the Waterberg Biosphere Reserve – the kind of bush I like, the birds I love, the dramatic seasonal changes

I've adapted to. It would still be home.

How fortunate we were. Unlike half of humanity, it seemed to me. We weren't ill, persecuted or hungry. We'd not been cast adrift by some natural disaster as many had been that year: hundreds of Japanese in the aftermath of a massive earthquake in July off the Niigata coast, thousands in Peru after an even bigger one that struck in August, thousands more a few days later when Hurricane Dean made its Category 5 landfall in Mexico. That very day as we were driving to Vaalwater, we were to discover later, there was untold misery in Bangladesh in the aftermath of Extremely Severe Cyclonic Storm Sidr. Thousands had died, thousands had gone missing, hundreds of thousands had lost their homes and would, for a time at least, swell the numbers of environmental refugees around the world.

In Africa the numbers were worse, always worse – the word refugee invariably accompanied by the word crisis. Millions of displaced persons in the Great Lakes Region and elsewhere, victims of an atrocious political environment, a natural disaster or both. Relief and other humanitarian agencies started talking about climate refugees. Drought, floods, deforestation; hunger, thirst, disease; people at the mercy of the elements and each other. Refugee camps became sprawling permanent settlements, for children perhaps the only home they'd ever known, while their elders still dreamt of repatriation, of going back home. A camp offered safety, food and medical care, but it was still exile. Displaced persons, asylum seekers, exiles – in 2007 the UN Refugee Agency estimated that there were over 31 million people in need of their support. Even when exile did not mean a life of danger and poverty, the siren call of home remained.

Despite the early hour, Vaalwater was already busy, with several vehicles queueing at the fuel station. "Might as well," Clive said and pulled in behind them. In the bush one learns to keep your tank topped-up. We had to stop in Vaalwater anyway – an errand we remembered late the previous evening. We were in a hurry to head north, so this was a nuisance, and then just when we were pulling off, Clive slammed on the brakes – he'd had another last-minute inspiration. There was a Pam Golding real estate agent in Lephalale, a man whom he knew quite well, and he wanted to phone him. "Might as well," he said, "He gets to hear of things."

Assis Pontes had indeed heard of things: that Lephalale property for which we were heading, for instance. He was blunt: it wouldn't work for us. We'd waste our time driving all the way up north to see something that he could tell us straightaway we'd find disappointing. Did we have our hearts set on the Lephalale district, or could he perhaps interest us in a neat 100-hectare parcel much closer to home? There was only one answer to that.

We drove out of Vaalwater, taking the same road that had brought us there, the same road we'd driven between the town and our homes in Lapalala and Melkrivier for over 25 years. "Now don't get your hopes up," Clive said. Too late, my hopes were soaring. A miracle it seemed to me that there should have been a suitable property available virtually on our doorstep, without us having the least knowledge of it.

"Stay on the tar for 25 kilometress," Assis had said. "You'll see a farm road going off to the left. I'll have my local farmer agent meet you there."

Of course it had always been there, that narrow gap in the screen of acacia thorn trees, and the track leading to it. After more than two decades of driving that road I knew every feature – every bend and what lay beyond it, every stream crossing, every turn-off, every signpost and fence, every view. I had my favourite stretches where I slowed down to see what was flowering, aloes or other succulents on small rocky outcrops by the roadside, or early summer lilies waving above the grass, or to watch the birds that visited, in large numbers sometimes, a seepage or small dam on the other side of a game fence. So I had noticed this track, one of a dozen such farm-tracks indicating that beyond the tree-belt there lay something that someone had thought worth getting to. In this instance, not an occupied homestead, I thought, nor an active farming enterprise, not with such a rutted, little-used access road.

The estate agent farmer was waiting, beckoned to us to follow, and drove across an ancient-looking cattle grid – rusted iron rails that rattled and clanked, tall grasses in between them that swayed in front of the Pajero's bonnet and then ducked under our passing.

With the bakkie leading the way in front of us, and bushes and trees in their summer foliage bracketing the track on either side, the place we'd come to see with such excitement, such hope, remained hidden – a breathless minute of being suspended between what I had known and what I was about to discover. Behind us lay all of our history; what lay ahead was without any personal connection, without a single memory, without any hurt or disappointment. All new. I realised that it had been a very, very long time since I'd looked at anything new the way my grandchildren did. If only I could enter into this next chapter – if this indeed was to be our next chapter – with their unclouded, uncontaminated enjoyment and appreciation. Perhaps I could manage it here: apprehensions and sadnesses left on the other side of that rickety cattle grid.

"Well, this is it," our guide threw his arms wide, "Raasmierfontein. Let me tell you what I know, and then I'll have to be off."

A young German lady, living in Pretoria, had acquired the land with the intention of opening a riding school there. Her plans hadn't worked out and she'd put the property up for sale. "The house isn't much, as you can see, but there *are* the stables..."

I glanced at Clive's pretend-serious face and I knew, I just *knew* what he was thinking: artist's studio. We'd be businesslike, discuss price and contracts, and probably consult with the children before signing, but the deal was basically done.

Electricity supply, borehole water, accommodation, fences and roads, neighbours, boundaries ... I was only half-listening. Those were not the most important features – they could be put in place, repaired, changed and improved. But that landscape ... now *there* was something you couldn't negotiate or create. *That* was the real selling point. Stretching away from us, all the way to a low ridge far away to the north, and another to the south, was almost-pristine savannah grassland. And scattered all over it were patches of rich green – vegetated islands, each 10 to 15 metres across. They were the remains of ancient termite mounds, the termites now gone but the enriched soil supporting at least 25 different tree species. I saw several kinds of acacia, wild figs, Cape beech, African wattle, Savanna sugarbush, weeping boerboon and *bergsering* (mountain syringa) – that great favourite tree of mine which had so often been beautifully portrayed by the late South African landscape artist Pierneef. So that single property offered grasslands, mixed bushveld leading onto rocky ridges, mini forests on more than a 100 treed islands, a little river (the Crocodile) and two small wetlands. With such a habitat range I knew the birdlife would be extraordinary. I loved it.

When we left, though we still held on to the fiction that no decision would be made until the children had seen the place for themselves and given their blessing, the property had a new name. On the title deed it was marked as Krokodilrivier (Crocodile River). The estate agent had it listed as "Raasmierfontein", referring to those ancient termites, the original creators of the vegetated islands, whose activities, especially in advance of big rain, resulted in a loud rustling as they hurried through dry grass and fallen leaves. Noisy ants: "Raasmiere". But for us, as we crossed back over the rusted cattle grid, it had already become "Walker's Islands".

At the end of the next winter I drove up to that cattle grid on my own, and stopped. I'd been trying to keep a promise I'd made to myself more than six months earlier: I would shed whatever burdens or bad moods I'd brought from the outside world, and enter Walker's Islands with as open and light a heart as I could manage. Usually it wasn't that hard – we were so delighted to have been able to buy the place and so captivated by its charms that it easily eclipsed other, less happy preoccupations. But that day I sat facing the cattle grid for a really long time before I felt peaceful enough to drive on.

My clothes, my hair, the vehicle I was driving, everything smelled, overwhelmingly, of smoke. Despite frequent applications of drops my eyes still smarted. Every so often a relentless irritation in my chest sent me into an exhausting coughing fit, hurting my already raw throat.

It had been the third fire around our home that season, and like the two before it, it had been started by (apparently) negligent activities across the road from us, at the erstwhile Melkrivier Museum complex. Of course, once you have a raging bush fire to contend with you put blame and resentments aside and focus on first saving lives and property. But once the fire is out, or at least contained, and you're left contemplating the aftermath, it is inevitable that you would calculate the culpability of the fire-starter: the destruction of property, the suffering and death of animals, the cost and danger to everyone called upon to fight the conflagration.

I'd survived many fires in the Waterberg, including a truly terrifying one in Lapalala in the 1990s when an unstoppable inferno raged for five days and laid waste to a third of the Waterberg. We all knew exactly what to do, who to call, whom we could rely on to help, and I had no doubt as to my own ability to deal with such crises. As foster mother of large wild animals, my biggest concern had always been on their behalf. When I worked with them, sometimes with thick, acrid smoke enveloping the bomas, I had to be confident and calm enough to reassure them that, despite what their senses and instincts were telling them, they were not in danger as long as they stayed with me. A rhino in a panic would have been disastrous, so I could not afford to let my fears get the better of me.

With multi-day fires, while staying in radio contact with the fire-fighting teams, and with Clive who'd usually be helping to coordinate efforts from a command post, I'd make sure that I had routine tasks to do around the bomas, to keep things as reassuringly normal as possible. Throughout the night, at regular intervals I'd take the torch and go out in the smoky dark to check on the animals. And then, like everyone else affected by that fire, I'd resume my vigil in front of a window or on the verandah, watching the jagged golden-red lines as they moved up or down or across a mountainside, or came ever closer – a fiery serpent advancing across the veld, devouring everything in its way. Flames would suddenly shoot up as some patch of vegetation virtually exploded in the extreme heat. A favourite stand of trees gone; a grassy field, a reedbed with birds' nests... We'd watch for the slightest change in wind direction and wait for first light when the teams would reassemble and the battle resume.

If you'd wanted to see a Waterberg community at its best, that would be your opportunity. As soon as the alert goes out, all neighbours rally around with their teams of workers and their water tanks; in no time at all there'd be a command post with a communications protocol; there'd be refreshment stations with plenty of drinking water and first-aid necessities; vehicles on standby for emergencies. I imagine it's the same in all farming communities: men and women who spare no effort in helping their neighbours, knowing that they'll be able to rely on the same level of generosity when it is their turn to appeal for help.

Whenever some unthinking, cruel action by humans upsets me enough to want to condemn the human species, in its entirety, to perdition, I have to remember this. Humans destroy, but they also rescue. They have the capacity for savagery, but also for kindness. It is humans who begin wars, but it is also humans who stop them. Dresden's Frauenkirche fell because of humans, but it also rose again, because of humans. While I'll probably always maintain that *Homo sapiens* is a flawed species, as long as we continue to create, nurture and love, we probably deserve our place in the vast, wondrous ecosystem of the earth. All of us, yes, even those who started the fires that threatened my home.

So I sat there, facing the cattle grid that guarded the entrance to Walker's Islands, and tried to argue myself into accepting that while I condemned their actions, I could regard the people with compassion. I could observe and assess, but would try to refrain from judgement. With a cynical nod at my own fallibility, I decided that, just for that day, just for the couple of hours I'd be spending at Walker's islands, I would refrain from judgement. I took a deep breath, precipitating another coughing fit, but when it had subsided, I drove on down the winding track through the trees and parked next to the little house. I'd come to take measurements.

As enthusiastic as Clive and I both felt about Walker's Islands, the inescapable reality was that we were still awaiting the land claim settlement for our Melkrivier investment. Until that had been finalised I felt that we had to remain at Magog's, and in truth we couldn't really afford any development anywhere else. Moêng was settled and happy there, and to my great joy there was now another rescued black rhino from Lapalala. None other than Meetsi, whom Anton and his crew had found as an 18-month-old calf, lying injured next to a waterhole in 2005. In his Lapalala boma Meetsi had recovered perfectly and we often visited him there, perhaps with, in the back of our minds, the possibility of taking him under our wing one day. His translocation to us at Melkrivier went smoothly and while he was still recovering, Moêng was already showing great interest in the new arrival. Anton had devised Meetsi's boma in such a way that it abutted part of Moêng's paddock, so they could interact while still each having their own space. Meetsi had developed into a handsome, strong young bull, with a proud bearing. Calm, friendly, very responsive to us – he instantly came when called and was happy to be petted and fed. He accepted all of us, Lazarus included, without any problem. Even so, Bwana had taught us not to be overconfident and underestimate the strength and instincts of such a powerful wild animal. I did notice that our little Jack Russell, Button, who had taken liberties with all my other animals, did not do so with Meetsi. They didn't have issues, but while she entered Moêng's enclosure and drank from her water supply, she never did so with Meetsi's. Of course, Button was older now than when she used to race Bwana and took hazardous shortcuts between his galloping legs. She still accompanied me on all my visits to the rhinos, and was at her post there while I was lecturing to the public. But when we were done, she'd quietly go back home to find a favourite spot to lie down and sleep – usually under Clive's desk, her head on his feet.

The sight of Meetsi and Moêng lying snuggled up together on either side of their shared pole fence, or face to face, rubbing their noses, more than compensated for the negatives of still being at

Magog's, and across the road from what was going on at our old Melkrivier Museum site. I knew the immense distance, in terms of healing and adjustment, both these rhinos had travelled, so their wellbeing and contentment, and their friendship, gave me enormous pleasure. Not for anything would I have wanted to uproot them; we'd only move them to Walker's Islands when all necessary facilities had been put in place and that would have to wait for the eventual Land Bank payout. In the meantime, we'd remain at Magog's and Anton and René could, should they wish, move to Walker's Islands.

But then the fires started, and after one which took 20 fire trucks and 70 firefighters to bring under control, I found myself longing to escape. I still didn't know how we could possibly afford to finance our move and get Walker's Islands ready to receive rhino, but I was ready to begin with the small preparations – measurements to determine how much, or how little, of our furniture we'd be able to fit into our new home. "Compact" the estate agent said; compared to our former homes, it seemed like a doll's house. I didn't mind. Clive and I would manage perfectly well with the minimum indoors, as long as we had plenty out of doors. And sufficient storage space. The stables would be a godsend for everything we had to salvage from the Melkrivier Museum, for Clive's collections and art materials, and of course his studio. In addition to the work he was required to do for the organisations he served and conservation causes he supported, it was in my view imperative that he should keep writing and painting.

In his almost eight decades he has not escaped the challenges we all have to face, the losses, disappointments and betrayals. Everyone finds his or her own way of wrestling with those. Sometimes one simply needs to escape, to take a few breaths of different air. For Clive that usually meant Botswana. Once he'd crossed the Limpopo River into the Tuli wilderness, tracking and observing his beloved elephants, he'd return a new man. As a family we'd sometimes undertake a much-needed exodus to the south coast. A different world with its tropical vegetation and the ever-present sound and smell of the ocean. Since 1978 we've had a cottage there,

Lomé, named for my father's birthplace in Togo. It was in a nature conservancy that gave us the pleasure of seeing small game and brilliantly coloured birds, like the purple-crested turaco, which we'd never see in the Waterberg. As a child of the dry hinterland of Africa, I was never strong on water sports myself, but loved watching the others as they swam and surfed, flew their kites in the fresh salty breeze, or were happily engaged for hours as they discovered the fascinations of marine life in rock pools. I had a favourite walk there, up to a view point above two small beaches. There were benches there donated in memory of loved ones that had passed away, and I'd sit in that blue serenity, every cobweb blown away as I gazed out to sea.

But one couldn't always take the time to go away; you needed your small escapes at home too. At Doornleegte I walked with Bwana on his hill behind the house, or with Mothlo across the floodplain down to her rockpool in the Palala, or sat watching Munyane's thriving little baby, Mokibelo, as she grazed alongside her mother, playing and learning under Doornleegte's umbrella thorns. At Melkrivier I could walk up Lonetree to the silence of my rock ledge above the world, or across to Moêng's boma to tend to her care, until her brave, sweet presence brought me back to peace. For Clive, I believe, it was his art that provided him with that therapeutic breathing space in his daily round. In front of his easel in the various studios he'd had over the years, or in some beautiful wild place, sitting alone with his sketchbook – that's where he quietly worked his way back to equanimity. That is how he was able to present to me, and to the world, a cheerfully philosophical acceptance of life's vicissitudes, and always find a way to regard events, and people, with a vision that opened up something bigger, something more hopeful and inspiring. I looked across to the stables. If we were to move to Walker's Islands, it wouldn't be long before I'd see him emerge from his studio there, stride up to our little house, walking stick swinging, and calling out as he saw me on the veranda, "You know, I've been thinking..."

And why not? We were not ready to retire, certainly Clive

wasn't – probably never would be. Slow down a bit, by all means. My back was certainly giving me occasional reminders that 70 years of hurrying, stooping and lifting, and driving over spine-jolting corrugated roads have not gone unnoticed. But to be in such a stunning place and only spend our time sitting on the verandah? Without any effort at all I could picture my rhino enclosures there, with the treed islands providing shade and interest and fresh browse. And should we wish to expand...

I stopped myself. Let Clive do the dreaming – he had had plenty of experience in that department and his schemes have always had a way of working out. For the present I had my hands full enough with my two black rhinos in their bomas at the foot of Lonetree. When the time came to move, we would know. When we were ready for a new beginning, we would surely know. And in the interim I'd give myself the pleasurable challenge of preparing to arrive at our new sanctuary one day with a cleansed, lightened spirit. No more baggage to shed, no more demons to battle at that rusted cattle grid. No more scar tissue to blunt my joy in the blessing of being granted another new beginning.

When I drove away from Walker's Islands that day it was with a profound sense of gratitude, for many things, of course. But there was one thing in particular, which I'd never seen so clearly before, although it had been a characteristic of our lives together: Clive and I had always been able to begin again.

Difficult as it is sometimes to be impressed with the human race, there is one thing that I know to our credit: we are, most of us, good at beginnings. Let our lives implode in a sorry mess, but somehow, more often than not, we will summon up enough grit and backbone to begin again. It must be coded somewhere in our DNA: we have to begin, again. I think that's because we are so poor at endings, and so afraid of them. As long as we can we'll hold on to a belief that things are yet possible. We'd rather try, risk and lose again if we must, than not begin again just one more time. There is surely no disgrace in doing as nature does: break open yet another day, a chrysalis containing possibilities that exist as yet only as hope.

Our story has been a story of beginnings. Perhaps, like life really, it is merely the story of a beginning in search of its appropriate, appointed ending. A bearable ending. One which will legitimise all the effort, courage and pain it had required to make those beginnings en route to the final one where everything could come to rest.

I could not have foreseen the cost of this final beginning.

10 August, 2008. A leisurely Monday morning – my one off-day per week. I could take care of household chores without hurrying, knowing that Lazarus would be out cutting fresh browse for the rhinos, and then – since Mondays were more leisurely days for him too – he would get stuck into his tasks at the bomas with the kind of thoroughness for which he didn't always have time on busier days of the week. At around 11 o'clock I became aware of someone making an awful lot of noise, shouting, screaming hysterically. It was rapidly coming closer. Then I knew: that desperate voice was coming for me. As I reached the backdoor and yanked it open, there was a piercing cry. Lazarus rushed up, shaking, seemingly on the point of collapse. He had his hands over his face, weeping uncontrollably, trying to tell me something. With some difficulty, and then in utter disbelief, I heard in between his shuddering wails: "Moêng is dead! Moêng, my Moêng is dead!"

Clive manhandled me away from the door and forced me to sit down. "Stay here, until I come back. Conit, listen to me, please! You're to wait, here. Understand?"

He left me there, absolutely stunned.

Much later he finally acceded to my raging demands and allowed me to see her. The poachers had lured her to the furthest corner of her 10-hectare enclosure, offered her some of her favourite game feed pellets and when she opened her mouth, as she had always done to take the treat, shoved a handgun in her face. The bullet went through the back of her mouth, into her brain. My little black rhino, finally perfectly healthy after her long, agonising healing journey, was killed for the two modest lumps of hair that had grown on her nose. I sank down on the blood-stained grass. Her ears were filled with thick coagulated blood. So were her eyes, her nostrils, her mouth and the jagged wound where her small horns had been gouged out. Moêng – brave, trusting soul – was gone. Murdered.

From that point on, my memory splits in two. On the outside my world had gone quiet. A lifeless hush had descended, like a fog, to blanket everything and mute the stream of events that I only peripherally experienced. The authorities called in to try to track down the poachers; Moêng buried in her enclosure; Meetsi relocated to his former boma in Lapalala; Clive and I packing up and moving to Walker's Islands; my family clustering protectively around me. I went through the motions, but I wasn't there. A disconnected witness, I heard their voices and saw their concern, but as if from a great distance. There was an unbridgeable divide between their world and the dark, icy place where I, alone, was being mauled and buffeted in an emotional storm such as I had not experienced before, but of which I have a much clearer memory than of the outer reality of that time.

Skewered by my guilt: I was the one who had taught Moêng to be so trusting, to respond so willingly, so unsuspectingly to human hands held out to her. Judging by the state of Meetsi's enclosure, he'd gone berserk when Moêng was killed. The poachers would have had no chance to get to him too, not with the kind of weaponry they carried. He was far too swift and aggressive, and not nearly as trusting around strangers. And there was something else: in the early hours of that Monday – still dark – I had heard a shot, and thought nothing of it. Neighbouring farms had to deal with nocturnal raids by bush pigs, so we'd become used to hearing the odd rifle shot with which they scared away the pigs. Even so, how could I not have sensed something was terribly wrong? I had been as naïvely trusting as Moêng who had now paid for it with her life.

I was consumed with anger, wildly railing at the poachers and whoever assisted them. It had become as clear as day that Moêng's killers must have had help from the inside, someone who knew her, and us. Someone we trusted. Someone who knew that, with this particular black rhino, all they'd need was a handgun. The sickening sense of betrayal was more than I could bear.

So it was that when, before the end of August, I crossed that cattle grid to Walker's Islands again, I did so without even registering the fact. Clive was driving and in the passenger seat the only real thing I was aware of was warm, chunky little Button sitting on my lap, breathing against my tightly clenched, exhausted body. Just as she did up on Lonetree the morning after Bwana's death, she comforted me again, simply by being there, by being alive. A small, sanity-saving link between my two realities: the outer one of arriving at our new life at Walker's Islands, and the inner one of the turbulence and despair with which I arrived there. The shock of Moêng's death had gathered other troubles and heartaches into a leaden, bitter depression that drained the life out of me.

Where was the resolution I'd made just weeks earlier, to keep Walker's Islands free from such psychological burdens? What had happened to that woman who had had the determination and confidence to stop at the cattle grid, and boldly declare that she would not take any historical baggage into her new home, that she would not make this transition while weighed down by sadness and shadows?

She was sitting on her new verandah looking out over a grassfield, a pale ochre breeze-ruffled expanse which stretched for 300 metres to a low hill which, if she were to stand there, would allow her to look all the way down to the Melk River. It was that close. But if it had been a thousand times that distance it would have made no difference. Moêng's entire range of vocalisations, the small puffs of dust that she kicked up as she played her pretend-chase-and-be-chased game, the feeling of her solid weight as she affectionately leaned against her favourite human, her dear, irreplaceable personality – they were all right there on the verandah. So was that single gunshot in the night, and her grave. And Bwana's. And the ruin of what used to to be the thriving Melkrivier Museum, the one and only cultural and natural history centre in the entire Waterberg Biosphere Reserve. The urgent scramble of the move from Magog's. The unbearably touching little cards of condolence that her grandchildren had made for her, and their drawings of Moêng, the way they remembered her – alive. A small child's tears at the upsetting realisation that such horrific things can happen.

After what might well have been hours of sitting, staring out over the dry grass, I got up. "Start by doing what is necessary," said St Francis of Assisi, that favourite saint of all nature lovers, and officially declared Patron Saint of Ecologists. "Start by doing what is necessary; then do what is possible, and suddenly you'll be doing the impossible."

There was a row of plant pots on the edge of the verandah, still just as they'd come from Magog's. I selected one of the larger ones, with a climbing creeper, now limp and drooping, and carried it over to a position where I thought it might do well. There was a dry branch, shaped almost like a cross, on the table where I'd put it down on the day we arrived. It had come from the rhino enclosures at Magog's. On the day we finally left there, Clive and I walked across the road to what was left of the garden of our Melkrivier Museum, to stand for a few minutes at Bwana's grave. It was so quiet there. The trees and plants had not been tended, the buildings not maintained. More had been buried there than just a most beloved mature black rhino bull. Then we walked back across the road and up to the now empty rhino enclosures at the foot of Lonetree. Right at the top of Moêng's enclosure was her grave. When it had been covered over, dead branches had been laid over the loose soil. There too, so much more had been buried than a rescued, healed and adored little black rhino. We were already walking away again when I turned back to break off a piece of one of those branches. This I now stuck deep into the potting soil, and then untwisted the plant's fragile tendrils and wound them all the way up the branch, as high as they could go.

My life at Walker's Islands had not begun the way I'd intended. I'd wanted it to be a sanctuary; a Shangri-La, I suppose, free from the stain of sufferings encountered elsewhere. I hadn't wanted to allow myself to bring in anything but my best. A foolish ambition. Circumstances, seemingly so cruel, had been more merciful. I'd been brought here just as I was, with all my inner chaos. Anger, resentment, pain and anguish – all unresolved. Walker's Islands was to be my place of healing.

EPILOGUE

The good remains

It's morning, and I'm looking east. A perfect wilderness sky – nothing to dim or dirty that clean, crisp break of day. All around are the rustlings and calls of birds: weavers, hornbills, francolins, glossy starlings, orange-breasted shrikes, black-crowned tchagras, a lone crested barbet, its unbroken *chirrrr* like a thin thread unspooling over the grass. And further away, reaching me from a rocky ridge still dark and featureless against the pale sky, the descending cadence, hurrying as it falls, of an emerald-spotted dove.

When I approached 80 years of age I discovered the unsuspected pleasure of lying-in in the morning. Without feeling guilty I could wait, cosily in bed, for the sun to strike the bedroom windows before getting up. But on some mornings, like this one, my love of the fresh, complex fragrance of Waterberg air still lured me out to greet the day as the other-than-human residents of Walker's Islands did, out-of-doors.

The sun arrives and with it the many greens of rainy season savannah. The grassy field this morning very still – a pale lake in which the treed termite mounds rise like dark green shadowy islands. At the closest one, two giraffe are browsing, leisurely and delicately picking off the soft new growth in the canopy. Not visible now, but they're there: the rest of our giraffe family, kudu, grey duiker, impala, warthog, blue wildebeest, mongoose, jackals, many others. Last night I heard lions roar.

There's a sudden burst of activity on the veranda behind me as two small dogs come racing out of the house: Jelly and Dinky, the Jack Russells that joined the family after Button left us at the age of 14. She's buried here at Walker's Islands, as are our children's and grandchildren's pets that have passed away. Astounding as it seems to me, my grandchildren are now teenagers, old enough to have experienced the grief of losing a pet that had reached the end of its natural life.

With Jelly and Dinky around I knew that Clive was up, and after invoking a silent blessing on all the lives at, and connected to, Walker's Islands, I turned and went indoors to begin the day. It was to be a busy one because, as I'd anticipated, there had come the moment when Clive hurried across from his converted-stables studio and called out, "Conit, listen, I've been thinking..."

As I'd expected, it was not to be retirement. Many friends cautioned us, with tactfully worded concerns about the physical fragility that comes with advanced age. Surely we'd done enough; it was time to leave the battles to the younger generations; we're out of step with a changed, less-safe world ... They were right of course, and also dead wrong. Who better to fight than those who'd been tested, bloodied and strengthened in many battles before? Who better to fight for the preservation of some precious, threatened thing than those who knew, in their bones, through their own hard experience, that such fights *can* be won, that they *have* been won before? Who better to lead the herd than the old matriarch who preserves – on behalf of all the others – the memories of routes and resources and survival?

In 1945 it was the war-scarred people of Dresden who were best equipped to inspire the eventual rebuilding of the Frauenkirche. Weak, wounded, and starving, they were the ones who began the work by facing the ruins and vowing that that would not be the end of their story. They knew the value of what had been destroyed there and would keep it alive until it could rise again, 66 years later. They had nothing left, just that dream, and the pieces of blackened stonework they began to gather.

Perhaps that is all one needs: a few basics and a dream that is big enough.

So at Walker's Islands we set about creating the Waterberg Living Museum. We've always believed that many people tend to forget just how important such places are. Museums are a repository of a society's memory and awareness, they curate collections that are a resource for research and study, they preserve knowledge and history, and help us to understand our place in the world. Like botanical gardens and art galleries, museums are tranquil havens in a busy, noisy world.

It took all the stamina, determination, wisdom and especially patience acquired during our many decades of fighting against the odds. And it took courage. I cannot deny that the obstacles were considerable, and the temptation to become discouraged was, for a while at least for me, a foe to be fought and defeated. But this daughter of stoic Lutheran missionaries found that enough of their grit and, yes, missionary zeal, had remained in her veins.

Our wildlife manager son, Anton, somehow found the time to take the lead in concept and design. We roped in our old-time builder and friend from Lapalala days, Klaas Mashasha, and construction began. It was to take some time, because the Walkers, true to form, were not about to start dreaming small: a main public area and tea garden with five individually themed museums spread out over a 1.2-kilometre botanically informative garden walk. We were enormously heartened by the fact the Parker family (through Mapula Trust), joined us in the project. Duncan Parker, son of the late Dale Parker, and his board have enabled a more extensive level of educational resource than would otherwise have been possible.

Then we began constructing the bomas, because it was meant to be a *living* museum. This phase of the project was extremely sobering for me because these days, if you want to keep wild animals in a setting that allows some measure of public access, your first concern has to be security. Fences and a locked gate are no longer enough. I listened as Clive and Anton talked about bringing in various endangered species – wild dog, roan antelope, rhino – and felt my heart clench.

If ever there was a time for a conservationist like myself to do battle with the big questions it surely has to be now, when the news that assails me most acutely is that of the relentless drive to extinction of wildlife species – elephant, lion, leopard, cheetah, pangolin, many others, and especially rhino. Moêng's poaching in August 2008 signalled the beginning of the greatest rhino war we'd seen. Terrible as the previous rhino war had been, conservationists had won and the rhino was saved. The current situation seems to me more dire, with threats more wide-spread and varied and intensifying all the time. Gone are the days when one looked forward, with undiluted pleasure, to news from your conservationist friends and colleagues. Now I dread it. It has become a news of numbers: so many rhino slaughtered; so many more rhinos poached during the course of this year, this month, this day; so many rhino calves orphaned, rescued, lost; so much closer to extinction. Whereas I used to love full moon nights in the bush, I now fear them, because that is now the Poacher's Moon, when the deadly tally of daily rhino losses invariably increases.

With the honour and morality of the South African political regime, under President Jacob Zuma, seemingly plummeting towards extinction at an even faster rate than the rhino, there seems little chance of our environmental and conservation concerns being prioritised. But whenever I feel despairing about what seems to me like our country's tragic slide into chaos, Clive will not encourage that mood. In fact, at Walker's Islands he appeared to have gained a second (or third, or fourth) wind. With Anton as co-author he wrote *The Rhino Keepers* telling the story of rhino conservation in Africa, and outlining the threat to their survival as this latest rhino war gathers momentum. It wasn't an easy book to write. Much more enjoyable was the completion of a 10-year co-writing project documenting the life of, and around, the Limpopo River.

And then, perhaps even more enjoyable than *Limpopo: River of Gold*, came *Baobab Trails* in which he charted his own adventures through Africa searching for, photographing and painting the biggest, oldest, most majestic baobabs. Some of those journeys I'd shared with him, so it was a particular pleasure for me to follow the writing as it progressed.

He documented another journey of ours in a book. The Management of the Lapalala Wilderness Reserve wanted a publication that would be both a record of its genesis and a celebration of the stunning wild sanctuary that it had become. My Lapalala years had been such a crucial part of my life that this book, with Clive's text and photographs by Dana Allen, is deeply meaningful to me. And what a solace it has been to know that it isn't simply a historical record of something that had been, but is no more. Lapalala is still there, still negotiating its way through the tricky socio-political and economic climate of the day, always with the aim of preserving that original dream, jointly held by both Clive and Dale Parker, which became the Lapalala Wilderness Reserve. And there, on the banks of Dale's beloved Palala River, our other dream, the Wilderness School, also still continues.

As I look back on our journey from Doornleegte to Walker's Islands I accept that some things were lost, but not all. Of the Waterberg Cultural and Rhino Museum at Melkrivier, nothing remains. For me it is now simply the place where Bwana and Moêng were buried, along with those parts of me that died with them.

When you work with animals, as closely as I had done, you sign on for much more than the duties of a conservationist. It is not a job. It is an investment of your heart and soul. Perhaps this is why it was best that I'd stumbled so naïvely into rhino care. Had I known the risk of pain and heartbreak that would come with little baby Bwana I wonder if I'd dared. But I didn't know, and will be eternally grateful that I did dare, because I've learnt – and I had to learn it the hard way – the answer to that most challenging of the big questions facing conservationists today: Why? Why keep on fighting? When everything seems to point towards destruction and loss, why keep on hoping?

Because the good remains. Life will find a way. It is the way nature works. One generation dies but another will have been seeded and life continues. So make sure the seeds are there. There's a rhythm to things. We don't always see it, because sometimes the scale is too large for us with our short life-spans. Conservationists know this: it is foolish to look for rapid outcomes. The rehabilitation of an animal can take weeks, or months, even years; the recovery of a wildlife population, or an ecosystem, can take decades; a shift in public perceptions and policies may take a generation or more. It requires our endeavours to be sincere and sustained and hopeful. That is how wars are won.

And this is why Clive, while fully aware of the perilous state of affairs in rhino conservation, refuses to despair. He wields his hope for a better outcome like a weapon – a deliberate effort of will and of goodwill that strengthens his resolve and mine.

So we will dedicate our Living Museum to that cause. We'll keep on pouring as much of ourselves as we can into the fight for the preservation of what is precious, and wild, and voiceless in a callous world.

Because it matters. Because I believe that we are diminished by the loss of so many of the other-than-human lives who share this planet with us. Every rhino that is killed, and killed with cruelty, is an accusation – a black mark against our capacity to be fully, responsibly, human custodians deserving of our place on Earth. I believe that the rhino war is not just about rhinos; in the final analysis it is a call to the human species to rise to a higher understanding of what it means to be human.

I have to believe that we can rise to that call.

About the author

CONITA WALKER IS THE WIFE of South African conservationist Clive Walker and has been a driving, dedicated force behind their combined conservation careers almost as long as their 50-year marriage. Since the founding of the Endangered Wildlife Trust in 1973 Conita has been the backroom engine of his long career. She became co-director of their adult wilderness trails organisation, which operated in the Okavango Delta, the Mashatu Game Reserve and Klaserie in the eastern Lowveld, managing organisational functions, charter flights, catering and professional field guides.

With the founding of Lapalala Wilderness Reserve in the Waterberg of Limpopo in 1981 she became the Alternate Director to the owner, Dale Parker, and managed what was to become the 'bush camp' operations for more than 23 years. As a trustee of the Wilderness Trust she was instrumental in establishing the Lapalala Wilderness School, which to date has seen more than 80 000 children, teachers and university students pass through its doors.

With the introduction of black rhino to the reserve in 1990 she took on a role she never thought she would have to face and that was to become the surrogate 'mother' to wild orphans. An abandoned black rhino male calf named Bwana grew to adulthood in her back garden; a female hippo calf grew up in her washroom and eventually returned to the Palala River where she has produced numerous offspring; a white rhino female calf was rescued, re-wilded and eventually returned to present her own calf to Conita.

The supreme test of her mothering skills was the raising of a very seriously injured black rhino female named Moêng who was saved in the nick of time by the dedicated work of veterinarian Dr André Uys. This rhino calf along with her predecessor 'siblings' were to be viewed up close by thousands of school children who came to her garden while attending the environmental school nearby. In August 2008 Moêng was poached, marking the commencement of South Africa's latest, most deadly rhino war. Since that date, more than 6000 rhino have suffered a similar fate.

A Rhino in my Garden chronicles Conita Walker's life as mother of two sons, foster mother of wild orphans, and supporter of her husband's conservation work. Always in the background, seldom in the limelight, her story reveals an extraordinary life, from fleeing the advancing Russian army as a war refugee in 1945, growing up in the realm of Modjadji the 'Rain Queen', flying all over the world with Trek Airways, to sharing a life with her husband in the Waterberg. There she still resides today on a small sanctuary where her family is creating a 'living museum' and botanical garden.